Major Short Stories
of D.H. Lawrence

GARLAND REFERENCE LIBRARY OF THE HUMANITIES
VOLUME 1948

Drawing of D.H. Lawrence by Mary Kearney-Danboise.

Major Short Stories
of D.H. Lawrence
A Handbook

Martin F. Kearney

Garland Publishing, Inc.
A member of the Taylor & Francis Group
New York and London
1998

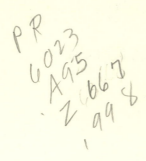

Library of Congress Cataloging-in-Publication Data

Kearney, Martin F.
    Major short stories of D.H. Lawrence : a handbook / by Martin F.
Kearney.
        p.   cm. — (Garland reference library of the humanities ;
vol. 1948)
        Includes index.
        ISBN 0-8153-2135-X (alk. paper)
        1. Lawrence, D.H. (David Herbert), 1885–1930—Criticism and interpre-
tation. 2. Short story.   I. Title. II. Series.
    PR6023.A93Z63667 1998
    823'.912—dc21   97-35670
                                                            CIP

Printed on acid-free, 250-year-life paper
Manufactured in the United States of America

37426437

To my mother; my wife, Charlene;
and my daughter, Caitlin

Contents

Acknowledgments

Thanks are extended to the Office of Sponsored Research and Grants at Southeastern Louisiana University for two research grants that allowed me to travel to Lawrence archives both in this country and abroad. I should also like to acknowledge the support for this project given me by my dean, Dr. John Miller, and my department head, Professor Anna Sue Parrill.

I am grateful to the following people and institutions for their generous and kindly assistance with my textual research: Ms. Cathy Henderson and staff at the Harry Ransom Humanities Research Center, University of Texas; the staff at the Bancroft Library, University of California, Berkeley; Mr. Wayne Furman and the Berg Collection at the New York Public Library; Mr. Vincent Giroud and the Beinecke Rare Book and Manuscript Library at Yale University; the staff at the University of Nottingham Library; and the staff at the Nottinghamshire County Library.

To my mentor, Daniel J. Schneider, for sharing his insight into Lawrence and for his encouragement, I express deep gratitude. I am most appreciative, also, to Keith Cushman for his kind words about the need for such a study and to James C. Cowan for making the initial suggestion, probably long since forgotten, that I embark upon this project. To my sister, Mary Kearney-Danboise, heartfelt thanks for the Lawrence frontispiece. Last but not least, I am greatly indebted to the hundreds of Lawrence scholars and critics who have made this book both possible and necessary.

Introduction

This reference guide is designed for those who would be knowledge-
able readers of major short stories by D.H. Lawrence when the store of
scholarship, investigation, and appraisal is far too vast for all but the
expert. An inclusive examination of what has been written about these
short stories, each chapter deals with a different short story and consists
of five distinct sections: (1) the complete publication history, including
all revisions and variants; (2) a thorough examination of recognized and
hitherto unrecognized sources, as well as the influences at work on
Lawrence in the creation of the story; (3) the story's relationship to
Lawrence's other writings; (4) acknowledgement and summary of all
extant critical studies; and (5) a bibliography of works cited.

FOCUS OF THE STUDY

This study concentrates on six short stories culled from Lawrence's
more than fifty works of short fiction. Two significant criteria were
considered in determining these six short stories as "major": (1) their
having been the focus of many critical studies and (2) their consistent
appearance in anthologies through the years. While it is expected that
some might question the omission of such respected works as "The
Blind Man" or "The Man Who Loved Islands," the six short stories
herein have been chosen both for their consummate artistry and for the
accurate cross section they present of Lawrence's entire career. Thus,
"The Horse Dealer's Daughter" was picked because it is among the
very best representatives of Lawrence's writing during World War I,

just as "The Rocking-Horse Winner" serves best to illustrate the fabular stories Lawrence wrote in the last five years of his life.

It is no accident that the first four short stories are the products of Lawrence's younger years that culminated in the *annus mirabilis* of 1914, when he wrote some of his very best short fiction. Of the six chosen, only "The Shadow in the Rose Garden" might occasion some surprise. The close examination which follows of this short story in relation to its fellows in *The Prussian Officer and Other Stories*, however, casts new light on it. The second chapter of this book also illustrates that this tale is in the vanguard of Lawrence's short fiction. Indeed, the deft touch of the artist in association with the philosophical and psychological complexities of the story's rose garden scene indicate Lawrence's best work.

All available criticism written in or translated into English has been consulted in the preparation of this study. Virtually all studies published before 1992 are included, as are some later studies. Criticism published only in foreign languages is omitted, but since such studies are relatively few, this research volume's comprehensive focus is intact.

INFLUENCES ON LAWRENCE'S EARLY SHORT FICTION

Though Lawrence would eventually travel through much of the world, he never would, nor could, leave behind him completely his birthplace, the small mining town of Eastwood, where ugly industrial technology squatted upon resplendent countryside. His social situation as a miner's son and this English Midlands' setting were major influences on Lawrence, the man, and on Lawrence, the artist.

However, one would commit a grave error to suppose, as did an early critic, that Lawrence was merely a "chronicler" whose art presents the working class he knew so well (Bates [1941] 1945, 198). Indeed, much closer to the truth was Sherwood Anderson (1930), who noted that Lawrence was hardly an English gentleman ("Sir D. H. Lawrence. Impossible, thank God") for Lawrence's literature was forged in a laborer's workshop. To Anderson, Lawrence was a prose artist: "one of a very few of his time" (22–23). But the issue arises as to just how he came to be so.

Another major influence upon Lawrence's art during the early years of his writing career was his reading. For example, the avant-garde *English Review*, first published in December 1908, impressed Lawrence enormously. Lawrence purchased each issue as it appeared and encouraged Jessie Chambers's family, as well as Louie Burrows's, to do likewise. In an October 1909 letter to Louie he sang the journal's praises, lauding its fineness, its "newness," and the fact that it was a showcase for "the new young school of realism" (Boulton 1979, 139–140). Lawrence's reading therein of such writers as Joseph Conrad, Henry James, John Galsworthy, and Leo Tolstoy was most influential, as were the journal's critiques and endorsements (Boulton 1979, 11).

Ford Madox Ford, the founder and first editor of the *English Review*, stated in the initial issue that the periodical was devoted to ideas and to the arts. The "ideas" were largely the general political and sociological issues of the day. Its slant was distinctly left-wing. Thus, the cordial and instant regaling of this miner's son, this "genius" colliery lad as Ford liked to call him, by the "inner coterie" of the *English Review* becomes quite understandable (Boulton 1979, 11–12).

Keith Cushman (1978b), an expert in the area of Lawrence's short fiction, found that the short fiction of Maxim Gorky and Guy de Maupassant influenced Lawrence's own short stories perhaps more than that of any other writers. Gorky's focus on life among the working class and his candid treatment of sex interested Lawrence greatly, and Lawrence may well have thought of himself in these early years a British Gorky. Thematically, Maupassant looks ahead to Lawrence's own central concern with the manner in which middle-class conventions and attitudes contribute to the deadening of sexual passion. Lawrence told Jessie Chambers how much he admired Maupassant's style, and in tales such as "Odour of Chrysanthemums" one can see that Lawrence had studied to great effect Maupassant's use of economy, dramatic quickness, and impersonal point of view. In this tale, Lawrence endeavors rigorously to attain "narrative objectivity." However, in only two years, by 1916, Lawrence's admiration of Gorky and Maupassant would wane, and he would find the latter obvious, coarse, fabricated, and self-consciously literary (Cushman 1978b, 102–05).

Janice Harris (1984) disagrees somewhat with Cushman on this point and argues that Lawrence's goal in such early work as "Chrysanthemums" was to write about a working-class community from within. In this way, the identification between narrator and community would be readily apparent. Gustave Flaubert and Maupassant's detached and occasionally ironic voices would not do. Chekhov and Tolstoy's would, however, asserts Harris, who believes that Lawrence subsequently modified these Russian voices to English subject matter so as to similarly make no apparent differentiation between the points of view of narrator, character, and community (6).

Lawrence also followed the Continentals' lead in the area of techniques employed to establish "unified effect." Like Chekhov, Lawrence restricted the number of significant scenes and images in his stories, filling them with meaning. Images, thus, convey the intricacy and the course of human experience that in a long work could be convened by means of a gradual buildup of data and impressions. For example, in "Odour of Chrysanthemums," the flowers are an intensely charged "image cluster," for they simultaneously intimate the perplexity of Elizabeth Bates's existence and strengthen the story's unified effect (Harris 1984, 27–8).

LAWRENCE'S FIRST COLLECTION OF SHORT FICTION: *THE PRUSSIAN OFFICER AND OTHER STORIES*

Following the June 1911 appearance of "Odour of Chrysanthemums" in the *English Review*, English publisher Martin Secker, with whom Lawrence would work from the 1920's onward, wrote the young author. So impressed was he with Lawrence's first novel, *The White Peacock* (1911), and with "Chrysanthemums" (in its early form) that he offered to publish an entire book of Lawrence's short fiction. In a letter of June 12, 1911, Lawrence responded that he had only written a few short stories because it seemed to him that few people were interested in them. He had six complete stories, two already published in the *English Review* ("Goose Fair" and "Chrysanthemums") and "several slight things" (Boulton 1979, 275). In the midst of writing his second novel, *The Trespasser*, Lawrence offered Secker these works for a fall publication, but they did not amount to enough material to interest the publisher at the time.

Austin Harrison continued to solicit tales from Lawrence for the *English Review*, and in August 1911 Lawrence exchanged letters with an editor who would play a monumental role in the young writer's development, Edward Garnett. A representative for the American magazine *Century* and an editor for the English publishing firm of Gerald Duckworth, Ltd., Garnett offered Lawrence three invaluable services: help in placing the short fiction, editorial advice concerning manuscripts, and influence with his publisher, Duckworth. Lawrence welcomed Garnett's interest, and virtually all of Lawrence's work between August 1911 and May 1913 came under his critical scrutiny (Boulton 1979, 15–16).

Garnett's firm, Duckworth, arranged to publish Lawrence's next novel. However, in late June of 1914 the publisher agreed to Lawrence's proposal that they accept a volume of short stories in the novel's stead (Boulton 1981, 187). (Lawrence wished Methuen to publish this next novel, *The Rainbow*, for they had offered him 300 pounds down for it, whereas Duckworth was offering considerably less.)

As a possible title for the collection of short fiction, Lawrence suggested *Goose Fair*, the title of one of the shorter tales therein. Lawrence, perhaps, thought this title appropriate due to the Midlands' setting shared both by a local fair of the same name and by nine of the twelve tales (Worthen 1983, xxx). Then, too, this title might have been perceived by Lawrence as Bunyanesque, in that each story depicts folly of one kind or another.

Accompanying a letter of July 14, 1914, Lawrence sent to Garnett a reworked "Odour of Chrysanthemums" and other tales likewise revised for the short-story collection and presented his preferred order for the stories:

1. "A Fragment of Stained Glass"
2. "Goose Fair"
3. "A Sick Collier"
4. "The Christening"

5. "Odour of Chrysanthemums"
6. "Daughters of the Vicar"
7. "Second Best"
8. "The Shadow in the Rose Garden"
9. "The Shades of Spring"
10. "The White Stocking"
11. "Vin Ordinaire" retitled "The Thorn in the Flesh," and
12. "Honour and Arms," retitled "The Prussian Officer"

In a follow-up letter of July 17, Lawrence sent Garnett the revised "Vin Ordinaire," now called "The Thorn in the Flesh," an appellation which Lawrence liked so much as to suggest it to Garnett as "a good title for the book" (Boulton 1981, 199). Lawrence argued that this 'thorn-in-the-flesh' concept applied directly to most of the stories. As critic and scholar John Worthen (1983) has suggested, Lawrence, no longer perceiving the work linked only in terms of common setting, now saw it thematically concerned with "pain 'in the flesh'" (xxx). Lawrence's suggestion clearly intimated his awareness that the stories of the collection were thematically bound.

In a subsequent October letter, Lawrence suggested yet another title for the book—one that would reflect the book's overriding theme and the great war that had commenced in August: *The Fighting Line*. Explained Lawrence, "After all, this is the real fighting line, not where soldiers pull triggers" (Boulton 1981, 221). This title for the volume was Lawrence's last and reflected, as Keith Cushman noted (1978), Lawrence's awareness that these stories were an assault upon commonly held beliefs and forms of perception (46). November 26, 1914, saw Duckworth's publication of the volume under the title *The Prussian Officer and Other Stories*; "Odour of Chrysanthemums" was situated dead last.

The January 9, 1915, edition of *The Saturday Review* first evaluated the collection. Although finding the colliery tales less powerful and not as poignant as the title story, dealing as they do with the drab and depressing lives of those living in a mining district (and not at all anticipated from the book's title), the reviewer did acknowledge two great strengths. Lawrence's intense earnestness was praised as was his "singular ability" to convey to readers that sense of the human soul's complete isolation (43–4). Two weeks later, January 23, 1915, *Athenaeum* discerned in Lawrence's presentation of countryside "a keen and poetic understanding," wherein not only Mother Nature, but human nature, too, seethes with instinct (68). Nevertheless, initial sales of *The Prussian Officer and Other Stories* were disappointing. A close analysis suggests a possible explanation.

In a letter of December 5, 1914, to his American agent J.B. Pinker, Lawrence vented his spleen at Garnett for the latter's unsolicited retitling of his book *The Prussian Officer*. He called Garnett "a devil" and asked, "What Prussian Officer?" (Boulton 1981, 240–41). Lawrence's point was that not only did he not title a story "The Prussian Officer," but that the retitled "Honour and Arms" concerned the *Bavarian* Army, which prior to World War I was not part of the Prussian Army (Worthen 1983, 249).

What could explain Lawrence's intense animosity toward Garnett? What exactly had Garnett done in the way of restructuring the volume that might have raised the rancor of Lawrence? The tales were reordered by Garnett in the following manner:

1. "The Prussian Officer"
2. "The Thorn in the Flesh"
3. "Daughters of the Vicar"
4. "A Fragment of Stained Glass"
5. "The Shades of Spring"
6. "Second Best"
7. "The Shadow in the Rose Garden"
8. "Goose Fair"
9. "The White Stocking"
10. "A Sick Collier"
11. "The Christening"
12. "Odour of Chrysanthemums"

Garnett began the volume with three of the strongest stories. Thereafter, he seems to have alternated a comparatively weak tale with a much stronger story until numbers ten and eleven, "A Sick Collier" and "The Christening," which are both relatively minor tales. The collection concludes with yet another masterpiece, "Odour of Chrysanthemums," which simultaneously establishes it as the capstone piece for both the two preceding mining tales and for the book itself. The order is not ineffectual. Opening the volume with the two German military stories both groups them and separates them from the other tales, which are set in the environs of the English Midlands. The question arises, however, as to whether such an arrangement might make the reader expect a number of German stories to follow the first two.

Garnett's order may have reflected sound publishing strategy. It is generally thought that Garnett's changing the titles of Lawrence's story and volume, as well as his rearrangement of the tales therein, was an effort to be both topical and commercial (Worthen 1989, 38). The First World War had only begun the previous August, it must be recalled. But as James Boulton (1981) has noted, Edward Garnett's changing the title of the first story from "Honour and Arms" to "The Prussian Officer" shifted the focus of the story from a critical examination of militarism in general to a criticism of German militarism specifically (6). In addition, Garnett's change of title shifts the focus of the entire volume. The collection's new title is a poor representative of the bulk of the book's content. It is possible, of course, that when the book was printed in November of 1914, Duckworth Publishing might have been on better terms with Lawrence. After all, that summer Lawrence had taken away from them his latest novel, *The Rainbow*, and given it to another publisher. Nevertheless, it would have made no business sense to place on the market a deliberately weak publication, so it must be assumed that Garnett and Duckworth did what they felt was necessary to put forth a successful book.

Apparently, they did not feel that paying close attention to the author's preferences in this matter was necessary. As a result, Lawrence was seething. In fact, his indignation over these unsolicited changes effectively marked the end of his association with Garnett. For this reason, the debate as presented by such critics as Helen Baron, Paul Eggert, Mark Sexton, and David Thompson over the relative worth of Garnett's editing of such earlier Lawrence works as *Sons and Lovers* is not as pertinent in the case of *The Prussian Officer and Other Stories*.

Without a doubt Garnett had given valuable assistance to Lawrence when he was first composing these short stories, but equally certain is the fact that Lawrence thought Garnett had "crossed" him in the matter of *The Prussian Officer and Other Stories.*

Close to the time of the June 1914 revisions of these short stories, it should be recalled, Lawrence wrote the famous letter to Garnett, stating that the theme in his fiction was not diamond, not coal, not soot, but carbon. He told Garnett, subsequently, that he was concerned with what a character was "as a phenomenon or as representing some greater, inhuman will" (Boulton 1981, 183). Janice Harris (1984) thought this carbon metaphor denoted the elemental in humanity: the component in humanity that must participate in universal and cultural rhythms that extend beyond self or understanding (93). Keith Cushman (1978a) saw in Lawrence's letter his understanding of his characters "in terms of the elemental laws of matter and energy that govern the universe" (37). With this new perspective, man could be seen as one of the phenomena in a world of animate and inanimate matter, and Lawrence's major concern in 1914 was to successfully render this vision into his art (37).

Ultimately, Lawrence's discoveries at this time were personal and aesthetic in nature, as illustrated in the final revisions of these tales (Cushman 1978a, 194). Lawrence's artistic perception in 1914 tried to encompass "the larger ordering beyond the flux of time," that is to say, "the larger meaning beyond the everyday" (198). Consequently, the tales that had combined symbolism and realism eventually assumed visionary qualities, to which Lawrence added "abstract and idiosyncratic speculation embodied in the metaphysic" (199). The best tales within this collection, thus, became a perfect blend of art and metaphysic: they formed a "seamless whole" wherein "art and idea" became indistinguishable" (200).

With regard to this, Lawrence's final suggestion to Garnett for the book's title, *The Fighting Line,* becomes particularly appropriate, for this phrase also appears in Lawrence's *Study of Thomas Hardy,* begun that September of 1914. Therein, Lawrence stated the aim of self-preservation was to "carry us right out to the firing-line, where what *is* is in contact with what is not" (Lawrence [1936] 1980, 409).

Lawrence continued, "Is not [man's] own soul a fighting line, where what is and what will be separates itself off from what has been?" (425).

Surely, this philosophy and newly found technical mastery influenced Lawrence's arrangement of the contents. A close study of the collection's original structure reveals an ingenious and forceful thematic design.[1] When Edward Garnett changed the order of these short stories and retitled "Honour and Arms," he did Lawrence no favor.

The initial story, "A Fragment of Stained Glass," is largely a tale-within-a-tale set in the fifteenth century. However, the frame tale's current vicar of Beauvale tells his guest that he is writing "a Bible of the English people—the Bible of their hearts—their exclamations in presence of the unknown" (Lawrence 1961, 110). Keith Cushman (1975) noted that the best tales in this collection concern a person who "achieves harmony with his deepest self by going through an intense experience of passion" (188). In so doing, the person makes "contact with the unknown" (189), his soul a fighting line. Obversely, other stories in this collection expose failed contact that results in general isolation (190). Lawrence's vitalistic theme, however, lies in both types of tale. Thus, it would appear that Lawrence's and the vicar of Beauvale's compositions coalesce: *both* present exclamations in the presence of the unknown.

The story proper of "A Fragment of Stained Glass" serves to frame the Vicar's tale of a serf in charge of the stable who is flogged by his master for having "brought down" one of the overlord's horses. The master of the stables then burns down the master of the manor's stable and house. Wounded but avenged, the serf and the flame-haired Martha steal away to the wood seeking safety. That night, he chips out a section from a radiant stained-glass window that depicted Christ's crucifixion. He is soon disenchanted with the stained-glass fragment, though, for by the cold light of a winter's morning it seems only a black, rough stone. However, when sunlight shines through it, he beholds its transformation. He sees the garnet-hued glass as a bloodstone, symbol of his lifestone. Martha, whose hair was described as the color of a red squirrel, demands this mystic talisman of him. He grants it her; she gives herself to him. Then, the short story's interior tale concludes with the sound of wolves approaching.

The transformation embodied within the stained glass and implicit within the lovers and their relationship is always a possibility in the subsequent stories. Like Laocoön, who warned the Trojans against the Trojan Horse and whose statue adorns the vicar of Beauvale's study, both the vicar and Lawrence perceive beyond the apparent in this modern world, beyond the superficial. Their vision distinguishes what lies within, the life force that enlivens and makes quick. When their characters experience this vision, they form a vital connection. But at work also within some characters' psyches are contrary forces such as will-to-power (an urge to control) or will-to-separateness (a self-imposed isolation) which refuse to acknowledge the 'unknown' in nature or the 'otherness' of another person. The consequence of such a denial in these stories is a death-in-life existence, making transformations impossible.

As Lawrence structured *The Prussian Officer and Other Stories*, this thematic motif masterfully unites the collection, as is illustrated by juxtaposing the first story with another. The tale which most closely parallels "A Fragment of Stained Glass" Lawrence placed last, "Honour and Arms," or "The Prussian Officer" as Garnett would have it. This last story parallels the first in: (1) its master-servant relationship, (2) the servant's warm emotional response to a woman, (3) the physical abuse of the orderly in the form of a beating by a master who, significantly, is identified with ownership of horses, (4) the servant's deep-seated resentment at such treatment that leads to subsequent revenge, (5) the orderly's flight from the scene of vengeance into a wood where he wanders, lost, and where forces of nature will end his life, (6) the orderly's last earthly sight, very much like "the light which stood bright and thick on the tree-tops" witnessed by the serf at his story's end, is "the mountains in a wonder-light. . .gleaming in the sky" (1961, 120, 24), and (7) the servant's violent retribution results in the waste of his young, potentially vital life.

Important differences between the two tales must be noted, as well. "The Prussian Officer" is a much more effective tale, and it focuses on the mechanical and deathly nature of life in the modern world. In this story, it is the military rather than the feudal system that is life-thwarting and abusive to the individual. Life is governed by the officers' will-to-power, which can nullify the common soldiers' sense of selfhood. Martha and the serf's loving, passionate embrace in the wood is mirrored by the officer and Schöner's deadly struggle in a similar forest. Also, the image of blood disfiguring the serf's face, caused by the "master," contrasts with the servant spilling the blood of his "superior." Not wolves, as in the case of the serf and Martha, but perversity, savagery, and alienation from self and the natural world band together to bring down the orderly, Schöner.

Despite these mirrored reversals, however, "The Prussian Officer" presents a world that is the direct descendent of that evident five hundred years earlier in "A Fragment of Stained Glass." The squirrel the serf thinks he sees on Martha's shoulder, for example, reappears as the chattering squirrel that so terrifies the dying Schöner. Such opposition of similar images and plot devices develops the collection's overall theme and creates six dualistic two-tale sets from the twelve stories.

Lawrence's polar placing of these two stories intimates a clever design that weaves this transformation theme throughout the collection. However, before this can be thoroughly explicated, one must consider whether Lawrence's order establishes an additional order in the work. For example, implicit in Lawrence's arrangement is a literal chronological time frame that depicts the world as unchanged from the Middle Ages into the modern period. A violent world is ubiquitous and although not always physical, the violence that occurs in the stories is no less brutal in its various mental (psychological) manifestations. Most violence is a display of will-to-power, and in these twelve stories the greatest hindrances to the formation of a vital connection between people are will-to-power and will-to-separateness. Characters are isolated unless, by means of a love relationship, they perceive a person's "otherness" and defer their own will to it.

Lawrence's second tale in his arrangement provides more illustrations of such isolation and violence. "Goose Fair" opens with a timeless scene of a young country woman taking her geese to market. The streets are cobblestone, torches illuminate the damp evening, and the geese recall those that "sat out like stones" in the previous tale, "A Fragment of Stained Glass" (Lawrence 1961, 190). For an instant, this place seems to be the same medieval setting of the previous story-within-the-story. The noise of the hosiery frames in the second paragraph, however, destroy that impression and introduces an industrial setting. But some things never change, despite the passage of 500 years. Not a horse stable this time, but a factory burns, and arson is suspected once again. Physical violence, paralleling the era's brutal economic conditions largely responsible for much of the town's grinding poverty, breaks out late in "Goose Fair" with a literal fight between the goose girl and the wealthy capitalist's son suspected of burning down his father's failing business for the insurance money. Victimization of the laborer by a member of the privileged class links "Goose Fair" with "A Fragment of Stained Glass" and is implicit, to one degree or another, in all the stories of this collection.

Complementing this pervasive thematic thread is another that concerns how such a world affects love relationships or potential love relationships where will-to-power and withdrawal into oneself obstruct vital connection. Motifs of fragmentation, incompleteness, thwarted transformation, isolation, and death—major themes Lawrence took great care to introduce in "A Fragment of Stained Glass"—run through the collection. Lawrence's first tale, it becomes apparent, is that keystone fragment which, when restored to its proper place, merges the other collected tales into a whole work of art, just as the replacement of the glass fragment into its original setting would reconstruct the stained-glass window in Beauvale Abbey. Thus, in the same way that a dull stained-glass window is radiantly transformed by sunlight, the collection of short stories continually delineates characters who have the potential for a vital transformation through a successful love relationship.

Now we can turn to another facet of Lawrence's intricate design for this collection. The first six tales and the last six form a very definite duality. Michael Black (1986) noted how two sets of stories, "Odour of Chrysanthemums"-"Daughters of the Vicar" and "The Thorn in the Flesh"-"The Prussian Officer," might be viewed as two diptychs in Lawrence's arrangement, for they are placed side by side (208, 241). This apt configuration of the diptych, however, fails to encompass the entire collection, for every tale is not arranged beside a counterpart story. Neither does the traditional carved diptych configuration match Lawrence's design, which is dualistic. The lower division of the duality (tales seven through twelve), in fact, mirrors the first. That is to say, its stories are arranged contrapuntally in *reverse* order to those first six tales in the duality's upper division. An image that helps to envision this arrangement is a tree that is reflected upside down in a pool of water at its base. This metaphor captures Lawrence's structure of the collection: the first six tales form "the tree" and the last six works "the reflection." In this manner, the base of the real tree, the sixth tale, is reflected in the seventh story. The top of the actual tree, the first tale, is reflected as the twelfth story. Tales two through five in-between are reflected by their counterparts, eleven through eight, respectively.

Lawrence's arrangement of the tales masterfully couples contrapuntally the first and last tales: "A Fragment of Stained Glass" and "The Prussian Officer." In addition, the first and second stories, "A Fragment of Stained Glass" and "Goose Fair," initiate the lineal (chronological) order that links the remainder of the tales. Furthermore, identical themes progress coherently from the first two tales, Group One, into the next four stories as arranged by Lawrence, Group Two. Four turn-of-the-century stories about coal mining and miners, Group Two is comprised of: (3) "A Sick Collier," (4) "The Christening," (5) "Odour of Chrysanthemums," and (6) "Daughters of the Vicar."

The next four works, all set later in or near England's Midlands, form Group Three. Containing the familiar Lawrence themes, too, they are: "Second Best," "The Shadow in the Rose Garden," "The Shades of Spring," and "The White Stocking."

Two pre-World War I German military tales, positioned last by Lawrence, "The Thorn in the Flesh" and "Honour and Arms" ("The Prussian Officer"), comprise Group Four and possess the same themes as the preceding ten stories.

An examination of these four groups shows that the skillful contrapuntal quality mentioned above between the first and last tale is also present between the two tales of Group One and those of Group Four as well as between Group Two's four tales and those of Group

Three. Thus, with Groups One and Two opposite Groups Three and Four, the initial six stories in Lawrence's order are mirrored in reverse order by the last six stories. A close analysis of the remaining dualistic two-tale sets, initiated already with the comparison between the first and the twelfth stories, "A Fragment of Stained Glass" and "The Prussian Officer," is most revealing.

The second story, "Goose Fair," and the eleventh, "The Thorn in the Flesh," set off each other nicely. Whereas the goose girl is attacked by Will, a willful "son of industry" whose relationship with the well-to-do Lois seems to be rather shallow, in the latter tale it is Bachmann who is the working-class "victim" attacked and humiliated by a "superior." A young soldier forced to climb the side of a fortification, he is so terrified that he loses control of his bladder. Hauled up to the top of the battlement, he is set upon by an abusive sergeant. He instinctively raises his arms to defend himself, striking the officer inadvertently and knocking him into the moat below. (Lawrence's use of water in the commission of Bachmann's "crime" contrasts nicely with the use of fire in "Goose Fair.") The mortified and fearful soldier seeks solace and safety with his girl Emilie, an officer's maidservant. Both know he will be arrested if found.

Will Selby, on the other hand, *is* arrested but not for his graver crime of arson. He is jailed overnight for his run-in with the goose girl, and the tale ends with him walking arm-in-arm with his lady of quality, Lois, who has maidservants of her own. Her knowledge of Will's moral turpitude—she accuses him point blank of burning down his father's business, and she sees the black eye given him by the goose girl—temporarily gives her the upper hand in this relationship. Will knows it, submits to her will, yet is contemptuous of the entire situation.

Unlike this unvital couple, Emilie and Bachmann acknowledge each other's "otherness" that night when they become lovers. Thus, they connect with life. However, they are forcibly separated at the story's end as Bachmann is arrested and led away. The lovers realize, nevertheless, that the authority of their superiors cannot destroy the knowledge they share, the integrity of their relationship, or their vital bond.

"Goose Fair" and "The Thorn in the Flesh" contain themes central to the collection, which accounts for Lawrence having suggested each as the volume's title tale. Their contrapuntal placement effectively displays the vitalistic theme by means of two opposite relationships: that of the monied class is willful and dead—that of the working class is tender and alive. In addition, the forced separation of the vital lovers by those in power in "The Thorn in the Flesh" is set off nicely in "Goose Fair" with the continuation of Lois and Will's perverse relationship. Furthermore, the arrest of Bachmann for defending himself becomes all the more ironic when contrasted with the arsonist who walks free, Will. Lawrence indicts the society where this could occur and simultaneously illustrates how modernity encourages and reinforces willful, unvital relationships.

Concurrently, Lawrence adroitly sets off thematically Group One with Group Four. Each contains a successful love relationship that is born of the most dire circumstances. Each contains a deadly relationship as well, made so by willful behavior. The two groups seem to thematically echo one another in the manner of musical counterpoint. (One is reminded that Lawrence loved most types of music, and took an avid interest in opera during these early years.) Thus, the Gregorian chants of the Cistercian monks in Beauvale Abbey in the opening story that is read in a "sing-song" manner by the vicar of Beauvale form an ethereal harmony line for the closing tale for Händel's oratorio *Samson*, the origin of Lawrence's original and preferred title, "Honour and Arms."

The stories comprising Groups Two and Three are also topsy-turvy correlatives that place the two groups in opposition and set off the first story of Group Two, "A Sick Collier," with the last story of Group Three, "The White Stocking."

The first of the four mining tales that comprise Group Two, "A Sick Collier" concerns the working-class marriage between Willy and Lucy Horsepool. He initially dotes on her, but after his health is ruined by a mining accident, Willy begins to resent Lucy's resilience. A tiff initiated by Willy's disdain for a white handkerchief that he discovers Lucy had placed in his pocket leads to his irrational demand that he be permitted to walk nine miles to Nottingham to see a football match.

Lucy's opposition only strengthens his resolve, even though the jaunt is impossible. Driven mad by his ineffectualness and the pain of his injury, Willy blames Lucy for both. Ranting and raving that he will kill her, he clumsily staggers after her and is stopped from doing Lucy violence by the intervention of Ethel Mellor, daughter of a well-to-do mine employee. The story ends with Lucy's fear that their injury compensation will be discontinued if word gets out of Willy's madness.

This unvital marriage of the opening tale in Group Two finds its counterpart in the closing story of Group Three, "The White Stocking." Unlike Willy Horsepool, who married a woman many thought too good for him, Ted Whiston is lower middle class and perhaps married somewhat beneath himself when he married former factory girl Elsie. Yet she is full of life, and her cheerful little songs contrast effectively with the clamor of machines and the ranting of the lunatic found in the Group Two story. Nevertheless, all is not well with the Whiston's relationship either. When Ted learns on Valentine's Day that Elsie has secretly accepted jewelry and white stockings from Sam Adams, who owns a lace factory, he is incensed. The threatened physical violence between man and wife in "A Sick Collier" explodes into being in "The White Stocking." Maddened momentarily by Elsie's taunts and her vindictive little dance performed in Adams's white stockings so as to humiliate her husband (a reverse reenactment of Willy Horsepool's mad shouts of "Kill her!" and his clumsy pursuit after his wife), Ted, too, wants to kill his wife. His forceful blow across her mouth brings blood, which signals his own return to sensibility. Elsie's terror and her feeble effort to defend herself against his superior strength bring both nausea and shame to Whiston. A fitting conclusion to this Valentine's Day story, each forgives the other and they embrace.

Not a white handkerchief but a pair of white stockings, sent to Elsie by Adams to commemorate her having once mistaken a white stocking for a handkerchief, initiates the battle of wills between husband and wife in "The White Stocking." Also opposed are the roles of the wealthy Ethel Mellor and Sam Adams. Whereas Ethel interrupts the Horsepool row, thus saving Lucy from harm, Sam's interference in the Whiston relationship is the impetus for Ted and Elsie's fray. In both stories, however, the mine and factory owners come off badly, for they use the working class to make their fortunes and for their own selfish pleasure. The self-indulgent and destructive will-to-power that lies behind their "success" is beyond class, of course, and is found in many personal relationships, as well, like the Horsepool's and the Whiston's. Lawrence shows us its destructive and unvital nature in these two stories. Yet, of the two marriages, the Whistons' holds the more promise

"The Christening," Group Two's second tale, and "The Shades of Spring," the penultimate story of Group Three, also form counterparts with one another. Hilda Rowbotham of "The Christening" is almost the alter-ego of Hilda Millership in "The Shades of Spring." The daughter of a wealthy dominating collier, college educated, and a school mistress, Hilda Rowbotham is also middle-aged, single, and delicate. The twentyish and vibrant Hilda Millership, on the other hand, lives on a farm, has never attended university, has a close affinity to nature, and is having an affair with a local gamekeeper. Whereas prim and proper Hilda Rowbotham is detached from life because of her social position and her father's overprotective nature, Hilda Millership decides to live her life fully. Thus, she rashly consummates her affair with the gamekeeper on the very night John Adderley Syson, a sensitive lad she had once loved, married. Her illicit relationship that she boasts of to Syson is mirrored by Hilda Rowbotham's sister's scandalous affair with a baker that has resulted in an illegitimate child and in Hilda's overwhelming sense of shame for the family name.

The two male protagonists in both stories are also counterparts. Joseph William Rowbotham, Hilda's father in "The Christening," is uneducated, wealthy, and willful. He speaks in a broad Derbyshire dialect, and his children fear him despite his failing health. As he acknowledges at the child's christening, he has kept his daughters from life. In fact, his prayer after the christening, where the fatherless infant was blessed in the name of the Father, the Son, and the Holy Ghost, begs God the Father's forgiveness for his having been a poor father. The focus on the figure of father in "The Christening" thus prepares the way for a focus on the figures of son and spirit in the contrapuntal tale.

In direct contrast to this archetypal father figure of Joseph Rowbotham is John Adderley Syson of "The *Shades* of Spring" [italics mine]. Weak and ineffectual, Addy Syson seems a perpetual lad, someone's son, as his name intimates. From a poor family, he attended Cambridge through the kindness of a local wine merchant. His local dialect, consequently, was replaced with an educated inflection. Unlike the patriarchal Rowbotham, whose christening prayer falls on the deaf ears of his family, Syson is clever with words. He composes poetry, much of which he had sent to his once-adoring Hilda. Hilda had regarded his engagement and marriage, however, as a betrayal of their mutual regard for one another. So, this male protagonist, in effect, has inadvertently nudged this Hilda from the safe world of self-delusion into the risky realm of life. At the end of "The Shades of Spring," after Hilda has told Syson that the person he had come back to find had never existed, had only been his perception of her, and was thus only a shade, she views herself as independent, with her whole life before her. Having forced Syson to lay this shade-spirit to rest, she dispenses with the son figure just as the Rowbothams do with the father figure.

Lawrence's *Study of Thomas Hardy*, written at the same time as these stories, presents God the Father as a Female symbol of Law and Nature, God the Son as a Male symbol of Love and Knowledge, and the Holy Ghost, to whom society should be erecting altars in Lawrence's opinion, as the Reconciler of the two. When these two contrapuntal tales are considered in this context, a clear pattern emerges. Joseph, the father in "The Christening," represents both law and nature, but he denies his daughters vital lives. John, the son-figure of "The Shades of Spring," though not involved in a literal christening does undergo a metaphorical baptism where he learns that his previous conceptions regarding knowledge and love were false. In contrapuntal fashion, the Female force in "The Christening" is thwarted by the father, Joseph's, domination over his daughters. The Male force represented by the "baptized" John Syson in "The Shades of Spring" is weak, deferring to the willful Hilda. Consequently, no Holy Ghost reconciles the two situations nor the two love relationships.

Hilda's having forced the affair with the gamekeeper into being and her refusal to marry him, contrasting nicely with the unwed

forsaken mother's situation in "The Christening," suggests that her
willfulness may cause her and others trouble in future. Yet she is so
much more vital than her counterpart, Hilda Rowbotham. A victim of a
repressive society, the humiliated school mistress with the weak heart
will live out her days serving others and thus trying to regain her
family's good name. Consequently, Hilda Rowbotham experiences no
transformation—she forms no connection with life. Hilda Millership,
obversely, could form a such vital relationship if she can give up her
class-consciousness and her willfulness.

The next two-tale set, Group Two's third story, "Odour of
Chrysanthemums," and Group Three's second tale, "The Shadow in the
Rose Garden," sustains Lawrence's pattern of opposition. Autumnal
chrysanthemums contrast with summer roses, both literally and
symbolically. Two different senses—smell and sight— are used to
develop Lawrence's vitalistic theme in these two stories. The drab and
dreary mining-community backdrop of "Chrysanthemums" contrasts
dramatically with the coastal resort in "The Shadow in the Rose
Garden" where Frank, the laboring mine electrician, and his unnamed
bride have temporarily escaped from their own colliery community on
their honeymoon. The most significant contrasts between these two
stories, of course, concern the love relationships.

"Odour of Chrysanthemums" begins with the news of Elizabeth's
father's impending wedding and ends with the demise of Elizabeth's
own marriage. Set in the fall, nature itself, the Bates's relationship,
even the modern world seem in decline. A proud and willful woman,
Elizabeth Bates believes she has married beneath herself and is
determined not to let her husband, Walter, bring her or her children
down to his bestial level.

On the other hand, in "The Shadow in the Rose Garden" the
couple's marriage is recent, providing readers with an embarking
relationship, in contrast to the Bates's foundering marriage that is about
to expire. Frank's nameless bride is socially and educationally above
Elizabeth. Just as willful and even more class conscious than Mrs.
Bates, this newlywed not only never loved Frank but finds him rather
contemptible. Thus, she brings him to a place laden with romantic
memories of her love affair with a rector's son, Archie. Wanting,

indeed expecting to marry him, she had been devastated when Archie threw her over. Having heard of his death, however, she married "second-best" Frank and returns to the rectory's rose garden to try and recapture those deliriously happy moments when she had thought herself engaged to her social superior.

News of her "master's" death, however, has the reverse effect on Elizabeth Bates in "Odour of Chrysanthemums." As she bathes Walter's corpse, Elizabeth experiences a revelation concerning life that, ironically, results from this death. Brutally honest with herself, she acknowledges her guilty role in the demise of their marriage. Neither mate had seen the "otherness" of the other. They had reduced each other in their own minds to "a shrew" and "a drunkard," respectively, just as Elizabeth had associated the odour of chrysanthemums with the pain and disappointment of her marriage to Walter and thus refused to acknowledge the flower's unique otherness. Elizabeth's revelation teaches her that each person is "other" from her and, thus, each person must be respected as such. She and Walter had never formed a vital connection, even in their most intimate moments, because they had been too willful to temporarily sacrifice their own "otherness" for the other. Self-consciousness, a desire to be dominant, and a refusal to let go of these facets of themselves had condemned them to lives of complete separateness.

With her newfound knowledge at the end of "Odour of Chrysanthemums," the widowed Elizabeth might someday form a vital love relationship. However, the outlook is more bleak for Elizabeth's counterpart, the bride in "The Shadow in the Rose Garden." She returns to the site of her and Archie's courtship, the rose garden, where a most revealing glimpse into her psyche is effected. (In a nice mirror reversal to Elizabeth Bates, her sustained interior monologue occurs immediately *before* her "dead" would-be husband appears.) She sentimentally loses herself in reverie and in the roses themselves, imagining herself "nothing but a rose." With a shock, however, suddenly she sees Archie, her former lover, standing before her! The obverse of the coal-blackened and disheveled corpse of blonde, mustachioed Walter Bates that Elizabeth must bathe, the "resurrected" Archie is "scrupulously dressed," well groomed, his black mustache waxed. Exactly like Walter's corpse, however, Archie's eyes stare without seeing. With a start, she realizes that he is completely mad and does not know her. Yet, like Elizabeth, she examines the shape of this "dead" would-be husband. She focuses upon his "compact, soldier's head," his hands, and his once-handsome figure, now diminished. And like Elizabeth, she realizes that it is not he.

In continuing reverse parallels to "Chrysanthemums," the newlywed waits to see if her former lover will recognize her. Drawing his face near to her, the one-time love of her life, now lunatic, claims to know her. She is horrified and flees. Her subsequent self-imposed isolation from Frank upon her return to their lodgings at once parallels a major flaw of the Bates's marriage and contrasts with Elizabeth's desire to claim Walter as hers alone in the small parlor as she embraced his corpse. Realizing that she and Archie are now forever dead to one another, the bride feels that her being has lapsed, that she is, if fact, dead. Her eventual confrontational confession to Frank, the result of the revelation she had just experienced, serves as this tale's second revelation, for in "Shadow" it is the husband who learns that he does not know his wife at all. As in "Chrysanthemums," however, where Elizabeth becomes aware of the infinite gap between her dead husband and herself, both the wife *and* the husband at the close of "Shadow" have learned of the wide gulf that separates them. Whether they will eventually share Elizabeth Bates's vital lesson before it is too late is questionable.

The concluding two-story set consists of "Daughters of the Vicar," Group Two's fourth tale, and "Second Best," Group Three's first work. Once again, each story mirrors the other. Set in England's midlands, both tales focus upon the courtships of two sisters. Mary Lindley, the older daughter of the vicar, marries the wrong man, an Oxfordian Master of Arts, for the wrong reasons, insuring an unvital relationship. The blonde, fair Louisa Lindley, Mary's younger sister, courts and all but proposes marriage to a coal miner, Alfred Durant. Louisa's lack of class consciousness and her recognition of Alfred's "otherness" bodes well for their marriage.

Anne, the younger sister in "Second Best," is fourteen and has a crush on a local farmer, Tom Smedley. Her older sister, Frances, has just been dropped by a Doctor of Chemistry, whom she had hoped to marry. Willful and elitist, Frances grudgingly settles for the farmer even though she does not love him. The opposite of Louisa Lindley and modeled physically after another Louisa, Lawrence's onetime fiancée Louisa Burrows, the dark-haired, dusky, and warm-complexioned Frances will marry the laborer whom her sister likes more than does she. In another plot reversal, following their avowals of love, it is Louisa who tells Alfred that he must ask her father for her hand, whereas Tom Smedley reminds Frances that they will have to tell her mother.

Thematically, as well, the two stories form counterparts. In "Daughters of the Vicar," Louisa's vision of coal miner Alfred's "otherness" is vitalistic, and her subsequent sacrifice for him of her will-to-power, social position, family, home, and country is positive. In marked contrast is Frances's doleful return to the provinces and her willful killing of the literal and symbolic mole (a Lawrentian emblem, like miners, for man's vital and dark level of sexuality) as well as her determination to marry a lad she deems beneath her. There is no question which relationship will be the more vital.

So, there it is. "Daughters of the Vicar" and "Second Best" enjoy the same kinds of correlatives evident in the five other two-tale sets of stories, placed in precise opposition by Lawrence's arrangement. With this design, Lawrence presents a perfect duality. Tale mirrors tale and group reflects group so precisely as to contribute significantly to the overall unity of the work. (In fact, balance, unity, and "radiance," characteristics usually associated with James Joyce's aesthetic, are very much in evidence in this short story collection, though it was published five months after *Dubliners* and two years before *A Portrait of the Artist as a Young Man*.) Lawrence favored the dualistic configuration: his psychology and philosophy testify to that fact. In 1921, Lawrence himself examined his art up to that juncture to try and determine just what it maintains. His subsequent psychological-philosophical treatise in which he lauds vitalism, *Fantasia of the Unconscious,* is based on a number of dualistic configurations. Sun-moon, fire-water, day-night, mountain-valley, male-female, the list goes on. Each facet mirrors the other, and each facet needs the other in full complementation before unity can be achieved. This conviction is embedded in his structure of his first collection of short stories.

Lawrence's design also establishes by means of the first and the last tale both a thematic and a chronological framework for the remaining stories. Viewed in this manner, the Prussian officer's orderly, Schöner's, fleeting impression as death approached assumes increased significance when read as Lawrence would have had it—last in the collection: "He [Schöner] was divided among all kinds of separate beings. There was some strange, agonized connection between them, but they were drawing further apart. . . . Then they would all split. . . . Then they would all fall, fall through the everlasting lapse of space" (1961, 25). Surely this realization encompasses Lawrence's 1914 view of humanity. An amalgam of the many characters who preceded him in the collection, Schöner's ultimate alienation from himself, mankind and the natural world is a chilling conclusion—and a warning. Lawrence implies that such is the fate of all mankind unless changes are made.

Edward Garnett's arrangement of the stories, if uninspired, was somewhat reasonable. It is debatable, however, as to how deeply Garnett understood Lawrence's art in 1914. A 1916 article implies that Garnett's grasp of Lawrence's themes was limited. Writing in the *Dial* on the collection's title story, Garnett asserted that "The Prussian Officer" revealed passion's triumph over "the material of life," as the former arose from darkness to light. Thus, in both the officer's enduring "lust of cruelty" and the servant's revenge, the merging of pleasure and pain that lay at the bottom of sexuality was presented as a combination of senses and soul (380). Garnett's rather limited reading supports the assertion that he missed the subtle artistry of Lawrence's arrangement for the twelve tales.

Ultimately, these short stories are about perception. From the first tale onward, Lawrence makes it evident that one's ability to always "see" clearly is imperfect. Thus, the Cistercian monks see a devil trying to enter their monastery, whereas, the bloodied serf sees double-faced angels looking up at him in fear. Both perceptions are mistaken, of course. As the figure of Laocoön in the vicar of Beauvale's study implies, one must look beyond the surface to discover "otherness," like

Louisa Lindley, who witnesses Alfred Durant's "otherness" radiate forth in what becomes both a transformation and a revelation. Once "otherness" has been perceived, a vital connection might be formed if self-consciousness, a need to dominate, and an urge to fortify oneself within oneself (will-to-be-separate) can be temporarily sacrificed.

In the final analysis, Lawrence's theme in each of these stories pertains to elemental humankind and their need to experience a vital transformation, such as the serf and Martha's in "A Fragment of Stained Glass," Bachmann and Emilie's in "The Thorn in the Flesh," Elizabeth Bates's in "Odour of Chrysanthemums," and Louisa Lindley's in "Daughters of the Vicar." By means of Lawrence's masterful design for this collection of short fiction, form and theme unite. Each complements the other in a blaze of illumination, like light radiating through a gemstone or a piece of stained glass.

Although Lawrence's extant letters to Garnett are without rationale for his placing of the stories in their very particular order, there seems to be no great mystery therein. Lawrence might have felt it would be impertinent to do so. After all, Garnett was an experienced editor. What is certain, however, is that Lawrence expected his tales to be organized in that very specific fashion, for he had been led to believe that they would be so.

The inevitable question as to whether Lawrence purposely designed this dualistic arrangement is impossible to answer with certainty. However, Lawrence himself has made such a question irrelevant. In his *Studies of Classic American Literature*, when considering which was the more important, an artist's intent or the finished work of art, Lawrence made his famous adjudication that one should always trust the art, never the artist ([1923] [1964] 1977, 8).

Ultimately, Garnett's reordering of Lawrence's arrangement left the volume in such a state of disorder that it well may have contributed to the book's initial slow sales. By placing topical and commercial interests ahead of artistic, Garnett sacrificed not only the ingenious symmetry of a great work of art, but also his friendship with its author.

LAWRENCE'S MIDDLE PERIOD

Lawrence's second collection of short fiction, *England, My England and Other Stories*, was published in October of 1922 in America by Seltzer and January 1924 in England by Secker. The ten stories therein had been written and revised between 1913 and 1921, and "The Horse Dealer's Daughter" is the acknowledged masterpiece of the collection. Other strong entries include the title tale, "Tickets Please," and "The Blind Man." The remaining tales are: "Monkey Nuts," "Wintry Peacock," "You Touched Me," "Samson and Delilah," "The Primrose Path," and "Fanny and Annie." As was often the case with Lawrence's short fiction, "The Horse Dealer's Daughter" was first published in a magazine, the *English Review* having printed it in April of 1922.

These ten short stories share with those in Lawrence's first collection both realism and a visionary quality, but these features are closely linked herein with myth and ritual. All of these stories are set in England, and their time period covers roughly those years when they were written, 1913–1921. World War I is witnessed first hand in the title tale, and the war's negative effects upon individuals, the general populace, and relationships appear, to one degree or another, in seven of the ten tales.

As with the first collection, love relationships in "the modern world" are the focus in *England, My England and Other Stories*, and once again, most are unsuccessful. Will-to-power, will-to-be-separate, self-consciousness, and sentimentality are the major culprits. Sometimes misunderstood or oversimplified and reduced to an advocacy for male dominance that some critics believe Lawrence touted during his Leadership Period in the early 1920's, the relationships in these tales go awry for more reasons than a woman's refusal to defer to a man. In fact, the modern lovers in most of these tales like Annie and John Thomas of "Tickets Please" and Winifred and Egbert of "England, My England" refuse or are unable to metaphorically "die" with the other in a death that is also life. "Sex-in-the-head" reigns; there is no mystical sexual union and thus, no communion with "the absolute," no vital connection between the lovers.

Of course, such failure is not new to this second collection of stories. One need think only of Walter and Elizabeth Bates's unvital relationship in "Odour of Chrysanthemums" for a correlative. Indeed, the necessity for the vital in love relationships is Lawrence's constant theme.

The most powerful story of the second collection, "The Horse Dealer's Daughter," cleverly portrays the birth of the relationship between Mabel Pervin and Jack Fergusson. Myth and ritual are rife in symbolic renderings of resurrection and baptism. Readers, immersed in Jack's psyche, share his agony as he battles a fear of drowning, a will-to-power, a desire to remain separate, a class consciousness, and a terrifying horror of commitment. But he crosses the gulf. He defers to Mabel. The doctor's old self dies, and he is delivered by this woman whom only moments before he had saved from suicide. "The Horse Dealer's Daughter" is the capstone of the second collection because it provides the all-important consummation of a love relationship that is nonexistent in the other stories. At last, with this alliance where the lovers have momentarily sacrificed themselves for the other, have willingly and completely given themselves over to the other, there is cause for optimism. Love *can* exist even in this modern world, proclaims Lawrence, once humanity stops being so damned willful and self-absorbed.

LAWRENCE'S LATER PERIOD

"The Rocking-Horse Winner," perhaps the best known of these six major short stories, was published twice during Lawrence's lifetime. It was written in February of 1926 for his friend Lady Cynthia Asquith's *The Ghost Book*, where it appeared that September. It had also been printed in the American magazine *Harper's Bazaar* that July. Following Lawrence's death in 1930, "The Rocking-Horse Winner" was published in 1933 by Viking Press in the fourth collection of his short fiction, *The Lovely Lady and Other Stories*. (The third collection was 1928's *The Woman Who Rode Away and Other Stories*.)

"The Rocking-Horse Winner" was accompanied in this volume by six other short stories: (1) the title tale, "The Lovely Lady," (2) "Rawdon's Roof," (3) "Mother and Daughter," (4) "The Blue

Moccasins," (5) "Things," and (6) "The Overtone." Written after 1925, with the exception of 1924's "The Overtone," these seven stories are set primarily in England, and they focus on the way facets of modernity, specifically the same miscreants responsible in the first two collections, undermine the vital in relationships.

Lawrence is caustic in his presentation of society in these tales, incorporating facets of realism, fable, myth, and satire. The later the story, the more fabular and satirical it is. Thus, the earliest of these tales, "The Overtone," contains much realism and myth. "The Rocking-Horse Winner," written in 1926, is perhaps the first major fable of Lawrence and is the most successful of this group of stories because realism, myth, and satire are effectively balanced. The later tales in this collection such as "The Blue Moccasins" and "Things" lack that harmony and, thus, suffer from a surfeit of sarcasm.

Parental repression and victimization is a common thematic thread running through several of these stories, including "The Rocking-Horse Winner," but Lawrence's concern is universal. As he said in his final major essay *Apocalypse*, mankind must learn to live breast-to-breast with the cosmos if humanity is to survive. Thus, these stories in general, and "The Rocking-Horse Winner" in particular, indict greedy, self-serving people and the avaricious materialistic unvital society in which they live. These stories reflect a world where "things" such as antiques, residences, and even a pair of symbolic blue moccasins assume such an ascendancy of importance to their "owners" that the lives of those "possessed" by these "things" and the lives of those closest to them become less real, less vital, than these material objects. In what might be seen as a modern psychological variation of a Dickensian signature, characters in these tales such as Paul's mother in "The Rocking-Horse Winner" become less human as their "things" become more so. Thus, Paul's house has a voice with a most insistent message. Paul's mother, Hester, is so taken with her financial windfall that she is completely oblivious to her neglected son's despair and subsequent heroic effort to "save her" by giving her a fortune. In this condemnation of a once-nurturing mother-child relationship that has become murderous, Lawrence incriminates all of modern society for its misplaced values, its unnatural self-absorption, and its deathward direction.

No doubt, Lawrence was hard on humanity, but that is because he loved it so. When Lawrence presents a symbolic "worst-case scenario" in his short fiction, its purpose is to shock and rouse what is best in humanity. F.R. Leavis (1930) noted that in reading Lawrence's best work, such as his short stories wherein his art is most unfailing, one assimilates a new perception as he experiences a rejuvenation of "sensuous and emotional life" (32).

Ever the advocate for vitalism, Lawrence's last tales, like his first, are intended to nudge mankind in the direction of life. His belief that there still existed an opportunity to move lifeward reveals an optimism that sets Lawrence apart from many of his contemporaries. The rich tapestry of his major short fiction is woven of the very stuff of life. To experience it fully is to come to life's gate. As Lawrence noted in his 1926 novella *The Virgin and the Gipsy*, it is easier to break down prison walls than to unlock undiscovered doors to life. These short stories were designed as signposts to provide direction ever lifeward.

NOTE

1. Another study of the two arrangements of the tales in this collection is: Atkins, Anthony, ed. 1995. "Introduction." *The Prussian Officer and Other Stories*. New York: Oxford University Press. vii–xxix. Unbeknownst to Atkins and myself, these two original examinations were conducted simultaneously on opposite sides of the Atlantic, and although some of their facets are tangential, such as the division of the twelve tales into four groups, the importance of the placement of "A Fragment of Stained Glass," and its parallels with "The Prussian Officer," most are otherwise.

WORKS CITED

Anderson, Sherwood. 1930. "A Man's Mind," *The New Republic* May 21: 22–23.
Athenaeum. 1915. "Fiction," 23 January: 68.
Baron, Helen. 1992. "Lawrence's *Sons and Lovers* versus Garnett's." *Essays in Criticism* 42: 265–78.

Bates, H.E. [1941] 1945. *The Modern Short Story.* London: Thomas Nelson and Sons Ltd. Reprint. Same publisher.

Black, Michael. 1986. *D.H. Lawrence: The Early Fiction.* New York: Macmillan.

Boulton, James T. ed. 1979. *The Letters of D.H. Lawrence.* Vol. 1. Cambridge: Cambridge University Press.

————. 1981. *The Letters of D.H. Lawrence.* Vol. 2. Cambridge: Cambridge University Press.

Cushman, Keith. 1978a. *D.H. Lawrence at Work: The Emergence of the Prussian Officer Stories.* Charlottesville: University of Virginia Press.

————. 1975. "'I am going through a transition stage': *The Prussian Officer* and *The Rainbow.*" *The D.H. Lawrence Review* 8.2: 176–97.

————. 1978b. "The Young D.H. Lawrence and the Short Story." *Modern British Literature* 2: 101–12.

Eggert, Paul. 1990. "Opening Up the Text: The Case of *Sons and Lovers.*" *Rethinking Lawrence.* Keith Brown, ed. Milton Keynes: Open University Press. 38–52.

Garnett, Edward. 1916. "Art and Moralists: Mr. D.H. Lawrence's Work." *Dial* 61(November 16): 377–81.

Harris, Janice. 1984. *The Short Fiction of D.H. Lawrence.* New Brunswick, New Jersey: Rutgers University Press.

Lawrence, D.H. 1961. *The Complete Short Stories. Vol. 1.* New York: Viking Press.

————. [1923] [1964] 1977. *Studies in Classic American Literature.* New York: Thomas Seltzer. Reprint. New York: Viking. 2nd Reprint. New York: Penguin.

————. [1936] 1980. *Study of Thomas Hardy. Phoenix.* New York: Viking Press. Reprint. New York: Penguin Books.

The Saturday Review (London). 1915. [*The Prussian Officer and Other Stories,*] 9 January: 42–43.

Sexton, Mark. 1990. "Lawrence, Garnett and *Sons and Lovers:* An Exploration of Author-Editor Relationship." *Studies in Bibliography* 43: 208–22.

Thompson, David. 1994. "Calling in the Realists: The Revision and Reputation of Lawrence's *Sons and Lovers.*" *Novel* 27.3: 233–56.

Worthen, John. 1983. "Introduction." *The Prussian Officer and Other Stories.* Cambridge: Cambridge University Press.

————. 1989. *D.H. Lawrence: A Literary Life.* New York: St. Martin's Press.

Major Short Stories
of D.H. Lawrence

I

"Odour of Chrysanthemums"

PUBLICATION HISTORY

Lawrence first came into print in 1907 as the winner of a Christmas story contest held by the *Nottinghamshire Guardian*. He submitted three tales: "The White Stocking," "A Fragment of Stained Glass," and "The Prelude," which took the prize. (After extensive revision, the first two would appear in 1914 in Lawrence's first collection of short fiction, *The Prussian Officer and Other Stories*.) A year and a half later, Lawrence's good friend Jessie Chambers copied out several of his poems and sent them to Ford Madox Hueffer (the surname became "Ford" when the First World War fostered anti-German sentiment), the editor of the distinguished *English Review*. Accepted immediately and published that November, these poems presaged Lawrence's future success.

On December 9, 1909, Lawrence himself sent to Hueffer two recently completed short stories. He had co-written one of the tales, "Goose Fair," with his future fiancee, Louisa (Louie) Burrows; the other was an early version of his masterpiece "Odour of Chrysanthemums." Hueffer accepted both for publication.

In a testimony since questioned, Ford Madox Ford later took credit for recognizing Lawrence's genius in the very first paragraph of this early version of "Odour of Chrysanthemums." He said he saw therein a writer with character, courage of conviction, and a keen observational mastery. Lawrence could obviously be trusted, Ford recalled, as was witnessed by his use of rhythm in the opening sentence to capture a reader's attention, his ability to forge a flawless paragraph, and his knowledge of the life about which he wrote, set in a region effectively revealed by means of an arresting word here and there (Ford 1937, 74).

On March 9, 1910, Lawrence received from the *English Review* a 27-page set of proofs dated March 3, which he corrected with black ink on the proof-set pages themselves. These galley pages, before Lawrence's revision, embodied the tale in its earliest form. The major difference between this and later versions lay in the ending. In the initial version, Elizabeth Bates took comfort in her husband's death. She apparently preferred him home dead to home dead drunk. This first rendition much later appeared in *Renaissance and Modern Studies* 13 (1969) (Boulton, "Odour," 1969, 4–48).

Having been led to expect a May publication date, Lawrence wrote a friend on June 1 that he was rapidly losing faith in the writing profession and wondered if the journal's new editor, Austin Harrison, had forgotten or mislaid his story (Boulton 1979, 162). The proofs, however, came back again in July with instructions to cut the tale by five pages. Lawrence spent part of the summer of 1910 making this revision, but as he mentioned to Louie Burrows in a July 24 letter, it was "a devilish business" (Boulton 1979, 172). Still dissatisfied, Harrison further asked that Lawrence shorten the first part of the story: much of the Bates children's playing should be cut to accelerate to the climax (Boulton 1979, 252). In late March and early April of 1911, Lawrence revised these same proofs accordingly, but he also rewrote the ending by means of "delving . . . into cause and effect"(Boulton 1979, 250), which improved the story, but lengthened it by eight pages. In this version, focus shifted from Elizabeth as mother and emphasized her role as wife. No longer pleased that her husband is dead, Elizabeth now sees herself as a lady whose knight has returned to her, exquisite and pure, from a base existence precipitated by alcohol abuse. She feels that she has reclaimed the essence of his former innocence.

Lawrence sent this manuscript to Louie Burrows on April 2, 1911, with a request that she make a fair copy, leaving out all that he had struck. He subsequently sent the clean thirty-nine-page fair copy to the *English Review* before the end of April, and "Odour of Chrysanthemums" appeared on pages 115–33 of the June 8, 1911 issue. Some of Lawrence's latest revisions, however—especially those in the tale's first half—failed to appear at this time. The printers, it seems, used much of the standing type from the 1910 page proofs as the primary text (Worthen 1983, li). For his story, the *English Review* paid Lawrence ten pounds, rather more than he had anticipated.

At the time, the *English Review*, which would ultimately print more of Lawrence's short fiction than any other magazine, enjoyed a circulation of approximately 10,000. Since he knew he might make more money from periodicals with larger circulations, it is to Lawrence's credit that he recognized this magazine's dedication to literary merit and experimentation. He knew, too, that his fiction would find greater appeal and understanding among subscribers to such an avant-garde publication as the *English Review* (Van Spanckeren 1986, 296–97).

As Ford Madox Ford later recounted, editors during the early years of the century were eager to find "authentic projections" of working-class life that had yet to be voiced (Ford 1937, 74). "Odour of Chrysanthemums" was just such an expression, for it portrayed life as Lawrence knew it from his earliest memories in Eastwood, the Nottinghamshire colliery village where he was raised, and it offered an objective glimpse of working-class life, wherein humanity was presented universally (Leavis [1956] 1979, 308). Having found "a market," therefore, Lawrence began to receive solicitations for his stories from other magazines.

In July of 1914, Lawrence extensively revised the 1911 *English Review* text of "Odour of Chrysanthemums," rewriting the ending again and dividing the story into two numbered sections. With a letter dated July 14, 1914, he sent this manuscript to his mentor/agent Edward Garnett, of Duckworth Publishers, accompanied by others also revised for a short-story collection.

Another thorough revision of "Odour of Chrysanthemums" occurred when Lawrence worked over the Duckworth proofs dated October 6, 1914. In this draft, he reworked for the final time the passage into the well-known ending wherein Elizabeth Bates recognizes the shared responsibility for the failure of the marriage. This version shifted the weight of emotion of the earlier versions away from the mother's attempt to reclaim her child, as well as the wife's endeavor to claim Walter as though he were also a child (Black, 1986, 208).

When the collection of tales Garnett entitled *The Prussian Officer and Other Stories* was published on November 26, 1914, by Duckworth, "Odour of Chrysanthemums" appeared last in the volume, presumably so as to conclude the book with a particularly forceful work. This tale would not appear in America in its final form until 1916, at which time B.W. Huebsch published *The Prussian Officer and Other Stories* in New York (McDonald, 1925, 34–6).

A later and somewhat controversial text of this story appeared in 1983 in the Cambridge University Press edition of *The Prussian Officer and Other Stories* (Worthen 1983, 181–201). The editor of this volume, John Worthen, a preeminent Lawrence scholar, examined all of the existing manuscripts of all the included tales so as to emend any textual corruptions, his goal being to present the tales in a final form Lawrence's might approve were he alive. Although the textual changes in this edition were slight, some scholars have criticized Worthen's well-intentioned work on the grounds that Lawrence was not, in fact, alive either to condone or condemn the so-derived text.

Also, appearing in this Cambridge edition of *The Prussian Officer and Other Stories* is a fragment of "Odour of Chrysanthemums" that seems to have been a working draft with an ending much briefer than in any of the other variants (Worthen 1983, 201–07).

CIRCUMSTANCES OF COMPOSITION, SOURCES, AND INFLUENCES

In the latter part of 1909, when D.H. Lawrence first composed "Odour of Chrysanthemums," he was teaching at the Davidson Road School in Croydon, a suburb of London. He lodged at 12 Colworth Road, the home of Mr. and Mrs. John Jones, and he would work there on his fiction after his tiring days in the classroom. During vacations, Lawrence stayed with his parents at Lynn Croft, Eastwood, Nottinghamshire.

This living arrangement continued through 1910. In the summer, as we have seen, Lawrence revised the March 3 proofs of the tale for the *English Review*. Then, owing to his mother's illness in late August and her death from cancer on December 9, Lawrence took increasingly more time off from teaching. During the year-end term break, he found it too painful to return to his family home, now empty, and stayed at the

Quorn in Leicestershire with the family of Louie Burrows, who had become his fiancée on December 3.

Lawrence made an April, 1911, revision of "Chrysanthemums" before its June publication in the *English Review*, then began his new career as a full-time writer. He had broken his informal engagement with Jessie Chambers the previous November, and his mother's death the following month had severed his strongest tie with his birthplace. The attractions of being a teacher with a secure and a stable domestic life were giving way to his fascination with the adventure and self-development that he associated with the writing profession. By 1911, he had completely immersed himself in the literary world (Boulton 1979, 15).

The publication that year of *The White Peacock*, his generally well-received first novel, and the appearance of "The Odour of Chrysanthemums" in the *English Review* that June had attracted the flattering interest of editors Martin Secker, Austin Harrison, and Edward Garnett. Letters from the latter part of 1911 to his fiancée, Louie Burrows, with whom he would soon break up, expressed his discontent with teaching and his desire to become a full-time writer. Garnett's encouragement played a major role in his decision to indulge that desire.

He was welcome at Garnett's Kent home, the Cearne, which soon replaced the Quorn, Louie Burrows' home, as the axis of his new career. He was heartened by the popular success of *The White Peacock*, but his health finally sealed the matter of his future occupation. In November of 1911, Lawrence caught a chill while working with Garnett in the Cearne's garden; the severe pneumonia that followed forced him to resign the teaching post at Croydon, and he never taught in a classroom again (Boulton 1979, 15–17). He recovered from his pneumonia, and in the three years before "Odour of Chrysanthemums" appeared in *The Prussian Officer and Other Stories*, he ended his engagement with Louie Burrows on February 4, 1912, and took up residence in Italy with a married woman, Frieda Von Richthofen Weekley, whom he married in July, 1914, following her long-pending divorce.

Lawrence and Frieda returned to England in June of 1914, and during the July revision of "Chrysanthemums" and other tales for the short story collection, they resided at Selwood Terrace, South Kensing

ton, London. He returned briefly that month to the English Midlands
for a four-day visit to Ripley, where his sister Ada lived. Then, during
the October revisions of the book proofs, the Lawrences stayed near
Chesham, at a residence called The Triangle.

Growing up in a colliery town where the deprivations outnumbered
the festivals, Lawrence remained keenly sensitive to "daily sensory
experience," and he infused in all of his early work the pulse of nature's
rhythms—bliss and suffering, birth and dissolution, creation and
disintegration—which drive and permeate class conflict (Freeman
1955, 18.) Lawrence had to look no further than his own family to find
a principal source for "Chrysanthemums." He was seven when he first
heard his Aunt Polly tell how in 1880 her husband, Lawrence's Uncle
James, had been killed in a mining accident at Brinsley Colliery
(Boulton 1979 199). As was the case with the fictional collier Bates, a
common name around Brinsley in the 1870's, Lawrence's uncle bore
no marks of violence or suffering (Worthen 1983, 272). The Bateses'
cottage, too, may well be based on Aunt Polly's lodge in Brinsley
(Delavenay 1972, 107); thus, by extrapolation some critics assume
Elizabeth Bates to have been modeled on this aunt (Moore 1974, 18).

Later critics, like Keith Cushman, however, argued convincingly
that the Bates family more closely resembles Lawrence's own. Walter
and Elizabeth Bates do seem very much like Lawrence's own parents,
which makes the narrator's detachment all the more remarkable.
Feuding parents similar to Walter and Gertrude Morel of *Sons and
Lovers*, Walter and Elizabeth Bates may well reflect Lawrence's own
home life (1978a, 48–9).

Lydia Lawrence, like Elizabeth Bates, experienced a social
degradation of sorts in assuming her station among the working class,
and she appears to have transferred to her children her desperate desire
to regain the middle class again where she might develop her mind and
spiritual nature. This longing both resulted from and contributed to her
disaffection for her husband, Arthur, whose own family came to resent
him and treat him as though he were a stranger at his own hearth
(Delavenay 1972, 6).

One can have little doubt that Walter Bates and Walter Morel of
Sons and Lovers took after Arthur Lawrence. In fact, as L.D. Clark has
noted, the Bates' cottage may not be based upon the aunt and uncle's

house at all, but rather on father Arthur's birthplace, a small house in a quarry hollow very near the level-crossing at Brinsley (Clark 1980, 350).

One result of a childhood spent in this tense and hostile household was Lawrence's major preoccupation revealed early in "Chrysanthemums": the indifference of his parents' sexual relationship, and the powers women hold over men (Holbrook 1992, 78). As Janice Harris observed, "Odour of Chrysanthemums" mines a vein of familial recollections that influenced all of his work, although an acute awareness of his own sexuality exerted another strong influence (1984, 36).

Over the years when "Chrysanthemums" took shape (1909–14), Elizabeth and Walter Bates, then, became an amalgamation of Lawrence's parents and his aunt and uncle. Nora Stovel (1983) argued convincingly that Polly and James Lawrence were sufficiently distant from their nephew to inspire objectivity in his portrayal of their conflicts. The years that had passed between James's death and Lawrence's first version of his story also encouraged an unprejudiced portrait. Following his mother's death in December of 1910, however, the variants of the tale—especially the final version—became infused with Lawrence's new sense of the utter separation death imposes, as depicted in Elizabeth's sense of "intense alienation" as she washed her husband's corpse. From his mother's death, Lawrence came to understand this sense of separation implicit in the later versions of "Chrysanthemums" (60–73).

Moreover, one must always account for the influence Lawrence's wife, Frieda, had on his personal and artistic growth between 1912 and November, 1914, when "Odour of Chrysanthemums" came out in *The Prussian Officer and Other Stories*. Critic J.F.C. Littlewood examined the various conclusions and decided that the later revisions must have been written during or after 1913, when Lawrence began his first version of *The Rainbow*. Littlewood sustained his position by comparing the later variants with the final version and with passages in the second and third version of *The Rainbow* composed in 1914, passages that revealed a new insight into "otherness" in the sense that Lawrence made his characters respond in concert with their essential selves. This artistic development resolved a personal integration problem present in earlier versions. Littlewood attributed this

development both to the several drafts of *The Rainbow* and to
Lawrence having "come through" his often tumultuous relationship
with Frieda (Littlewood 1966, 112–24).

The final 1914 text of "Odour of Chrysanthemums" contained a
dual vision: man's being seen as it relates to the eternal rhythms of the
cosmos, and this vision of radiance emerging from the prosaic base of
the workaday world. This dual vision reflects the deep personal
fulfillment Lawrence found with Frieda and a relationship that freed
him from the difficulties of early manhood (Cushman 1978, 44).

Scholars like Keith Cushman and Janice Harris who investigate the
young Lawrence's reading interests find still more influences upon his
growing conceptions of art and artistry. Cushman saw Lawrence in the
early variants of "Odour of Chrysanthemums" employing formulas
peculiar to the symbolic realism of the late nineteenth century as a
strategy for placing the piece in a magazine. Similarly, Lawrence
explored the traditional form of tragedy in this tale. Like John
Millington Synge's *Riders to the Sea*, which Lawrence admired greatly
for its genuine dramatic pathos, "Chrysanthemums" concludes with a
corpse-washing scene accompanied by a woman's sudden intuitive
understanding of the true human condition (Cushman 1978a, 47–9).

Another critic, Ute-Christel Wulff (1988), found close similarities
among the first version of "Odour of Chrysanthemums" (1909) and the
stories of two German authors: Johann Hebel's (circa 1811) tale
"Unverhofftes Wiedersehen" ("Unexpected Reunion"), and Hugo von
Hofmannsthal's 1900 story "Das Maerchen von der verschleierten
Frau" ("Fairy Tale of the Veiled Woman"). Lawrence is known to have
been interested in Hofmannsthal's work, and his avid reading of
German literature dating back to 1908 possibly included the coal-
mining story by Hebel. Wulff believed that Lawrence consciously
borrowed details from the German stories for "Odour of Chrysanthemums" in 1909. Like Lawrence's tale, the two earlier stories used
the motif of a trapped miner with a lover left behind. From Hebel's tale,
Lawrence may have created Elizabeth Bates and her mother-in-law to
represent the dead miner's young and, later, aged lover. In both
instances, the reuniting of dead miner and lover evoked a sense more of
joy than sorrow in the lover's heart. In Hofmannsthal's tale, meanwhile,
Lawrence may have found the idea of using a flower (carnation, in

Hofmannsthal) and a brook to achieve a tone of anxiety and portend the miner's death. From these literary models, Wulff noted, Lawrence soon freed himself, as the later versions of the story prove (287–95).

But Lawrence's influential reading interests extended well beyond fiction. From 1913 through 1916, Lawrence read deeply into ritual and mythology. Sir James Frazer's *The Golden Bough* and *Totemism and Exogamy*, as well as Jane Harrison's *Ancient Art and Ritual*, and works by E.B. Tylor and Gilbert Murray interested him greatly. These works provided the characters, references, conceptions, and rituals that infused his stories with "archetypal significance" and with symbolic journeys of transformation through crisis (Piccolo 1979, 88).

In "Odour of Chrysanthemums," Piccolo argued, Lawrence focused on the primary human crises of marriage, birth, and death using such "ritual symbols of transition" as chrysanthemums, and presenting the dead miner as the representative "archetypal stranger" and the "scapegoat god," who poses a threat to an insulated family or society. Just as a king in decline is killed by suffocation to preserve his person, so was Bates asphyxiated, his body remaining unmarked. Just as in Frazer, wherein a society kills a physically impaired king to protect its future well-being, Lawrence's presentation of Bates's death implies society's culpability, especially in the 1911 *English Review* version, which attributes Bates's excessive drinking to a changing modern world into which he does not fit (Piccolo 1979, 90–92).

THE RELATIONSHIP OF "ODOUR OF CHRYSANTHEMUMS" TO OTHER LAWRENCE WORKS

Lawrence viewed himself in the early phase of his career as a member of the incipient school of realism, and he focused on a new area for British realism: collier life and the countryside of the Midlands. He evoked this milieu with "rare emotive power" in early variants of such tales as "Odour of Chrysanthemums," "Daughters of the Vicar," and "A Sick Collier," all of which appeared in *The Prussian Officer and Other Stories* (Cushman 1978b, 110).

Philip Hobsbaum (1980) noted Lawrence's forceful realism in Lawrence's accurate illustrations of collier life (41). The collier strikes in 1912 reawakened Lawrence's interest in industrial themes, as the tales he wrote in the early part of that year show—such tales, that is, as "A Sick Collier," "Her Turn," and "Strike-Pay." Lawrence revised "Odour of Chrysanthemums" shortly before, in 1911, and all these tales, in conjunction with "The Miner at Home" and "The Christening," formed his "collier group," which contain some of his best naturalistic work (Hobsbaum 1980, 28–31).

In fact, Janice Harris (1984) called "Odour of Chrysanthemums" the "first fruit" of Lawrence's adoption of realism. The subsequent yield included: "A Modern Lover," "Second Best," "The Shades of Spring," "The Old Adam," "The Witch a la Mode," and "Daughters of the Vicar" (26). Graham Hough (1957) found Lawrence's exemplary objectivity in "Odour of Chrysanthemums" present as well in the first part of *Sons and Lovers* and in the short story "The White Stocking" (169).

In regard solely to subject matter, no other work of Lawrence's came as close to "Odour of Chrysanthemums" as the drama *The Widowing of Mrs. Holroyd,* first written in 1910 and revised in 1913. An early critic suggested that this tale furnished the story line for the final act of the play (Fuller 1917, 238.) A much later scholar also believed that material from the short story had found its way into the drama (Widmer 1962, 225), but it was 1965 before Ford published a direct comparison of the two works. Both the tale and the play focused on domestic disharmony and a woman's inability to love her loutish miner husband. But Elizabeth Bates's major moment of recognition— her discovery of the distance that had separated them in marriage—was not shared by Mrs. Holroyd. Differences in both authorial intent and medium may explain this departure (71).

A more detailed examination in 1983 adduced more similarities between these two works and established their relationship with *Sons and Lovers*, as well. For example, each of the three pieces is set in a mining village and centers on a mining family's kitchen. Also, characters share the names Elizabeth and Walter as well as the characteristics of pride and sensuality, respectively. Similar conflicts precipitate crises that culminate in death. A deviation occurs in that the short story and play focus on a wife's growing awareness of her significant part in the demise of the marriage and her husband's destruction; whereas, the surviving husband in the novel is largely responsible. A most important parallel in these works, however, is the caring for the corpse by the wife-"lover." The two Elizabeths' grief over their husbands' dead bodies has a correlative in Paul Morel's lonely vigil with the body of his mother-lover. All three works are infused with Lawrence's "growing tragic recognition of the dignity of death" (Stovel 1983, 60–79).

Critic Mara Kalnins (1976) saw a close relationship between "Odour of Chrysanthemums" and *The Rainbow*, and she noted a parallel between Elizabeth Bates's attempts to grasp the full significance of her husband's death with those in *The Rainbow* of Lydia, who wrestled with the same profound grief when the drowned corpse of Tom Brangwen was brought home. In both instances, Lawrence relied upon the repetition and antithesis characteristic of a prose that, like scripture, seems organic, seems to grow, and achieves an evocation of sensations and emotions beyond the rational, conscious understanding. Another facet that linked the 1914 form of "Chrysanthemums" with *The Rainbow*—as well as with the short stories "The Thorn in the Flesh" and "Daughters of the Vicar"—was Lawrence's interest in the idea that each person's "otherness" or uniqueness should be acknowledged and respected by one's lover if the relation-ship is to succeed (147, 151). Accordingly, the appearance of such tales in *The Prussian Officer and Other Stories* marked Lawrence's efforts to take characterization beyond personality, self conception, and emotional response so as to fix the essence of that character truly. This philosophical and stylistic exploration subsequently linked these works with *The Rainbow*, wherein Lawrence attempted the same effect on a greater scale (150, 152).

Thomas McCabe (1972) became the first critic to note Lawrence's use of phrase repetition in "Chrysanthemums" and in "The Thorn in the Flesh" to establish a rhythmic unity (65). Similarly, Cushman (1978a) found repetition in Lawrence's mature work along with those facets of accretion and intensity of passion found in the conclusion of the final version of "Chrysanthemums." Cushman, too, mentioned the parallels between this short story and the scene in *The Rainbow* where Lydia and Anna Brangwen tend the corpse of the drowned husband and father, Tom, a scene written only weeks after the final draft of the short story. Less developed, this scene lacked the dramatic tension in "Odour of

Chrysanthemums," suggesting that Lawrence merely reused his earlier insights. Both the short story and the first part of the novel are, of course, studies of man's solitary condition. Both marriages—the Bateses' and the Brangwens'—are marked by separateness, except in the latter instance a unity that eluded the Bateses appears. Cushman believed that awareness of man's separateness, as seen shortly thereafter in *The Rainbow* with Rupert Birkin's idea of star-polarity, came to Lawrence from his early experience with Frieda (71–5).

Another parallel exists between this tale and "Daughters of the Vicar," as Michael Black pointed out. In both stories, a miner's body is washed by a woman struck by the "otherness" of another human being: Elizabeth Bates and Louisa Lindley both experience this visionary moment (1986, 208). Such mystical, religious insights recur in Lawrence's fiction from this early point into his last works, such as "The Escaped Cock" and *Apocalypse*, and he made these direct references to Christianity, less from denigration than from a desire, as Black phrased it, "to get back to a stage behind [Christianity]" (193). What Lawrence incorporated from the Bible into his own writings were Christian mythology and a linguistic apprehension of different manners of perceptual modes removed from "thought" per se. Thus, both Louisa Lindley and Elizabeth Bates experience an Annunciation of sorts while washing their miners' bodies. Louisa's new knowledge of Alfred's "otherness" leads to her rebirth. Elizabeth's Annunciation, however, amounts to "a negation of joyful prophecy" (205–06), for Black saw a bleak future for Elizabeth and the child she carried.

Keith Cushman, on the other hand, viewed the climactic corpse-washing scene as "a Lawrentian archetype" to which Lawrence returned repeatedly. Cushman presented as four examples: (1) the poem "A Man Who Died"; (2) Birkin's viewing Crich's corpse in the room at the mountain inn at the end of *Women in Love*; (3) Kate's response to the injured Don Ramon in *The Plumed Serpent*; and (4) Mrs. Bolton's memory of her deceased husband in *Lady Chatterley's Lover*. Other instances or variations include: Mabel Pervin's washing of her mother's gravestone in the tale "The Horse Dealer's Daughter," and in *Sons and Lovers* the arrival of the casket containing Ernest (1978a, 48–9).

Yet another relationship between this tale and others lies in the way that Lawrence used touch as a means for characters to find (or *not* to find, in some cases) true relatedness with themselves, with one another, and with the cosmos. James Cowan (1990) examined "Odour of Chrysanthemums," "The Blind Man," and "The Prussian Officer" from this perspective, illustrating convincingly how touch could be constructive or destructive (135–52).

Lawrence's presentation of social problems in "Chrysanthemums," as well as in "Daughters of the Vicar," leads to such important later works similarly concerned with "cross-class relationships" as *The Lost Girl*, *The Virgin and the Gipsy*, and *Lady Chatterley's Lover* (Worthen 1991a, 100–101).

Moreover, Graham Holderness's (1982) Marxist study of *The Rainbow* compared Lawrence's presentation of community, society, and individual characters in "Odour of Chrysanthemums" and *Sons and Lovers* with his approach in *The Rainbow*. Each work concerned members of a mining community; Lawrence's use of realism in the two earlier works allowed him to synthesize imaginatively individual life and factual history in "Odour of Chrysanthemums" and to show the complex, ambiguous nature of his personal existence and society in *Sons and Lovers*. The shift in style evidenced in *The Rainbow* sacrificed these strengths along with the informed-narrator technique wherein the mining industry, town, households and dependents are described from the inside (174–89).

Another study of mining communities in Lawrence's fiction groups "Chrysanthemums" with *Sons and Lovers*, *The Widowing of Mrs. Holroyd*, and *The Daughter-in-Law*. Each work depicts the battle of the miners with those whose ambitions are threatened by the limitations of a collier community. Consequently, the miners' families all undergo a crisis (Modiano 1987, 25).

Mark Schorer (1956) noted that Lawrence saw as a single process the corruptions of place and the corruptions of men, which resulted in their yielding to mechanical forms. Thus, a common theme of Lawrence's writings, one that certainly infused "Chrysanthemums," was the need to rediscover the vital connection between man and place (8).

One might now consider the matter of how Walter Bates as father and husband complements "The Odour of Chrysanthemums," and consider as well his relationship to similar characters in other works. Dervin (1984) saw the death of Walter Bates as the fulfillment of Paul

Morel's disturbing prayer in *Sons and Lovers* for the death of his father (116). Keith Cushman (1978a) noted that Lawrence treated the similar situation of a father and husband's death in three other works between 1907 and 1915: (1) "The Father": Part I, Chapter IV of *The White Peacock*; (2) Act III of *The Widowing of Mrs. Holroyd* with its conclusion fashioned upon the story; and (3) the "Marsh and Flood" chapter of *The Rainbow* where Lydia and Anna view Tom Brangwen's drowned corpse (53).

L. D. Clark (1980) noted that Lawrence used his father's birth-place—"in the cottage in the quarry hole just by Brinsley level-crossing"—to correspond with dark, unconscious maleness in "Chrysanthemums," *The Widowing of Mrs. Holroyd*, and *The Virgin and the Gipsy* (350).

John Vickery (1973) viewed Lawrence's father and husband figures in mythic terms, and saw in "Chrysanthemums"—as well as in the later stories "Samson and Delilah," "The Fox," and "The Border Line"—the sudden appearance of the archetypal stranger possessing either an "aura of fertility" or magical powers over others. Walter Bates's death, according to Vickery, transformed him for Elizabeth into a stranger "possessed of his own power of finality and completeness" (302). Vickery also classified this tale with such contemporary stories as "A Sick Collier," "The Christening," "Second Best," as well as with the later tale "Jimmy and the Desperate Woman" as stories of endurance, all stressing man's stoical efforts to endure hard times, pain and subjugation without surrender (324).

CRITICAL STUDIES

The only American review of "The Odour of Chrysanthemums"—the *Nation* of March 15, 1917—treated it in the context of *The Prussian Officer and Other Stories*. The anonymous critic found much of the detail in this story and others in the collection to be naturalistic and "in the Latin manner." "Chrysanthemums" portrayed the utter loneliness of the human spirit contending in a deathward direction "as an end of the coil, if not a solution" (313–14).

Having accepted "Chrysanthemums" for publication in the *English Review*, Lawrence's first editor, Ford Madox Ford (1937) would later say of his "discovery" that its form was, despite a certain influence from French writers, completely natural, and that its naturalness was stylistically the "most singular characteristic" of the piece (88). Despite moments of introspection, which to Ford were tiresome, he found the nature passages racing like fire through the work, infusing it with excitement and life. In one of his more apposite summaries of Lawrence's writing, Ford proclaimed it "rich and coloured and startling like a medieval manuscript" (87–89).

Thirteen years later, critic Anthony West (1950) called Lawrence's prose masterfully integrated, as evidenced in the opening paragraph of "Odour of Chrysanthemums" where visual image, action, and idea are in perfect harmony. Nevertheless, West found the opening rather stiff, like the initial paragraphs of a novel by Thomas Hardy, who had influenced Lawrence greatly. West noted that a subsequent skillful fusion of person and place would become a hallmark of such later work as *St. Mawr, The Virgin and the Gipsy,* and "The Captain's Doll" ([1950] 1977, 88–9).

Although the opening paragraphs of "Chrysanthemums" seemed to West the work of a self-conscious artist, he believed that Lawrence's best short fiction drew upon his subconscious which reveals itself more spontaneously in short fiction, novels being less likely to depend on bursts of subconscious fervor or insight. Accordingly, West judged Lawrence's tales generally superior to the longer works (90).

An important study by Graham Hough (1957) took issue with West's ambivalent assessment of "Odour of Chrysanthemums." Hough considered the tale both powerful and a complete achievement. He liked the contrast between Elizabeth and her mother-in-law's attitude as they tended Walter's corpse, that contrast adding "depth and complexity" (170).

Kingsley Widmer's (1962) study of Lawrence's short fiction, the first to focus solely on Lawrence's tales, mentioned the realism in "Chrysanthemums" as realized in the domestic scene. He also cited the poetic insight into the connection between death and passion. To develop this latter theme, Lawrence repeated images of darkness to equate with death, and of fire to signal passion (22–3). Widmer saw the story examining how "a knowledge of death and its absoluteness" rendered more acutely one's sense of living an unvital existence. Elizabeth, "the rigid and righteous wife," realized that she had denied Walter as both a sexual partner and an individual throughout. She saw, in short, her ultimate failure as lover and wife. Her husband's death also brought her an awareness of the isolated nature of life, which ultimately succumbs to death (Widmer 1962, 22–4).

A year later, E. W. Tedlock (1963) formulated the most thorough examination of "Odour of Chrysanthemums" to date. He believed the work illustrated Lawrence's art at its "organic best." Mood, setting, the characters' speech, and plot, combined with such images as an untended garden, autumn, and the scent of chrysanthemums to infuse the work with suggestions of death so as to convey a sensory apprehension of "a cumulative fatality" that comes into being climactically. Thematically, Tedlock noted a Lawrentian concern that Lawrence would later broaden: the inclusion of the attitudes and actions of an entire modern cultural milieu to show failures in relationships that focused in "Chrysanthemums" on only one family. Elizabeth's initial worries over her husband's skipping dinner to spend all their money in a pub bespeak moral and economic value judgments. When Walter is brought home for the last time—his corpse a symbol of her inability to perceive the "basic living man"—Elizabeth must move from such judgments to an appraisal of her own life, which she comes to recognize as a kind of death-in-life (26).

Ronald Draper's (1964) discussion of the story included a not-wholly-justified criticism of Ford Madox Ford's much earlier assessment. Deeming "Chrysanthemums" Lawrence's first masterpiece, Draper charged Ford with ignoring a quality in the tale that would eventually become to be a Lawrentian signature: animation and the infusion of the author's own personality into the opening scene. More perceptively, Draper observed that the vital background in this scene serves to emphasize more clearly the "bankrupt condition" of the Bateses' marriage, Elizabeth's recognition of the moribund nature of her marriage being skillfully integrated with descriptions of the bleak region (121–22).

Robert Hudspeth's (1968–69) subsequent examination of "Odour of Chrysanthemums" illustrated the fact that the story had yet to yield up all of its secrets. He praised Lawrence's skill in combining image, scene, and mood in the successful endeavor to illuminate a flash of reality. For example, Elizabeth Bates associated chrysanthemums with "moments of heightened passion," foreshadowing another insistent association when her husband's corpse was carried into the parlor. Largely by paralleling the Bateses' utter separateness with "technique of organization," Lawrence conveyed the idea that isolation consists of anguish and dread, which Hudspeth included among "life's defining characteristics." Similarly, he found that Lawrence's demonstrating isolation through the illustration of the miner's wife reveals the paradox of detachment: one must capitulate yet maintain one's integrity (Hudspeth 1968, 630–36).

Five years passed before another thematic study of "Chrysanthemums" saw print. Marred by the mistaken belief that the 1914 tale in its final form was the same story as the 1909 version published in the *English Review* in 1911, Tony Slade's (1969) work did recognize the story as a masterpiece and contributed some astute observations. For example, Slade noted how Lawrence first established an opposition between industry and nature, then Elizabeth Bates' dreary death-in-life existence. He recognized her irritation when her daughter Annie responded to the chrysanthemums she wore. Symbolic of Mrs. Bates' pregnancy, the miner's wife dismissed the flowers, an act that contrasts dramatically to Annie's delight in life. Anticipating sociological approaches to Lawrence's work, Slade noted that this parallel between flowers and pregnancy appears often in English folk songs, and thus links Lawrence with his working-class origins (101).

Embellishing earlier discussions of Elizabeth's moment of recognition while caring for her husband's corpse, Slade believed that she learned of life's mutability and the iniquity of her life as she had lived it, allowing life's day-to-day monotony to numb her emotional being and reduce her character. Walter's death brought home the reality of their uniqueness, which each had denied in the other (99–100).

Keith Cushman's (1978a) landmark textual study of Lawrence's early short fiction acknowledged in "Chrysanthemum's" opening paragraph, a superbly descriptive set piece fashioned so as to establish mood and tone, to convey the reader without delay into the writer's imaginative world, and "to produce a shock of recognition in [a reader]" (51). Cushman deemed this story—a powerful declaration about the condition of mankind, as well as one of the most carefully crafted of the early works—an embodiment of Lawrence's art "at its most dramatic, his vision at its most sympathetic" (Cushman 1978a, 47).

Addressing the occasional charge that Lawrence's short fiction lacks formal structure, Anthony Piccolo (1979) used "Chrysanthemums" to illustrate how Lawrence's work often took up emotional being and the evolution of human relationships. Piccolo argued that Lawrence's short fiction generally contained specific patterns of myth and ritual that created formal constructs. Subsequently, Lawrence's tales balance a logical and progressive "realistic narrative" with a "submerged ritual strategy" that by means of its "inevitability" promotes an unusual scale of norms (88). As a case in point, Piccolo showed how, in "Odour of Chrysanthemums," Lawrence leads up to the theme's objectification by means of the revelatory death of Walter Bates, effectively using imagery to foreshadow that culminating scene wherein Elizabeth ritualistically prepares her husband's corpse. In the initial paragraph, Lawrence presents the autumnal landscape, marred by the colliery, the pit pond, and the pit bank, in terms of death and disorder. The ever-present chrysanthemums, later to be connected with such life transitions as marriage, birth, and death, portend Elizabeth Bates's change of direction toward life "through the ministry of death" (89–90). Piccolo appears to have been the first critic to perceive potentially redeeming aspects in Elizabeth Bates's moment of recognition.

A study published a year later, in 1980, pursued this idea. Judging this tale to be flawless, wherein nothing is superfluous or tendentious, George Becker suggested that Elizabeth gained "fugitive spiritual sustenance" from the ragged chrysanthemums in her garden. While tending her husband's corpse, Elizabeth realized that their connubial hopelessness had developed long before her husband's demise. Forever separated from that facet of her existence, she became aware that she must give herself to life. Considering this to be Lawrence's most compassionate work, Becker was a bit hyperbolic in asserting that the tale dealt clearly with obstacles to happiness (114–15).

A study by Nora Stovel (1983) examined the integration of place and character in "Chrysanthemums." For example, she saw the pit itself as a central character. The pit fires mirrored the cottage hearth fires, and the spasmodic winding of an engine turning up the miners was anthropomorphically akin to the beating of the human heart. Elizabeth's garden of pink chrysanthemums served as the antithesis to the mechanized mining environment, but the odor of decaying chrysanthemums foreshadows Walter Bates's death (61–2). Addressing the characters themselves, Stovel noted that Walter had lost his battle of sensuality against Elizabeth's "proud puritanism." His essence diminished until he became quite hollow, and his physical demise followed his moral destruction at the hands of his wife. Implicit in Elizabeth's acknowledgment of this outcome was her awareness that the separateness imposed by death was but "the logical extension" of this apartness in life (67). Stovel's convincing concluding argument was that at the heart of this 1914 story was Lawrence's own increasing "tragic recognition" of death's dignity (Stovel 1983, 79).

Janice Harris's engaging 1984 book-length study of Lawrence's short fiction discussed aspects of style in relation to "Odour of Chrysanthemums." Harris began, however, with the skilled way in which Lawrence used the image cluster of the chrysanthemums themselves. An ambiguous symbol, the flowers suggested to Harris both hope and disappointment, experience of the present and of the past. A sensuous image that merges the senses of sight, touch and smell, the chrysanthemums anticipated the preparation of Walter Bates's corpse. Also, they connote a passing from autumn to winter. The tattered flowers in Elizabeth's apron waistband, noted Harris, represent the uncertainty with which she regarded the unborn child. Accordingly, these flower images, in conjunction with other images, convey the complications that comprised Elizabeth's life, and simultaneously support the story's unified conclusion (28).

Weldon Thornton's (1985) study of some of Lawrence's short fiction explained how his singular method of characterization surpassed in subtlety and complexity that used by such writers as Joyce and Flaubert. In "Odour of Chrysanthemums," as in stories like "The Prussian Officer" and "The Rocking-Horse Winner," Lawrence placed himself within each character as completely as possible, which permitted him to experience fully each character's situation and, subsequently, to depict each character's feelings, desires, thoughts, and confusions. The result, according to Thornton, is prose fraught with energy and intensity (46–47).

Thornton also focused on the importance of contextuality in Lawrence's work. The psychological context of a Lawrence character is unique and conforms to no superimposed Lawrentian code of conduct. As an example Thornton noted Elizabeth's realization concerning her denial of Walter's true self is her initial reaction to shock and grief, and as such, was probably less than lasting. Anxiety, self blame, and the need for a simplistic formula to hold onto for comfort can all be said to accompany her "discovery." In death, she could afford to grant her husband what would have been impossible to grant him alive. In this manner, Thornton convincingly argued, Lawrence's tale goes beyond didacticism: when viewed contextually, the story becomes a true-to-life psychological exploration of such a loss, replete with complexity and contradiction (1985, 54–5).

The most recent thematic treatment of "Chrysanthemums" was Volker Schulz's (1991) examination. Drawing upon the many previous studies, he noted that the detailed setting ably permits a reader to visualize the lives of the miners and their families. Structurally, the tale's external action unfolds in three segments: (1) the Bates family's anxious wait for Walter to return home; (2) the rising certainty that he has been killed in a mining accident; and (3) the mother and wife's caring for the corpse as they cope with their loss. The story focuses thematically on the internal process of Elizabeth Bates's recognition of the truth about her life with Walter, which radically reorients her. Having symbolized decay throughout the tale, chrysanthemums do so again when the vase is knocked from the table and broken by the men bearing Walter Bates's corpse. Elizabeth's hasty tidying up suggests a disposition of the shards of her destroyed marriage. Her awareness of the inescapable force of death underlies her new-found connection with the force of life represented by the child she carries. She appears, then, to abandon her failures as a wife and turn toward the chance of fulfillment as a mother (363–70).

The earliest psychological-mythological treatment of "Chrysanthemums" appears to be Frank Amon's (1953) study of Lawrence's short stories. Focusing on psychological changes during the stories, Amon saw that the result was often a transfiguration triggered by a significant emotional experience. Lawrence's characters often undergo a kind of symbolic *rite de passage*, like an initiation or baptism, which opens new perceptions of life. The theme of "Chrysanthemums"—essential loneliness and isolation, even among those with whom one is most intimate—develops largely through symbolism and ritual. The chrysanthemums become "talismans of change" that encompass marriage, birth, and death. Amon also noted how they pique readers' interest and help them focus (1953, 222–24).

The key scene involving the *rite de passage* is, of course, the washing and dressing of Walter's corpse. Amon saw the rites of consecration and purification enacted there. Elizabeth subsequently experienced her "moment of inner revelation" in which the essential loneliness of life is made manifest. Her discovery promotes her transition from wife and mother to widowed mother. In this manner, argued Amon, Lawrence integrates literal and symbolic action so as "to objectify his theme" (224–26). Similarly, with his use of ritual, Lawrence captures Elizabeth's moment of transition and reinforces it with the emotional-imbued symbol of the chrysanthemums (1953, 234).

Eighteen years elapsed before another critic applied the psychological approach to Lawrence's short fiction. R.E. Pritchard (1971) noted that "Odour of Chrysanthemums" presented a more insightful, sensitive, and mature view of Lawrence's parents than the view in *Sons and Lovers*. The mother-figure's loss and limitations are much more in evidence. Washing her dead husband's body, Elizabeth Bates recognizes the real beneath the superficial, apprehends life and death in a completely new way, and becomes aware of their similarities. Pritchard suggested that Elizabeth becomes attuned to the existence of "the dark body of life" lying below the surface of personality or individuality. Rather than being opposites, death and life are identical; Walter's dark, vital body is composed of the impersonal being's essence—"the nonhuman unliving source of life," as shown in the story's life-in-death and death-in-life polarity (62–4).

Subsequently, Shirley Rose (1975) contrasted physical trauma with the psychological effects upon characters in Lawrence's short fiction. In "Odour of Chrysanthemums," she saw how sorrow or remorse could lead to self-knowledge, whereas pain could not provide such insights. Elizabeth's instinctive sorrow over Walter's death leads her to two truths: (1) Walter was other than she; and (2) he was dead, not she. These two basic philosophical and psychological truths help ease her sorrow, providing more relief than remorse at the end of the unhappy marriage. Thus, her final awareness of "life's initial and death's final mastery over her" rested on her detached response to Walter's demise (Rose 1975, 79).

A 1986 book-length study by Michael Black examined the ritualistic aspects of this short story first noted by Frank Amon. Black's work focused mainly on the corpse-washing scene wherein Elizabeth encounters her moment of "withering self-recognition." Black called this scene "the greatest of all Lawrence's ritual lavings" and, in fact, "one of the great set-pieces in the language" (203–07). Tracing Elizabeth's tactile response to her husband's corpse, Black illustrated persuasively the psychic process that leads to her visionary experience. First, in "a movement of ego," she lays her hands upon Walter's body in an effort to claim what she fears to lose. Such an overt attempt at the possession of another, Black classified as stemming from hubris. She next touches her husband's body as she prepares to wash him. No longer possessive, she "ministers" to him, but again she is unsuccessful in her attempt to reach him. Only then does she see the truth. He was "other" than she; they are eternally separate through death just as they had been in life. Lawrence's language becoming biblical, the laving ensued. Pregnant, yet facing "an annihilating negation," Elizabeth undergoes a tearful, tragic Annunciation. Her earlier possessive gesture amended, Elizabeth is now aware of the integrity of one's being, and administers to Walter humbly. The truth that Black saw in this work was the accountablilty of oneself to oneself and to others. Also, he implied, any visionary moment we encounter will usually come too late to help us or those around us (203–10).

Daniel Schneider's (1986) penetrating study advanced R. E. Pritchard's thesis concerning man's essence while exploring Lawrence's concept of the self. Focusing upon Elizabeth's moment of recognition, Schneider noted that her illumination expresses a Lawrentian view of selfhood. Manners and ego only mask the true self. The soul's deepest desires, which lie beneath ego, formulate the self "as a manifestation of the greater inhuman will" that brings men and women together, and then forces them apart. As objectifications of will, men and women thus might be seen as beautiful, eternal, and immutable. This glorious selfhood beneath the ravages of time, Schneider maintained, Elizabeth discerned in Walter's remains (80).

An interesting psychological study by Vijaya Lakshmi (1987) unfortunately suffered from idiomatic difficulties and inconsistent referencing. The work seemed to center on the polarity between body and intellect, or the unconscious and conscious planes of man's psyche in Lawrence's short fiction. Lawrence's philosophy, according to Lakshmi, consisted of a tripartite paradigm, wherein the "egocentric absolute" could form an "exocentric connection" with the whole cosmos via "the lateral movement of the self." This passage of the unconscious self, as revealed in the tales by means of symbolism, became Lakshmi's main focus, and applied to "Odour of Chrysanthemums," the focus fell on Elizabeth's relentless "flights into the unconscious" following Walter's death, wherein she found the truths about her failed marriage, truths that took her to her exocentric self and her realization of cosmic reality (125, 131).

Citing earlier studies, Thomas McCabe (1987) preferred to call the "otherness" in Lawrence's fiction what critics generally term "separateness" and "isolation." Then deeming the latter two terms too negative, McCabe noted that too few critics mention the positive aspects of Elizabeth Bates's discovery: the comfort she takes in the lesson of her apartness and the sense of peace it bestows. "Otherness," for McCabe, concerns one's perception of life as existing beyond and apart from oneself. Although the realization that one was always separate and can never know completely another human being in this life is at first painful, McCabe argued that the obverse response could be one of joy for a world comprised of "unique individual separate men, women, birds, beasts and flowers" (150).

McCabe's study skillfully leads a reader through the tale toward the realization that the Bateses' marriage failed largely as a result of their inability to perceive each other's "otherness." Feeling familiar with one another, they assumed that the one's conception of the other encompassed the whole person (151).

McCabe next showed that by means of imagery, Lawrence paralleled Elizabeth's blindness to the truth with "an atmosphere of obscured sight" present in the opening paragraph and sustained throughout. At the same time, the darkness represents the "dark knowledge" of otherness that Elizabeth learns, paradoxically, through her sightless sense of touch. McCabe noted that the miner's wife twice touches her husband's corpse in an effort to lay claim to him and thus form a connection with him, but the failed attempts lead her to recognize his "otherness." Originating from her unconscious, this discovery registers as conscious knowledge, thus leading "to this double knowledge of otherness" (McCabe 1987, 155–56).

The most recent psychological treatment of "Odour of Chrysanthemums" was James Cowan's fine (1990) study where he argued convincingly that of the five senses, touch held the most significance for Lawrence. Through the tactile medium, whether it involved "unconscious motivation and insight, nurturance, bonding, intrusiveness, ritual, [or] sexuality," Lawrence developed his all-important concept of true relatedness (135–36). For example, Elizabeth's sight of her dead husband yields to an awareness that they had always been separate, even during their most intimate moments. Embellishing Michael Black's earlier thesis, Cowan observed that only when she clasped and bathed her husband's naked corpse could she apprehend the permanence of their separateness death had established. In this manner, touch activated into consciousness formerly unconscious needs or desires. The result is her deepening understanding of self and others (140).

Sociological investigations of "Odour of Chrysanthemums" began with F. R. Leavis's (1956) observation that the tale is both a portrayal of life as Lawrence knew it from his earliest memories in Eastwood, and a typically unbiased glimpse of working-class life, wherein humanity is presented universally ([1956] 1979, 308).

Seven years later, Julian Moynahan (1963) noted how the contrasts in the opening paragraph between such features as the colt and the locomotive, the pit bank and the pond, the clatter of machinery and the evening calm establishes the tension between mankind's will to survive, which encouraged the growth of the industrial system, and mankind's instinct to remain free and independent (182). The central image in the work, the chrysanthemum, comes into being and grows on its own, is picked, but will blossom again. Lawrence shows a reader both vital and deadening aspects of modern existence. Walter Bates's death, a complete waste of life, reveals the truth the unnatural and isolating facets of the industrial system had hidden. With Elizabeth's recognition of the "naive, inviolable, impregnable dignity" of a common laborer, Lawrence affirms life (184).

George Ford (1965) also followed the sociological approach but embraced aspects of autobiography and psychology, as well. Raised in a crowded household, Lawrence learned early how family life contributes to the alienation of the individual, and Ford suggested that a painful sense of isolation—of the profound separateness among all members of the human race—provides a central theme in Lawrence's fiction stemming from his own character (66).

In the latest sociological note to address this tale, Philip Hobsbaum's (1980) pointed out that Lawrence's collier stories introduce into English literature a realism that finally pictured industrial laborers as serious human beings in their own milieu (41).

Eight different formalist textual studies of "Odour of Chrysanthemums" have examined its variants. First came Royal Gettman and Bruce Harkness's (1955) essay that recognized Elizabeth's lesson about isolation as underscoring the aloneness within the framework of three living generations and the death of a lone man. The 1914 version, Gettman and Harkness wrote, depicts the two Mrs. Bateses far more forcefully than the earlier version printed in the *English Review*. Furthermore, the changes that occurred in the tale as it approached its final form accentuate the universal nature of the tragedy (18–21).

James T. Boulton's (1969) important textual examination printed for the first time the 1910 galleys of the tale and recounted the revisions made in the 1911 variant. Looking carefully at the three revised endings of the story, Boulton perceived a developing theme that gradually moved the emotion of maternal love to the story's center (44–48).

Focusing on Elizabeth's role as wife rather than mother, Emile Delavenay (1972) saw Elizabeth's reverie over Walter's corpse in the tale's earliest form as sentimental and unrealistic. She still loves the man and is thankful for his restoration to her in such a physically unblemished state. The much-revised 1914 tale, however, stresses Elizabeth's harshness. Delavenay astutely recognized that she does not weep over his body because to her it represents the breach that kept them apart in life (107).

Four years later, Mara Kalnins's (1976) analysis of "Odour of Chrysanthemums" took issue with James Boulton's emphasis on maternal love. Kalnins suggested that the passion of maternal love does indeed lie at the center of the earlier versions, but that subsequent changes shifted the focus from the momentary awakening of maternal feelings on Elizabeth's part to a profound and complex examination of herself as mother, wife, woman and, finally, as human being. Such an authorial tour de force illustrates how far Lawrence had advanced his artistic craft and vision between the initial ending in 1909, and the final revisions in 1914 (Kalnins [1976] 1988, 146).

Keith Cushman (1978a) produced the most complete and detailed textual investigation of the several variants of "Odour of Chrysanthemums." His comparison of the early version as it appeared in the proof sheets after its acceptance in 1909 in the *English Review* with the variant that finally appeared there in 1911 revealed the shift in focus from the waiting family (wherein the children, particularly, played a large role) to Elizabeth's mounting anger, eventual introspection, and the recognition as she ministers to her husband's corpse (57). For example, despite its charming nature, a long passage where the son and daughter pretend to be gypsies, then colliers, and then hear a Hans Christian Andersen bedtime story, disappeared in the 1911 version.

The "emotional climax" of the tale, the wife's thoughts over her husband's corpse, offered no revelation in either of the *English Review* versions. In the earlier form, the reinforcement of her previously held views shields Elizabeth from the truth about the emptiness of her marriage (58). She embraces death, for it has given her an unblemished husband, beautiful in death and as helpless as a child. Her love is reinstated and emanates throughout her interior monologue. Cushman identified Elizabeth's primary emotion stemming from the termination of her marriage as relief, which is implicit in the tone of the initial version (59).

Cushman found little better the 1911 reworking of Elizabeth's reverie, which depicts a bereaved wife imagining in her deceased husband the young knight she had married before he became the derelict she had so relentlessly battled. Cushman's observation that this entire reverie passage was overwritten certainly seems warranted (59–60).

Another change from the earlier variants and the final version occurs in the role of the mother-in-law. Supporting James Boulton's earlier view, Cushman acknowledged the miner's mother to be an archetypal figure (like Synge's Maurya in *Riders to the Sea*), and she retains this aura throughout all of the variants. But Cushman also agreed with Kalnins's assessment that some of the focus shifts from the mother-in-law in the final version so that Elizabeth can be more fully realized. This shift reflected Lawrence's constant "archetype of maternity" and changing "archetype of wifehood." After all, Cushman noted, the significance of the changes lies in Elizabeth's evolving response to Walter's death as revealed in her interior monologue (1978a, 59).

Cushman also saw that in the 1911 version Lawrence attempted to explain sociologically the miner's dissipation and, as with the former versions, the tale concluded firmly on the side of Elizabeth, who had done everything she could to save Walter from his baser instincts. Similarly, in the first published version of the tale, Elizabeth is thankful to death for having concealed the truth from her. But by the time Lawrence finished his final version, she is grateful for the truth and redeeming insight (61, 70).

Closely examining the 1913 and 1914 revisions, Cushman concluded that in the interim Lawrence himself had acquired insight into the man-woman relationship and human existence. He had, in fact, found "an unbridgeable gulf" between man and woman, even at their most intimate. This assumption, said Cushman, informed Lawrence's mature art. Thus, Cushman appraised the story in its final form, rather than its pre–1914 variants, the more aesthetically coherent revelation of man's irredeemable aloneness (68–9).

But what of this idea of man's basic isolation—an idea Cushman believed few other critics had noticed—in the context of "Odour of Chrysanthemums"? Cushman suggested that Lawrence used the tale to illustrate man as an inevitable isolate, a condition occasionally altered by love only to reassert itself, for people must always separate from one another and proudly walk "in their own fierce isolation" (76).

Janice Harris (1984), too, examined the tale's 1914 conclusion and found an obstacle in its form. Disagreeing with the majority of critics, she believed that Lawrence had been far too shrill and abstract in his delineation of Elizabeth's psyche in the final scene. She explained this deficiency with her theory that such visionary fictions as "The Prussian Officer" and *The Rainbow* that Lawrence wrote in 1914 employed rhythms, scenes, and image configurations portraying facets of human singularity unencumbered by direct realism. She considered "Odour of Chrysanthemums" a flawless realistic story until the last scene, where the intrusive visionary technique interferes with its rhythms (Harris 1984, 36).

Less controversially, Harris's judged the tale "an admirable pioneer in the art of realistic short fiction in England." She also observed, perceptively, that the 1914 revision of "Chrysanthemums" following the publication of *Sons and Lovers* reflected a quite different view of the Morel marriage from the one presented in that novel. Noting that this story begged the question of what Mrs. Morel might feel if her husband were killed, Harris found that the "Chrysanthemums" variants before 1914 seemed to present Elizabeth Bates's response as identical to the likely response shared by Mrs. Morel. But, Harris concluded, in the final version, Elizabeth's comprehension of the tragedy is far more complex (36).

Michael Black's (1986) study agreed that the later versions of the story shifted the weight of emotion away from the mother's attempt to reclaim her child, as well as the wife's endeavor to claim Walter as if he also were a child. Black's interesting contribution lay in his belief that through this pattern, Lawrence condemns all possessive females who would make men their own, be they mothers like Lydia Lawrence or wives like Elizabeth Bates (208).

Marko Modiano's (1987) examination of "Chrysanthemums" took a different tack with the observation that in the earlier variants Elizabeth is liberated by her husband's death. Modiano concurred, however, that the later variants moved the tale away from the realm of Lawrence's psychological "fantasy" into the sphere of social realism by means of this objective portrait of devastating dehumanization generated by industrial production juxtaposed to the marital discord of a collier and his spouse (45, 47).

The first full linguistic study of "Odour of Chrysanthemums" appeared in 1982, wherein Walter Nash examined the "distinctive linguistic features" to illustrate the way Lawrence deployed language to establish a sense of alienation in the text itself that paralleled the focus of the overall work. Accordingly, Nash found such linguistic facets as deixis, article changes, and distinctive verb types achieving the effects he specified (101–14). Following a procedure that would eventually become controversial, Nash then analyzed the style by means of an intuitive textual response, a delineation of the text's pattern, and the identification of the patterning based on linguistics and style that tautologically supported intuition and revealed patterning (Nash, 1982, 101–14). (Peter Barry's refutation of this complex approach follows here shortly).

Two years later, Janice Harris discussed Lawrence's linguistic ability to convey a convincing perception of such visionary characters as Elizabeth Bates as she appears at the tale's conclusion in the 1914 version. She credited Lawrence's success in this aspect of the story to his skillful use of long, intertwining sentences and paragraphs, verbs of being used in unusual and at times playful ways, definite in preference to indefinite articles, biblical imagery, and sentences with distinct rhythms. The result is a heightened diction in the character's speech that generally paralleled the entire linguistic tone of a visionary tale (1984, 92).

In 1985, Peter Barry took Walter Nash's earlier linguistic study to task. Barry vigorously argued that Nash's analysis was simply fallacious. First, he characterized Nash's apportionment of the text into independent units of study as arbitrary. Next, the passage Nash singled out for its symmetrical structure was, in fact, asymmetrical, and Nash's subsequent explication of the piece seemed to Barry "inherently and inescapably subjective" (53). Barry's next conclusion was that Nash's focus on the one passage produced a misreading of the overall work and, consequently, Nash's careful discrimination "between 'intuition' and the findings of stylistics should be rejected" (53).

Only two feminist studies of "Odour of Chrysanthemums" have been published to date. John Worthen's (1991a) examination made some astute observations about style and stressed, as well, his belief that the tale ultimately explored the tragedy of Elizabeth Bates rather than of Walter Bates. (Most critics assume that the tale's tragedy involves *both*.) In regard to style, Worthen asserted that in the final passage—Elizabeth's somber reflection over her husband's corpse—we see both the character and the narrator endeavoring to state their realizations in a manner comprehensible to readers. Thus, surmised Worthen, the difficulty for modern readers lies in this dual-purpose nature of the prose. As for the feminist theme, Worthen saw in the wife's acceptance of her own guilty role in the demise of the marriage her assumption of responsibility as a partner, an essential act in her process of self-realization (Worthen 1991a, 40–41).

David Holbrook's (1992) examination of "Chrysanthemums" offered several new observations. He noted the contrast between the mechanical world and the natural world—the former belonging to the male sphere, the latter to the female—established in the opening paragraph and continued through the tale. In this vein, Elizabeth's connection with creativity by means of her pregnancy is presented in terms of nature in full bloom, but the landscape in which she moves is besmirched, ragged, and even threatening as a result of local industrial pollution (78–9).

Most insightfully, Holbrook recognized that as she waited for Walter's return, remarking that a pub always held the right degree of warmth to suit her husband, she implies that his alcoholism sustained in the snug, comfortable pub at least partly rebuked her denial of warmth and comfort at the hearthside they shared. As she reaches up to light a lamp, the fire, the light, and the chrysanthemum in her waistband combine to imply promise in life, but a promise blighted by poverty, anxiety, and emotional-spiritual deprivation (81). Holbrook saw Lawrence limning life's mystery in this short story. All human beings must eventually leave their hearths and go out into the world where they will "live and die as creatures." Yet bonds exist that can transcend this utter separateness of a man's existence. At the tale's end, Walter's mother seems closer to the man; however, Elizabeth cannot bridge the gulf, having always been isolated from her husband (84).

The inaccessibility between Elizabeth and her dead husband becomes a manifestation of the situation wherein they had never known each other on the plane of being-to-being, an acquaintance with a potential for transcending death (83). The subsequent guilt she feels stems from "her own impulse to deny the male life in him, his fulfillment" (85). As he suffered in dying, so had he suffered by means of her daily denial of his body, his sex, and the existence of love. Elizabeth accepts blame because their beings had not been fulfilled in their life together as man and wife, largely because of her imperious disillusionment. Consequently, Walter's life and the Bateses' marriage come to an end, leaving the terrible message that a man and a woman's most intimate relationship had been devoid of meaning. Such a tragic predicament, asserted Holbrook, is shared by us all. That is, we must discover through love meaning in our lives when confronted with death (1992, 85–86).

Finally, Roger Ebbatson (1987) produced a curious scientific investigation of some of Lawrence's work. He became convinced that Lawrence's purported resistance to evolution fails to appear in the fiction. He argued that Darwin's view of natural selection, in fact, helps inform such works as "Odour of Chrysanthemums," *Women in Love*, and "The Woman Who Rode Away," wherein maladjusted organisms like Walter Bates, Gerald Crich and Mrs. Lederman, respectively, move toward extinction (90). The full significance of Ebbatson's tenuous thesis in relation to the full body of Lawrence's work never received a clear explication; rather, readers of the study are left to draw their own conclusions. Perhaps Ebbatson believed Lawrence's well-known distrust of science was, in fact, too general-ized to be accepted by modern critics. If, however, Ebbatson believed that facets of Lawrence's philosophy and psychology as rendered in the fiction result directly from contemporary orthodox scientific investigation, he ought to have presented a stronger—and more specific—case in support of such a position.

In any event, this masterpiece of short fiction, "Odour of Chrysanthemums," has received suitable appreciation in the Lawrence criticism, and readers now enjoy many useful approaches to the story.

WORKS CITED

Amon, Frank. 1953. "D. H. Lawrence and the Short Story." *The Achievement of D.H.Lawrence*. F.J. Hoffman and Harry T. Moore, eds. Norman: University of Oklahoma Press. 222–234.

Anderson, Sherwood. 1930. "A Man's Mind." *New Republic*, 21 May: 22–23.

Athenaeum. 1915. "Fiction," 23 January: 68.

Barry, Peter. 1985. "Stylistics and the Logic of Intuition: or, How Not to Pick a Chrysanthemum." *Critical Quarterly* 27.4: 51–8.

Bates, H.E. [1941] 1945. *The Modern Short Story*. London: Thomas Nelson and Sons Ltd. Reprint. Same publisher.

Becker, George. 1980. *D.H.Lawrence*. New York: Frederick Ungar Publishing Co.

Black, Michael. 1986. *D.H. Lawrence: The Early Fiction*. Cambridge: Cambridge University Press.

Boulton, James T., ed. 1979. *The Letters of D.H. Lawrence*. Vol.1. Cambridge: Cambridge University Press.

————. 1981. *The Letters of D.H. Lawrence*. Vol.2. Cambridge: Cambridge University Press.

————. 1969. "'Odour of Chrysanthemums': An Early Version." *Renaissance and Modern Studies* 13: 4–48.

Clark, L.D. 1980. *The Minoan Distance: The Symbolism of Travel in D.H Lawrence*. Tucson: University of Arizona Press.

Cowan, James. 1990. *D.H. Lawrence and the Trembling Balance*. University Park: The Pennsylvania State University Press.

Cushman, Keith. 1978a. *D.H. Lawrence at Work: The Emergence of the Prussian Officer Stories*. Charlottesville: University of Virginia Press.

————. 1975. "'I am going through a transition stage.'" *The D.H. Lawrence Review* 8: 176–97.

————. 1978b. "The Young D.H. Lawrence and the Short Story." *Modern British Literature* 2: 101–12.

Delavenay, Emile. 1972. *D.H. Lawrence: The Man and His Work*. Carbondale, Illinois: Southern Illinois University Press.

Dervin, Daniel. 1984. *A 'Strange Sapience': The Creative Imagination of D.H. Lawrence*. Amherst: University of Massachusetts Press.

Draper, Ronald. 1964. *D.H. Lawrence*. Boston: Twayne Publishers.

Ebbatson, Roger. 1987. "A Spark Beneath the Wheel: Lawrence and Evolutionary Thought." *D.H. Lawrence: New Studies*. Christopher Heywood, ed. New York: St. Martin's Press. 90–104.

Ford, Ford Madox. 1937. *Portraits from Life*. Boston: Houghton Mifflin Co.

Ford, George. 1965. *Double Measure: A Study of the Novels and Stories of D.H. Lawrence*. New York: Holt,Rinehart and Winston.

Freeman, Mary. 1955. *D.H. Lawrence: A Basic Study of His Ideas*. Gainesville: University of Florida Press.

Fuller, Henry. 1917. "Embracing the Realities." *The Dial* 62 (22 March): 237–38.

Gettman, Royal A. and Bruce Harkness. 1955. *Teacher's Manual for a Book of Stories*. New York: Rinehart. 18–21.

Harris, Janice. 1984. *The Short Fiction of D.H. Lawrence*. New Brunswick, New Jersey: Rutgers University Press.

Hobsbaum, Philip. 1980. *A Reader's Guide to D.H. Lawrence*. London: Thames & Hudson.

Holbrook, David. 1992. *Where Lawrence Was Wrong About Women*. Lewisburg: Bucknell University Press.

Holderness, Graham. 1982. *D.H. Lawrence: History, Ideology and Fiction*. Dublin: Gill and Macmillan.

Hough, Graham. 1957. *The Dark Sun: A Study of D.H. Lawrence*. New York: The Macmillan Co.

Hudspeth, Robert. 1968–1969. "Lawrence's 'Odour of Chrysanthemums': Isolation and Paradox." *Studies in Short Fiction* 6: 630–36.

Kalnins, Mara. [1976] 1988. "D.H. Lawrence's 'Odour of Chrysanthemums': The Three Endings." *Studies in Short Fiction* 13(Fall): 471–79. Reprint. *Critical Essays on D.H. Lawrence*. Dennis Jackson and Fleda Jackson, eds. Boston: G.K. Hall & Co. 145–53.

Lakshmi, Vijaya. 1987. "Dialectic of Consciousness in the Short Fiction of Lawrence." *Essays on D.H. Lawrence*. T. R. Sharma, ed. India: Shalabh Book House. 125–133.

Leavis, F.R. 1930. *D.H. Lawrence*. Cambridge, England: The Minority Press.

———. [1956] 1979. *D.H. Lawrence: Novelist*. New York: Alfred A. Knopf. Reprint. Chicago: University of Chicago Press.

Littlewood, J.F.C. 1966. "D.H. Lawrence's Early Tales." *The Cambridge Quarterly* 1: 107–124.

McCabe, Thomas H. 1987. "The Otherness of D. H. Lawrence's 'Odour of Chrysanthemums.'" *The D.H. Lawrence Review* 19.2: 149–56.

———. 1972. "Rhythm as Form in Lawrence: 'The Horse Dealer's Daughter.'" *PMLA* 87.1 (January): 64–69.

McDonald, Edward. 1925. *A Bibliography of the Writings of D.H. Lawrence*. Philadelphia: The Centaur Book Shop.

Modiano, Marko. 1987. *Domestic Disharmony and Industrialization in D.H. Lawrence's Early Fiction*. Sweden: Uppsala.

Moore, Harry T. 1974. *The Priest of Love: A Life of D.H. Lawrence*. New York: Farrar, Straus and Giroux.

Moynahan, Julian. 1963. *The Deed of Life: The Novels and Tales of D.H.Lawrence*. Princeton: Princeton University Press.

Nash, Walter. 1982. "On a Passage from Lawrence's 'Odour of Chrysanthemums.'" *Language and Literature: An Introductory Reader in Stylistics*. Ronald Carter, ed. London: George Allen & Unwin. 101–123.

Nation (New York). 1917. "D. H. Lawrence," 15 March: 313–14.

Piccolo, Anthony. 1979. "Ritual Strategy: Concealed Form in the Short Stories of D.H. Lawrence." *Mid-Hudson Language Studies* 2: 88–99.

Pritchard, R.E. 1971. *D.H. Lawrence: Body of Darkness*. Pittsburgh: University of Pittsburgh Press.

Rose, Shirley. 1975. "Physical Trauma in D.H. Lawrence's Short Fiction." *Contemporary Literature* 16: 73–83.

Sagar, Keith. 1979. *D.H. Lawrence: A Calendar of His Works with a Checklist of the Manuscripts of D.H. Lawrence by Lindeth Vasey*. Austin: University of Texas Press.

Saturday Review (London). 1915. [*"The Prussian Officer and Other Stories*,"] 9
    January: 42–43.

Schneider, Daniel J. 1986. *The Consciousness of D.H. Lawrence: An
    Intellectual Biography*. Lawrence: University Press of Kansas.

Schorer, Mark. 1956. "Introduction." *Poste Restante*. Harry T. Moore, ed.
    Berkeley: University of California Press. 1–18.

Schulz, Volker. 1991. "D.H. Lawrence's Early Masterpiece of Short Fiction:
    'Odour of Chrysanthemums.'" *Studies in Short Fiction* 28: 363–70.

Slade, Tony. 1969. *D.H. Lawrence*. New York: Arco Publishing Co., Inc.

Stovel, Nora Foster. 1983. "D. H. Lawrence and 'the Dignity of Death': Tragic
    Recognition in 'Odour of Chrysanthemums,'" *The Widowing of Mrs.
    Holroyd*, and *Sons and Lovers*." *The D.H. Lawrence Review* 16.1: 59–82.

Tedlock, E.W. 1963. *D.H. Lawrence: Artist and Rebel*. Albuquerque:
    University of New Mexico Press.

Thornton, Weldon. 1985. "D. H. Lawrence." *The English Short Story: 1880–
    1945*. Boston: Twayne. 39–56.

Van Spanckeren, Kathryn. 1986. "Lawrence and the Uses of Story." *The D.H.
    Lawrence Review* 18.2–3: 291–301.

Vickery, John. 1973. *The Literary Impact of 'The Golden Bough.'* Princeton,
    N.J.: Princeton University Press.

West, Anthony. [1950] 1977. *D.H. Lawrence*. Denver: Alan Swallow. Reprint.
    Norwood Editions.

Widmer, Kingsley. 1962. *The Art of Perversity: D.H. Lawrence's Shorter
    Fiction*. Seattle: University of Washington Press.

Worthen, John. 1991a. *D.H. Lawrence*. London: Edward Arnold.

———. 1991b. *D.H. Lawrence: The Early Years 1885–1912*. Cambridge:
    Cambridge University Press.

———, ed. 1983. *'The Prussian Officer' and Other Stories*. Cambridge:
    Cambridge University Press.

Wulff, Ute-Christel. 1988. "Hebel, Hofmannsthal and Lawrence's 'Odour of
    Chrysanthemums.'" *The D.H. Lawrence Review* 20(Fall): 287–97.

II

"The Shadow in the Rose Garden"

PUBLICATION HISTORY

Some question exists among textual critics as to the original composition date of "The Shadow in the Rose Garden," although it is generally thought to have been first written in 1907 or 1908. Lawrence Clark Powell (1937) described an early unpublished version entitled "The Vicar's Garden," a seven-page manuscript in Lawrence's own hand, in ink on ruled 7 1/2 by 9 inch paper (21). Two six-page carbon typescripts made from and identical to the holograph, also titled "The Vicar's Garden," survive, too (Sagar 1979, 256).

Although this first surviving version of what would become "The Shadow in the Rose Garden" amounted to only a sketch, it is a complete text and readily recognizable as a precursor of the tale. Because it was written on the same paper as that of the 1907 story "Legend" composed for the *Nottinghamshire Guardian* Christmas competition, Tedlock dated "Shadow" at 1907 (1948, 32). John Worthen (1983), a distinguished expert on Lawrence's early fiction, agreed with Tedlock, narrowing the date of composition to October of that year (xlv).

Keith Cushman (1975), however, himself an eminent authority on Lawrence's short fiction, placed the composition in the summer of 1908 (32). Keith Sagar (1979) agreed with Cushman, arguing that Lawrence had apparently written "The Vicar's Garden" too late for the local newspaper's 1907 Christmas story-writing contest and did not submit it for consideration (8). As John Worthen (1991) pointed out, however, only three categories of stories fell within the guidelines of the contest rules: tales of a pleasant Christmas, tales of a humorous Christmas, and tales of a legend about a historic building. Furthermore, the setting had to be the English Midlands. "The Vicar's Garden" met none of these criteria, would have been ineligible for the contest, and would probably not have been submitted (189–90).

The exact date of initial composition being moot, critics do, however, agree on the tale's nature. Tedlock was the first to summarize the sketch: a honeymooning couple exult over a beautiful rose garden in a vicarage and wonder about the owner's disposition. They learn from their landlady that the vicar no longer lives at the vicarage, but his son, who has returned from the Boer War mad, is kept therein. Tedlock regarded the manuscript's ending, wherein the young husband announces they will consequently not spend their honeymoon by that bonny northern cove, "amateurish" (32–3). Keith Cushman agreed, deeming this first version a slight piece (32). Janice Harris (1984), too, disparaged this early effort, calling it a "stock item in the storehouse of traditional short fiction" (16–17). She examined the brief story structurally, however, and found that it merged two major movements—the couple's visit to the rose garden, and the boarding-house owner's news that the vicar has abandoned the vicarage to his insane son—the second section serving to undermine the severity of the first (17).

Reasoning from Lawrence's correspondence, John Worthen (1983) suggested that "The Vicar's Garden" had been revised in August 1911 and sent to the *English Review*, which then rejected it (xlv). But no such revised manuscript has ever been found and no direct reference to a story with this title, or the title "The Shadow in the Rose Garden," in Lawrence's correspondence mentions such a submission in 1911. Critics concur, however, that Lawrence retitled and revised "The Vicar's Garden" in July 1913, sent it to his typist, and—thanks largely to American poet and sometime literary agent Ezra Pound, who received the tale in mid-August 1913—saw his story accepted by the American magazine *Smart Set*, where it appeared as "The Shadow in the Rose Garden" in March, 1914 (Worthen 1983, xlv).

The entire evolution of "The Vicar's Garden" into "The Shadow in the Rose Garden" is, of course, less simple. Returning to England in the summer of 1913, Lawrence made a concerted effort to shape existing short stories into publishable form (Cushman 1978, 150). In a July 14, 1913, letter to his agent Edward Garnett, he pictured himself "drudging away" on the revisions of some short stories, and "The Shadow in the Rose Garden" may have been one of them, given its appearance in revised form eight months later in America (Boulton 1981, 39). To improve the chances of placing his short stories by making them more professional in appearance, Lawrence hired Edward Garnett's nephew, Douglas Clayton, to type his manuscripts. By the end of August, Clayton had prepared some fourteen manuscripts, twelve of which were variants of the short stories that would comprise the November 1914 collection of Lawrence's short fiction, *The Prussian Officer and Other Stories* (Worthen 1983, xxvi).

In the summer of 1913, however, Lawrence was more interested in placing his tales with magazines—he eschewed Ezra Pound's proposal of a volume of stories—and four of the typed tales were accepted right off: "The Fly in the Ointment," "Her Turn," "Strike Pay," and "A Sick Collier." Five additional works—"The Shadow in the Rose Garden," "The Christening," "Vin Ordinaire," "Honour and Arms" and "The White Stocking"— were taken by magazines during the next eight months (Worthen 1983, xxvi–vii).

In a December 21, 1913, letter to Edward Garnett, Lawrence mentioned receiving ten pounds payment for "Shadow" from *Smart Set*, sent him by registered mail to his current residence, Lerici, per Fiascherino, Golfo della Spezia, Italy (Boulton 1981, 126–27). In March 1914, *Smart Set* enjoyed a circulation of 60,000, and although American magazine editors usually paid a penny per word for short fiction, *Smart Set*'s editor, "the generous Willard Huntington Wright" (Joost and Sullivan 1970, 6), would pay ten times that amount for stories he particularly liked (Van Spanckeren 1986, 295–96). Lawrence expressed pleasure in receiving a comparatively large sum for such a brief tale.

A week and a half after having received the ten pounds, Lawence wrote Garnett directing him to send Ezra Pound three or four copies of his 1913 poetry collection *Love Poems and Others*. Pound had received a sovereign from *Smart Set* as commission for recommending "Shadow," and loathe to keep money generated by another's work, Pound sent the money on to Lawrence and asked for the poems in its stead so that he could provide them to the Polignac Prize committee (Boulton 1981, 132).

The revised 1913 tale, critics agree, is a much better story than its earlier variants. The wife now visits the rose garden alone so as to reminisce about her earlier affair with the vicar's son. As she sits among the rose blooms and reflects, she all but becomes a rose herself. The former lover, now mad, discovers her in the garden, speaks with her, but fails to recognize her. Horrified, she flees and returns to the boarding house, where she coolly apprises her husband of her past and of her experience that day. He then makes his pronouncement about their imminent departure.

Several critics have compared this story with the initial 1907–08 version, most notably Emile Delavenay, Brian Finney, and Keith Cushman. Delavenay (1972) found the *Smart Set* variant still flawed. He objected to the routine opposition between husband and wife, the husband's honesty contrasting with his wife's dissemblance, and to a flat and dramatically ineffective conclusion (193). Finney (1975) noted that the latter version was three times the length of the former, and he heard in the husband's conclusive decree that the couple must leave an echo of the first variant's "bathos." But in this and subsequent versions of the tale, Finney found that Lawrence had replaced the early sentimentality with real emotion. Additionally, the revision relinquished methodical plotting for a deeper examination of the couple's unconscious feelings. The second version, furthermore, employed nature symbolically, whereas it had earlier served merely as scenery (332, 327–28).

Cushman (1975a) noted that the 1913 version was both three to four times longer and much better developed than the original. The first-person point of view had shifted to third person, a palpable tension had developed between the honeymooners, and the sentimental, descriptive flower garden of "The Vicar's Garden" had become fraught with thematic significance in "The Shadow in the Rose Garden." In addition, the vicar's lunatic son, never seen in "The Vicar's Garden," had become the wife's former lover, while the husband had become a mine electrician in "The Shadow in the Rose Garden" (31–46).

The ending of this 1913 revision as published in the March 1914 *Smart Set* appeared in the Appendix of the Cambridge University Press edition of *The Prussian Officer and Other Stories* (Worthen 1983, 264).

Other works Lawrence produced in 1913 include the play *The Daughter-in-Law*, the "Foreword" to *Sons and Lovers*, two hundred pages of a novel that would become *The Lost Girl*, the first draft of *The Sisters* (later to become the two novels *The Rainbow* and *Women in Love*), the travel piece *Twilight in Italy*, and a revision of the play *The Widowing of Mrs. Holroyd* (Sagar 1979, 35). But as profitable as Lawrence's 1913 work proved, all of his best tales, with the exception of "Honour and Arms" (to be retitled "The Prussian Officer"), remained just intimations of what they would become during their comprehensive revisions of 1914 when Lawrence readied them for the short story collection Duckworth would publish later that year. On July 8, 1914, Lawrence asked Douglas Clayton for a typescript of "The Shadow in the Rose Garden." But the very next day, contradicting himself, Lawrence sent another note asking Clayton instead for the manuscript of the tale so he could revise it yet again (Boulton 1981, 194).

Only days before, Lawrence had appointed J. B. Pinker as another of his agents and had given him *The Rainbow* for the publishing firm Methuen, which had offered an advance of 300 pounds—an amount that Duckworth, to whom the novel had been promised, would not match. Lawrence offered Duckworth this volume of short stories as compensation. The tales, however, remained far from their final form.

Working quickly and intensely, Lawrence sent Garnett a revised "Shadow" on July 14, along with some others for the Duckworth collection, having sent him another batch of stories the previous week. Lawrence asked that "The Shadow in the Rose Garden" appear as the eighth tale in the volume of twelve, desiring to position it between "Second Best" and "The Dead Rose" (later retitled "The Shades of Spring"). As for the volume's title, Lawrence suggested *'Goose Fair'* (Boulton 1981, 196–97).

Neither request would be fulfilled. "The Shadow in the Rose Garden" appeared in the Duckworth edition entitled *The Prussian Officer and Other Stories* between "Second Best" and "Goose Fair" as the seventh tale in the collection. Such positioning situated it between a strong entry in "Second Best" and one of the weakest stories, "Goose Fair."

In October, Lawrence revised the page proofs of "Shadow"

slightly, and he then suggested that *The Fighting Line* become the title of the short-fiction compilation. But Garnett presumed to change the title of "Honour and Arms" to "The Prussian Officer," to reposition the order of the stories, and to entitle the collection *The Prussian Officer and Other Stories*. (Lawrence would never forgive Garnett this presumption.)

With regard to the 1914 final version of "The Shadow in the Rose Garden" that appeared in the Duckworth volume, E. W. Tedlock (1914) was the first critic to note its great improvement over the 1913 variant in *Smart Set*, citing greater mastery and "a much more complex and dramatic situation" (33). Emile Delavenay viewed the final versions of this tale and the other short stories from 1914 as reflections of Lawrence's artistic development. He saw Lawrence's perspective becoming more objective, and his dialogue more natural, less wordy (205). John Worthen (1983) noted that the 1914 revisions of both "Shadow" and "Odour of Chrysanthemums" display even more artistic growth than do the revisions of his novels at this time (xix).

Brian Finney (1975) compared the 1913 and 1914 versions and found in both the wife's sense of becoming no more than a rose, followed by harrowing experiences with her past lover and her present husband. In the former, however, she is merely a sentimental woman with a kind of martyr complex, whereas in the latter, she progresses from past disinterestedness to a present "awareness" of the man she has taken for her husband (328–29).

Cushman (1975a) provided the most thorough analysis of the changes between the 1913 and the final versions of "The Shadow in the Rose Garden." In the tale's final form, the marriage is presented as a kind of battle, wherein facets of violence, separateness, and impersonality come into play. The husband is made more common and direct in 1914, a Midland's dialect replacing his earlier genteel speech. And in the husband's attempt with brutal interrogation to bring his wife forcibly down to his level, Cushman detected social class as the origin of the battle (31–42).

Other changes in 1914 concerned the intensity of the sensuous descriptions of nature and the destructive tone of the wife's confrontations with her former lover and her husband. Lastly, in 1914, Lawrence introduced many more sexual symbols. Cushman's examples included the lunatic's hands, symbols of erotic love, resting on his thighs, and the wife's panicky confusion as she bolts from the garden and then endures her husband's interrogation—as though her mind were a membrane torn in two (42).

In its final form, "The Shadow in the Rose Garden" appeared first in England out of Duckworth in November 1914 in the first collection of Lawrence's short fiction, *The Prussian Officer and Other Stories*. B.W. Huebsch brought out the same volume in America two years later. "Shadow" was reprinted in England in June of 1922 as part of the volume *Georgian Stories*, published by Chapman & Hall Ltd (McDonald 1925, 105). Putnam published the American edition of *Georgian Stories*. Periodically anthologized, "The Shadow in the Rose Garden" appeared in a 1950 American short-story collection, *15 Stories*, edited by Herbert Barrows. It next appeared in volume one of the three-volume *The Complete Short Stories of D.H. Lawrence* published in 1961 by Viking. In 1976, Penguin brought out this same edition. The tale remained in its 1914 Duckworth form until 1983, when Cambridge University Press published its edition of *The Prussian Officer and Other Stories* in what it considered to be the definitive version that incorporated all existing manuscripts, fair copies, typescripts, page proofs, and published variants (Worthen 1983, 121–33). (The Publication History Section in the "Odour of Chrysanthemums" chapter discusses this controversial "corrected" text.)

Other important works written by Lawrence in 1914 include a second draft of *The Sisters*, then called *The Wedding Ring* and to be retitled at Frieda's suggestion *The Rainbow*, the short-story revisions for the Duckworth collection, and the lengthy essay *Study of Thomas Hardy*.

CIRCUMSTANCES OF COMPOSITION, SOURCES, AND INFLUENCES

When "The Shadow in the Rose Garden" was first composed in late 1907 or early 1908, Lawrence was twenty-two and living at home on Lynn Croft Street in Eastwood. A student at University College, Nottingham, he hoped to become a school teacher. The emotionally unsettled young man both relished and despised the idea of marrying his long-time friend and confidant Jessie Chambers. The budding writer in him faced another kind of trial: the completion of a novel begun in

1906, *The White Peacock*, which would be published in 1911 (Harris 1984, 14).

On October 12, 1908, having received a teaching appointment at Davidson Road School in Croydon, a suburb of London, Lawrence moved to 12 Colworth Road and remained there until returning home for the Christmas holidays. He continued teaching until his severe pneumonia at the end of 1911, after which he abandoned his classroom career. Having published several poems and short stories, as well as a novel, and with his second novel due out momentarily, Lawrence chose to become a full-time writer. Accordingly, he left for Germany on May 3, 1912, discretely traveling in the company of his future wife, Frieda Weekley.

An early version of *Sons and Lovers*, titled *Paul Morel*, received an abrupt rejection from Heinemann in July of 1912, forcing Lawrence to rely yet more heavily on the income his short stories furnished. Aware that he could earn more if he published his stories in magazines rather than in a volume, he lost much of his former interest in Martin Secker's proposal that he collect his short stories. Thus, he began dispatching his stories, both old and new, to various magazines (Worthen 1983, xxiv).

Although busily revising *Paul Morel* into *Sons and Lovers* during the fall of 1912 and working on two new novels, early versions of *The Lost Girl* and *The Sisters* (*The Rainbow* and *Women in Love*'s former title), in the first part of 1913, Lawrence was encouraged in March of that year to see "The Soiled Rose" (revised and retitled "The Shades of Spring" in 1914) appear in *Forum*. It would also appear two months later in his friend John Middleton Murry's magazine *Blue Review*. Unlike his novels, Lawrence's early short stories made money—though not a great deal—and it was certainly welcome during these hard times.

Eager to see more of his stories into print, and more money into his meager bank account, Lawrence wrote to his agent Edward Garnett on June 10, 1913, explaining that he wanted to rework some of the manuscripts left with Garnett in England, so that he could send them off to such magazines as the *English Review* and *Smart Set* (Worthen 1983, xxvi).

Accordingly, when Lawrence and Frieda returned to England in late June of 1913 and stayed with Garnett at the Cearne, his house in Kent, Lawrence set about revising much of his earlier work. At this time—early July of 1913—Lawrence revised "The Shadow in the Rose Garden," as well as "The Christening" and "A Sick Collier," all of which Douglas Clayton then typed (Worthen 1983, xii). Lawrence remained at the Cearne until July 9, then resided at 28 Percy Avenue, Kingsgate, Broadstairs, Kent until July 29, when he returned briefly to the Midlands before departing on August 7 for Europe (Boulton 1981, xix).

When "The Shadow in the Rose Garden" appeared in *Smart Set* in March 1914, Lawrence and Frieda were living at Villino Ettore Gambrosier, in Lerici, Golfo della Spezia, Italy. They remained in Italy until June, at which time Lawrence returned to England to revise yet again the short fiction, this time for the November 1914 Duckworth collection. The Lawrences were married July 13, 1914, at the Kensington Registry Office and took up residence at 9 Selwood Terrace, South Kensington, London (Sagar 1979, 44, 51).

Several interesting articles have examined the various sources for and influences upon "The Shadow in the Rose Garden." Keith Cushman (1975a) observed that the story's original title, "The Vicar's Garden," might refer to a vicar's garden in Greasley Lawrence remembered. But more plausibly, Cushman thought the garden depicted the rose garden at Robin Hood's Bay, Yorkshire, he had visited with Jessie Chambers in August of 1907 (32).

Jessie Chambers's (1935) memoir recounts the particulars of that Yorkshire vacation, and it suggests that Lawrence connected his story with a passage from *Jane Eyre* where Rochester sits with Jane in a rose garden (98). Cushman acknowledged that the rose garden scene in which the wife finds her former lover, now mad, parallels Jane Eyre's discovery of Rochester, now blind and scarred, in a flower garden. The threat of fire implicit in the absence of curtains in the vicarage also echoes *Jane Eyre* (Cushman 1975a, 35).

In fact, Cushman saw Jessie Chambers's relationship with Lawrence as a major influence upon "Shadow" (32). But other critics found Frieda, not Jessie, in the story—especially in the 1913 and 1914 variants. Emile Delavenay (1972) suggested that the couple's quarrels in the *Smart Set* version appear to correspond to the Lawrences' own spats in Gargnano, squabbles that seem to have centered on Lawrence's placing great importance on their dinners and his annoyance that

Frieda, as yet undivorced, continued to wear Ernest Weekley's wedding ring (193).

John Worthen (1983), too, saw the often tumultuous relationship between Lawrence and Frieda pictured in "Shadow," focused as it is on disillusion, despondency, and incipient marital discord. Worthen observed that the name of the lover, Archie, had been Oswald in the *Smart Set* version, perhaps alluding to Oswald Alving of Ibsen's *Ghosts*, whose syphilis produced dementia. Lawrence changed the name again, however, in the July 1914 revision to Monty, Frieda's son's name. Although no ready explanation for this name choice presents itself, Frieda had been making concerted efforts to see her three children by Ernest Weekley. Frieda's children remained, in fact, a matter of continual contention in their marriage, Lawrence apparently resenting his wife's attachment to the children she had abandoned for him two years earlier (264).

Numerous critics point out that many of Lawrence's experiences with Frieda would find their way into print. In 1913, he wrote to Edward Garnett that he was making great strides in *The Rainbow*, and its subject—the relation between the sexes—seemed to him to be the major problem of the day: finding a new basis for the relation or some alteration in the current outmoded relation between the sexes (Boulton 1979, 546). Similarly, in 1914 he wrote to Garnett that he and Frieda had triumphed over their former resistance to one another; consequently, he noted, both he and she were in *The Rainbow*, which he called the work of them both (Boulton 1981, 164).

Frieda's own comments on her marriage to Lawrence occasionally reveal a marriage in stark contrast to the kind of love one finds in "The Shadow in the Rose Garden" between the protagonist and both her former lover and her husband. For example, in 1951, twenty-one years after Lawrence's death, Frieda observed that she and the great writer had resisted the shopworn idea of "being in love." Rather, the bond between them was their approach to life, with its freedom and openness to possibilities. They lived every moment rather than just existing day to day, and they approached everything as a new experience (F. Lawrence 1951, 14). By contrast, the willful husband and wife in the tale had no special connection, separated as they were by his social mores and middle-class morality and her cognitive approach to love based largely upon class consciousness.

Critic Kathryn Van Spanckeren (1986) merged the idea that Lawrence's life often paralleled his stories and the observation that his intense interest in the short-story genre (tempered by the realities of the publishing world) greatly influenced his writing style. She remarked astutely that Lawrence tended to view life as story and "as privileged text" (291). Accordingly, one finds the story form at the heart of Lawrence's poetry and essays, along with the novels and obviously the short fiction itself. In fact, Van Spanckeren continued, he thought of himself first as a writer of short fiction, and by means of identifying truth with art and art with short fiction, his work itself reveals how deeply he committed himself to this genre. Noting, as others have before her, how Lawrence's short fiction avoided certain weaknesses in his longer work, Van Spanckeren cited an important shaping force behind Lawrence's "clarity, economy, and control" implicit in the tales. Publication in the magazines of the day demanded such verisimilitude that Lawrence developed himself into a highly skilled writer of contemporary short fiction (294–95).

A very recent study of the tale by Brenda Maddox (1996) suggested that James Joyce's short story "The Dead" may have influenced "A Shadow in the Rose Garden." Citing similarities of language, scene, and situation, such as the husbands gazing up at their wives who are contemplating past lovers, and the wives' subsequent impassioned confessions to the shocked husbands, Maddox wondered if Lawrence had read "The Dead" in manuscript form before his June 1914 revisions of "Shadow" or after the June 1914 publication of Joyce's tale in *Dubliners*. Lawrence's letters from that period make no mention of Joyce or his work, but similarities between the two short stories are remarkable.

THE RELATIONSHIP OF "THE SHADOW IN THE ROSE GARDEN" TO OTHER LAWRENCE WORKS

E.W. Tedlock (1963) was the first critic to note that the hands of the mad ex-soldier in "The Shadow in the Rose Garden" once represented Eros to the new wife and that she had come to fear that they might do her violence. Tedlock, in fact, failed to discuss a striking example of the justification of this very anxiety in "The Prussian Officer," where the orderly's hands, which customarily massaged the officer, throttled him and finally broke his neck. Tedlock did note, however, that in Lawrence's post-World War I tales, the psyches of former soldiers are often shown to have been affected. Many of these military men—like Count Psanek of "The Ladybird," Maurice Pervin of "The Blind Man," and Joe Boswell and Major Eastwood of *The Virgin and the Gipsy*—become, however, resurrected men struggling for new life (25).

Emile Delavenay (1972) observed that the short story "Once," like "Shadow," concerns a husband's jealousy roused by an army officer. And, as in the tale "Fanny and Annie," "Shadow" involves a woman in love with a man above her in station, who must settle for second best (442). This same situation appears, as well, in two other tales in *The Prussian Officer and Other Stories*: "The Shades of Spring" and "Second Best."

Keith Cushman (1975a) thoroughly analyzed the relationships between "The Shadow in the Rose Garden" and Lawrence's other works. For example, Cushman found the first-person narrator of "The Vicar's Garden" similar to the protagonist, Cyril Beardsall, of *The White Peacock*. This resemblance to Lawrence's first novel, combined with the sentimental treatment of the rose garden scene, encouraged Cushman to place "Shadow" more in the world of *The White Peacock* than in that of *Sons and Lovers* (33–5).

As in *Sons and Lovers*, however, where Miriam takes Paul to see the white roses, and as in "The Shades of Spring," where Hilda conducts Syson on a tour of the wood, in "The Vicar's Garden" a young girl brings her young man into a rose garden to experience the blossoms with her. In fact, precisely like Syson in "The Shades of Spring," the protagonist of "The Shadow in the Rose Garden" returns to a specific natural place to relive or confront her past (Cushman 1975a, 35–6).

Then, too, Lawrence's description of the roses in the 1913 and 1914 variants of "The Shadow in the Rose Garden" is much like his presentation of plants in his book of verse *Birds, Beasts, and Flowers*. Moreover, the husband's occupation, mine electrician, parallels that of Tom Vickers in "A Modern Lover" and Blackmore in Lawrence's play *The Widowing of Mrs. Holroyd* (Cushman 1975a, 37–9).

Furthermore, the July and October 1914 revisions reflected various thematic concerns that appear in such other tales collected in *The Prussian Officer and Other Stories* as "The White Stocking" and "Odour of Chrysanthemums." All three tales address to some extent Lawrence's idea of impersonality between lovers, as well as with the reality of man's isolation obscured by "everyday living." These three tales hardly stand alone in this respect. Two additional stories from the Duckworth collection, "The Shades of Spring" and "Daughters of the Vicar," also focus on the essential "otherness" of individuals (Cushman 1975b, 40–44).

Cushman also perceived violence coming into play in both "Shadow" and "The White Stocking." Although more overt and literal in the latter, where Elsie feels the strength of her husband's hand, the confrontation between the husband and wife at the conclusion of "Shadow" approaches brutality and is, to a certain extent, cathartic (40–44).

Emile Delavenay (1972) discerned yet another close connection between "Shadow," "The Shades of Spring," and *Sons and Lovers*, a connection that recalls Lawrence's childhood. Lydia Lawrence, the miserable wife of a coal miner, remained keenly aware of a certain stigma attached to a working-class life. Thus, she instilled in her children her aspiration to return to the middle class, as well as her craving for "spiritual communion" with people of cultivated minds. Lydia's disaffection from her husband, Arthur, became the subject of the first part of *Sons and Lovers*, but it also seems implicit in the wife's disregard for her working-class husband in "The Shadow in the Rose Garden" (6).

The most recent comparison of "The Shadow in the Rose Garden" with other Lawrence works was Janice Harris's fine 1984 study. Harris, too, acknowledged similarities between this tale and "The White Stocking," but her examination extended to the early and late variants of both tales. In their initial forms, the stories shared unanticipated endings, sketchy character development, and a heavy dependence upon episode. Amended in their final versions, both tales place their couples at the center to struggle in strained marriages, and to see that struggle lead to new understanding (17).

Harris also found a key connection among four tales first written or revised in the summer of 1913: "The Prussian Officer," "The Thorn in the Flesh," "New Eve and Old Adam," and "The Shadow in the Rose Garden." The theme of each is the loss and discovery of self, though Lawrence used different styles to develop this central subject. Echoing critics before her, Harris attributed these stylistic and thematic inventions to Lawrence's integration of stylistic experimentation and to "the content of his new, often frightening experiences" in his personal life with Frieda (85).

These four stories thus exhibited Lawrence's recognition of the ambiguity implicit in an intimate relationship: one must flee the chains of community and confirm the self by means of a sympathetic connection with another; yet these four tales illustrate the complexity of such a choice. Self is not always sheltered in a relationship. One's "otherness" may overpower another's, leaving that person a specter in a virtual void. For example, as Harris noted, Peter Moest's horror of becoming a hollow shell in "New Eve and Old Adam" can be seen to be manifest in the vicar's insane son (100).

It becomes evident, Harris argued, that in the final revision of "The Shadow in the Rose Garden," Lawrence retained the hallmark of his fiction of 1913—the powerful fear of annihilation—and added the intense struggle and deliverance he experienced in his own marriage in 1914 (100). Accordingly, in both "New Eve and Old Adam" and "The Shadow in the Rose Garden," Lawrence figuratively presented the lovers of the early tale "Once" at a much later stage in their relationship: affairs and honeymoons now in their past, the couples in these two later tales find themselves in marriages complicated by apprehension, ache, and physical love (85).

CRITICAL STUDIES

Censorious at first, critical opinion of "The Shadow in the Rose Garden" became commendatory with time. Today, the tale enjoys high regard among critics for its many admirable qualities, although it has yet to be unanimously acclaimed as a masterpiece. A look at the early commentary, especially Katherine Mansfield's, may explain the lingering reluctance to acknowledge the story's greatness.

Allan Monkhouse (1914) of the *Manchester Guardian*, the first serious critic to review *The Prussian Officer and Other Stories*, conceded that the tales were "relevant,' if not "gentleman-like."

Praising certain stories, Monkhouse dismissed "The Shadow in the Rose Garden" as unrestrained and "dreadful" (95).

A January 1915 review of the short story collection in *Athenaeum*, though failing to mention "The Shadow in the Rose Garden" expressly, included it in the positive assessment that Lawrence's presentation of the countryside revealed "a keen and poetic understanding," wherein human nature seethed with instinct, as did all aspects of Mother Nature herself (68).

Lawrence's agent and advisor, Edward Garnett (1916), wrote in an essay on Lawrence's work that "The Shadow in the Rose Garden" reaffirmed the need to balance nature's morality, as evinced in sexuality, and worldly conduct (380).

But undoubtedly the most influential condemnation of the tale came in 1922 from one-time friend and fellow writer Katherine Mansfield as stated in a well-known and often misquoted letter to a mutual friend of Lawrence and her, S. S. Koteliansky. She first attacked generally the contents of *Georgian Stories*, in which "The Shadow in the Rose Garden" appeared, as "an extremely bad collection of short stories" (Nehls 1958, 159).

Mansfield's remark perplexes. One of her own stories appeared in the volume, along with works by such writers as Sheila Kay Smith and Alec Waugh. She went on to single out "The Shadow in the Rose Garden" as "perhaps one of the weakest [tales] that he ever wrote" (Nehls 1958, 159). But she concluded her assessment by remarking how she relished its difference from the other modern tales in the volume, specifically praising Lawrence's ability to evoke vital realism: the red ripe gooseberries on the gardener's tray were "real," as was the "sharp, sweet, fresh" apple from the landlady's garden eaten by the husband (159).

Mansfield's having twice damned the story—directly the first time and with "faint praise" the second—attracted those critics who valued the literary judgment of Lawrence's respected contemporary. Critic Lawrence Powell in 1937 recorded Mansfield's disapproval (22), as did Harry T. Moore in 1954 (367). Kingsley Widmer (1962) bolstered the negative view when he labeled the tale "atmospheric melodrama" (154). Keith Cushman (1975a), fully aware of Mansfield's earlier misgivings, took a more favorable, if guarded view of "The Shadow in the Rose Garden," deeming it "interesting" but "second-line" (7). Two years later, George Becker (1980) intensified Mansfield's negative evaluation by paraphrasing the 1922 letter so as to read that this tale was "the poorest story he wrote, but still better than what others were doing" (119). That same year, Philip Hobsbaum added reservations, tagging the tale extremely weak (26).

Mansfield's notorious appraisal appears to have been influential enough to raise questions about a possible "follow-the-leader" impulse among the earlier critics. Accordingly, one should understand some possible motives for Mansfield's disparagement. A scrutiny of the Lawrence-Mansfield relationship as it stood in 1922 when she wrote her letter raises reasonable doubt about Mansfield's inclination to be wholly objective in any matter involving Lawrence.

Having twice befriended the New Zealander and subsequently fallen out with her, Lawrence wrote her a hateful letter February 6, 1920, wherein he stated that he found the tubercular Mansfield loathsome and revolting (Boulton 1984, 470). In short, he was making a permanent break. (He had seen her for what would be the last time in October of 1918, and except for a final postcard sent her two months following the publication of *Georgian Stories*—a postcard mailed from Mansfield's birthplace consisting of one word, "Ricordi" ("Memories")—Lawrence would never write her again.) His letter so outraged Mansfield that she commanded "her man," John Middleton Murry, to strike Lawrence the next time that he saw him (Nehls 1958, 23). This plea from the distressed Mansfield prompted Murry's pugnacious note to Lawrence stating his "fixed intention" to hit Lawrence in the face when next they met, regardless of when or where that might be (Boulton 1984, 468).

Described by acquaintances like Dorothy Brett as a mercurial woman who could laugh one minute and be savagely caustic the next, Mansfield kindled her indignation (Meyers 1990, 137). In a February 10, 1920, letter to Murry, she expressed a desire to strike Lawrence herself, and deemed the former friend "somehow filthy" (Nehls 1958, 23). Mansfield's resentment toward Lawrence remained ten months later, as evidenced by her scathing appraisal of Lawrence's latest novel, *The Lost Girl*, which she said denied humanity, the imagination, and life. She judged it overall to be "false—*ashes*" (Nehls 1958, 52).

Although the July 1922 letter that disparaged "The Shadow in the Rose Garden" praised facets of Lawrence's newly released novel *Aaron's Rod* ("it is," she said, "a living book") capacity for objective assessment after the bitter split with Lawrence may well be questioned—especially since Lawrence had always presented himself as Mansfield's superior, never crediting her work, which the general reading public nevertheless embraced more readily than Lawrence's.

Lawrence's jealousy of Mansfield's popularity no doubt affected his assessment of her literary value, just as her uncharitable but understandable resentment and envy of Lawrence almost certainly colored her view of his work.

Still, Mansfield's dismissal of "The Shadow in the Rose Garden" may reflect more than just her personal resentment. After all, when her pique finally passed, Mansfield judged Lawrence's work more impartially. But, as Sylvia Berkman (1951) noted, a sharp division existed in Mansfield's response to Lawrence's art: she sincerely admired Lawrence's forthright passion and unique "poetic realism," but she could neither comprehend nor adopt his "doctrine of mindlessness" (229). Unable to appreciate Lawrence's use of the power of "the unconscious," Mansfield no doubt missed the masterful portrait of the wife's psyche as she sat in the rose garden, a portrait that illustrated her *potential* to form a vital connection with another being on that unconscious level.

An ability to pass freely from acute consciousness to the unconscious and back again suggested to Lawrence a balanced psyche crucial for any person able to connect, if just fleetingly, with the "otherness" of another human being. In her distrust of this "mindlessness," however, Mansfield may have stripped the wife's experience in the rose garden of its significance, thus rendering the overall tale, in Mansfield's view, slight. In any event, modern critics have been able to shed Mansfield's considerable early influence.

As early as 1950, Herbert Barrows recognized the worth of "The Shadow in the Rose Garden," including it in his short story anthology, *15 Stories*. He chose this tale of all possible Lawrence short stories because it was "a *good* story" that would reward attentive reading and foster productive classroom discussion (1950a, xi). Barrows, in fact, considered the tale remarkable for the powerful way it presented: (1) Eros viewed retrospectively, (2) the blow to the protagonist when she realized that her former love was lost even to her memory, and (3) the shared hatred between the wife and her husband that left them at an impasse. Barrows also praised Lawrence's economy of development as revealed in his use of such devices as symbolism (more of which will be discussed shortly) and the tension that builds the story's last scene (1950b, 29–31).

John Worthen (1983) made passing reference to Mansfield's letter, but his regard for the story was implicit in his use of the letter to register Mansfield's praise for Lawrence's ability to capture reality (264).

In the first sociological analysis of "The Shadow in the Rose Garden," E.W. Tedlock (1963) pointed out the significance of the husband's and wife's diverse social and cultural backgrounds. Aware that her husband was "second best," the wife retires to a rose garden that becomes emblematic of "the delicacy of sensibility and class" that sets the wife apart from her miner husband (25).

The next sociological study of "The Shadow in the Rose Garden" came from Emile Delavenay in 1972. He recognized two familiar Lawrentian themes in the tale: a husband's jealousy arising from an awareness of social inferiority, and a cultured woman's contempt for the laborer she has married. Delavenay also noted that Lawrence established characterization by means of dialogue, his word choice carefully attuned to social background, his ear, ultimately, contributing greatly to the powerful depiction of his characters' "moral isolation" (Delavenay 1972, 192).

The psychological approach to "Shadow" proved popular, the first such study appearing in 1924. Frances Newman's examination concluded by placing Lawrence in the Romantic school because he lent grace, form, and effulgence to the unconscious, even though Newman saw Lawrence as "a snarling romantic" ([1924] 1925, 244).

The 1962 analysis of the tale by Kingsley Widmer noted how Lawrence illustrated the contrast between love and marriage by means of "a brutal honeymoon episode." The "rose garden of love," Widmer asserted, plays an important part in the story, giving the wife a negative identification with a rose: she is the rose that cannot blossom. Widmer believed that Lawrence thus inverted the classic tradition of the allegorical rose, much as Blake's "The Sick Rose" showed how secret love could lead to a sickness of love (155 & 247).

Widmer saw the final discussion between husband and wife as cathartic and revelatory: they became aware of the gulf widening between them in marriage. In this story, Widmer perceived Lawrence's assertions that love and marriage are antithetical, that marriage never wholly satisfies the extremity of Eros, and that the opposition between spouses becomes the center of their relationship. Moreover, cosmic differences parallel the demands of relatedness in personal relationships, and conflict is essential; disparateness must be acknowledged if a transcendent union is to be achieved, for "relatedness demand[s] difference and polarity" (156).

E. W. Tedlock's 1963 study of "The Shadow in the Rose Garden" also drew upon psychology. Tedlock noted that the roses as natural objects correlate with the protagonist's psychic state, a device characteristic of Lawrence. Consequently, the soft intimacy once shared with a young gentleman is reawakened by the pink roses; whereas, the white roses, suggesting ice, symbolize her cold disappointment. After the confrontation in which husband and wife set out to humiliate one another, their relationship is left in a state of "traumatic suspension," like the relationships of many other Lawrentian couples (25–6).

In 1973, Roger Sale published his psychological examination of the father-figure in Lawrence's fiction. He noted there that Lawrence presented such characters as Baxter Dawes in *Sons and Lovers*, Tom and Will Brangwen in *The Rainbow*, and this "shadowy father figure" (the mad Archie in "The Shadow in the Rose Garden") much more sympathetically after 1912 than he had earlier. Sale concluded that Lawrence's unsettled life in Europe with the married Frieda Weekley urged upon him a need to make peace with his past. Consequently, Lawrence attempted in his fiction what he could not do in actual life: return his mother to her husband and, thus, complete his passion for his mother and release himself from its bondage ([1973] 1975, 38).

Cushman's (1975a) study of "The Shadow in the Rose Garden" called attention to the overt symbolism in the husband eating an apple while waiting for his wife to join him for breakfast; he is there an "old Adam" figure, a Lawrentian character whose strong unconscious impulses are barely repressed beneath a polite social veneer. The rose garden itself embodies the psychic state of the wife as she leaves her mundane daily existence and enters "a world circumscribed by her mind and emotions." As Cushman astutely observed, the rose garden is more than a mere representation of the woman's past. It *is* her past as she relives there the passion of a young soldier. Cushman viewed the appearance of that lover, now a lunatic, and his failure to recognize her as one more example of Lawrence's presentation of lovers as strangers. Moreover, this scene parallels the story's final scene where husband and wife, though intimate, hardly know one another. Her encounter in the garden leaves the wife "absent, torn" and widens the gulf between her and her husband, while his crude interrogation illustrates just how separate they are. Separateness and impersonality become thematically central, and the violence depicted in the husband-and-wife confrontation at the conclusion is cathartic. They are, however, not reconciled. Cushman saw little hope that their relationship would ever become vital. The breach between them, and between any two people, could not, in effect, be closed (44).

In a subsequent study that same year, Cushman (1975b) made yet another point concerning "The Shadow in the Rose Garden": at the story's end, the verbal battle between husband and wife over, the husband is left with the knowledge that he will always be second best in the eyes of his dominant wife. Consequently, a creative polarity would never be established between them (1975b, 192).

In 1976, Donald Ross analyzed Lawrence's skillful representation of the wife's psyche and milieu in "Shadow": Lawrence's narration provides a well-developed mental life for the inarticulate woman by means of the author's articulations representing her thoughts (1222–42).

Janice Harris's (1984) study of "The Shadow in the Rose Garden" noted as the thematic foundation of the tale the contrast between the vacuous, blank son of the vicar and the married couple involved in a battle against the annihilation of each individual self, the pitiful son symbolizing just such an annihilation. Harris saw Lawrence employing sight and blindness through image patterns of eyes and windows to develop the central contrast and to stress his point that self-realization frequently depends on one's acknowledgement by such a "significant other" as a lover or a spouse. Thus, this tale illustrates the danger of the characters becoming but shadows should they fail to see or be seen. In an interesting analysis of the argument at the story's conclusion, Harris saw husband and wife as each beginning the "process of shedding an old self." Each has seen the other's "otherness" and will now retreat from the relationship into himself and herself, making it possible one day to reapproach one another with new insight and sensitivity. Thus, the scales fall from the eyes of the couple largely as a result of the assault upon their individual senses of self and upon their world views. Although the story possesses no tidy conclusion, Harris believed it sufficient that the couple is left to see more clearly now that the floodgates of their stream of consciousness have been opened (100–03).

Weldon Thornton's fine 1985 study of Lawrence's work examined his presentation of the protagonist's psyche in this and other Lawrence stories. Agreeing basically with Donald Ross's earlier similar examination, Thornton took issue with Ross's idea that Lawrence's records of the wife's thoughts in the rose garden gave the reader access to her mind. Thornton believed that by representing her psychical experience, Lawrence had offered much more than a mere glimpse into her mind; rather, a reader acquired a masterful portrait of the woman's entire state of being (50).

A 1990 study of "The Shadow in the Rose Garden" by Martin Kearney discussed the way in which Lawrence used his "pollyanalytics"—his psychology and philosophy—in conjunction with his concept of spirit of place to express his vitalistic views. Using Lawrence's *Fantasia of the Unconscious* as the basis for this pollyanalytic approach, Kearney traced the psychical process whereby the protagonist temporarily becomes "no more than a rose" herself in the rose garden. Kearney thus emphasized the unique way Lawrence interrelated place and character so as to form a psychic correlative, which, in turn, advanced the development of character and theme. Such an application of pollyanalytics to this tale demonstrated how much the wholly unconscious psychology and philosophy, which took Lawrence until 1921 to formulate, permeated his spontaneous art (1–15).

At last the time comes to examine the rose garden as symbol in "The Shadow in the Rose Garden." L.L. Martz (1947) adduced a previously unnoticed debt T.S. Eliot owed Lawrence in connection with this tale. Familiar with the story, having lectured on it and discussed it briefly in his book *After Strange Gods* (wherein he asserted that the story contains "an alarming strain of cruelty") Eliot certainly knew the rose-garden scene well (Eliot 1933, 79). In fact, according to Martz, the powerful and resonant rose-garden image Eliot used in *Burnt Norton*, the first of his *Four Quartets*, as well as in his *The Family Reunion*, derives from "The Shadow in the Rose Garden." As in Lawrence's story, Eliot used the rose-garden image to present in these two poems an object of desire transfixed in "a moment of timeless reality" perceived, however, in a world fraught with time (Martz, 131–33).

A later essay by Giorgio Melchiori (1954) further examined the connections between Eliot's *Burnt Norton* and "The Shadow in the Rose Garden." The images drawn from Lawrence's tale, he noted, were "fundamental" to the *Quartets*. The rose garden, as presented in the latter work, is the foremost "objective correlative of Eliot's moment of revelation," wherein concentrates a mystical experience of unity with the entire physical and spiritual cosmos (204). Lawrence's protagonist, too, formed in her rose garden a momentarily transcendental connection with the natural world before the sudden appearance of Archie rudely brought her back to "reality."

Frances Seidl's (1973) examination of the story noted the symbolic importance of two contrasting gardens therein: the rose garden and the garden adjoining the cottage where the couple lodges. Seidl asserted that the twisted apple tree in the latter garden intimated the couple's frail and contorted love. The brownish rosiness of the apple the husband eats suggests their wilted and spoiling passion. Their love is over-ripe; the time for them to form a vital connection is passed. Similarly, the over-ripe gooseberries the gardener carries insinuates that the ardor the protagonist and Archie had shared is now "past its peak." To the wife, the rose garden represents enchantment; whereas, the cottage garden exemplifies her blighted marriage. After Archie's appearance, however, the rose garden becomes blemished, leaving the wife a sterile life bereft of the resplendence of love presented symbolically in the dual gardens (9).

Janice Harris's 1984 study of "The Shadow in the Rose Garden" offered both a close look at the garden as symbol and an analysis of the male narrator in the tale's earliest form, "The Vicar's Garden." She acknowledged Martz's 1947 perception of the rose garden as a symbol for a lovely past lost to the protagonist forever. Then Harris made the additional point that Lawrence intentionally projected a sense of the ominous in the garden with its great weight of memories to imply that this path led only to lunacy (272.) She supported her argument with the observation that in "The Vicar's Garden" Lawrence had linked the young male protagonist's terror of annihilation with the surging flowers and with his demanding, elated female companion. The sea beyond the garden represented for him the serenity and security of detachment; while, the intense emotion in the rose garden could lead him not only to extreme joy, but to insanity as well, for an unsuccessful love relationship could disrupt his integrated being (19). The young man's great fear in this earliest version came close to reality for the protagonist and her husband in the tale's final form.

In 1956, celebrated Lawrentian F. R. Leavis highly praised Lawrence's artistic range in the short fiction. He made a particularly apt point in regard to "The Shadow in the Rose Garden": although not yet fully recognized, the consummate skill that infused Lawrence's short stories rendered them of such significance as to place Lawrence among the great writers (307).

After a respectable, but less than enthusiastic critical greeting, "The Shadow in the Rose Garden" gradually attracted admiration, until today it has attained general recognition as one of Lawrence's moving and masterful artistic expressions.

WORKS CITED

Athenaeum. 1915. "Fiction," 23 January: 68.

Barrows, Herbert, ed. 1950a. *15 Stories*. Boston: D.C. Heath.

———. 1950b. "The Shadow in the Rose Garden." *Suggestions for Teaching 'Fifteen Stories.'* Boston: D.C. Heath. 29–31.

Becker, George. 1980. *D.H.Lawrence*. New York: Frederick Ungar Publishing Co.

Berkman, Sylvia. 1951. *Katherine Mansfield: A Critical Study*. London: Oxford University Press.

Boulton, James T., ed. 1979. *The Letters of D.H. Lawrence*. Vol.1. Cambridge: Cambridge University Press.

———. 1981. *The Letters of D.H. Lawrence*. Vol.2. Cambridge: Cambridge University Press.

———. 1984. *The Letters of D.H. Lawrence*. Vol.3. Cambridge: Cambridge University Press.

Chambers, Jessie [E.T., pseud]. 1935. *D.H. Lawrence: A Personal Record*. London: Jonathan Cape.

Cushman, Keith. 1978. *D.H. Lawrence at Work: The Emergence of the Prussian Officer Stories.* Charlottesville: University of Virginia Press.

————. 1975a. "D.H. Lawrence at Work: 'The Shadow in the Rose Garden.'" *The D.H. Lawrence Review* 8: 31–46.

————. 1975b. "'I am going through a transition stage.'" *The D.H. Lawrence Review* 8: 176–97.

Delavenay, Emile. 1972. *D.H. Lawrence: The Man and His Work.* Carbondale, Illinois: Southern Illinois University Press.

Eliot, T. S. 1933. *After Strange Gods: A Primer of Modern Heresy.* London: Jonathan Cape.

Finney, Brian. 1975. "D.H. Lawrence's Progress to Maturity: From Holograph Manuscript to Final Publication of *The Prussian Officer and Other Stories.*" *Studies in Bibliography*: 321–32.

Garnett, Edward. 1916. "Art and Moralists: Mr. D.H. Lawrence's Work." *The Dial* 61(November 16): 377–81.

Harris, Janice. 1984. *The Short Fiction of D.H. Lawrence.* New Brunswick, New Jersey: Rutgers University Press.

Hobsbaum, Philip. 1980. *A Reader's Guide to D.H. Lawrence.* London: Thames & Hudson.

Joost, Nicholas, and Alvin Sullivan, eds. 1970. *D.H. Lawrence and the 'Dial.'* Carbondale: Southern Illinois University Press.

Kearney, Martin. 1990. "Pollyanalytics and Spirit of Place in Lawrence's 'The Shadow in the Rose Garden.'" Paper presented at the Fourth International D.H. Lawrence Conference,University of Montpellier, France, June 25, 1990.

Lawrence, D.H. 1961. *The Complete Short Stories.* 3 Vols. New York: Viking Press.

————. 1976. *The Complete Short Stories.* 3 Vols. New York: Penguin Books.

Lawrence, Frieda. [1951] 1968. "Note." *'I Rise in Flames,' Cried the Phoenix.* Tennessee Williams. New York: New Directions. Reprint. *Ramparts* 6(January): 14–19.

Leavis, F.R. [1956] 1979. *D.H. Lawrence: Novelist.* New York: Alfred A. Knopf. Reprint. Chicago: University of Chicago Press.

McDonald, Edward. 1925. *A Bibliography of the Writings of D.H. Lawrence.* Philadelphia: The Centaur Book Shop.

Maddox, Brenda. 1996. "Lawrence's 'Shadow in the Rose Garden' and Joyce's 'The Dead.'" Paper presented at the Sixth International D.H. Lawrence Conference, University of Nottingham, UK, July 13, 1996.

Martz, L.L. 1947. "The Wheel and the Point: Aspects of Imagery and Theme in Eliot's Later Poetry." *The Sewanee Review* 55: 126–47.

Melchiori, Giorgio. 1954. "The Lotus and the Rose: D.H. Lawrence and Eliot's *Four Quartets." English Miscellany* 5: 203–16.

Meyers, Jeffrey. 1990. *D.H. Lawrence: A Biography*. New York: Alfred Knopf.

Monkhouse, Allan (A.N.M.). [1914] 1973. "Review of *The Prussian Officer and Other Stories." Manchester Guardian* Dec. 17. Reprint. *D.H. Lawrence: A Critical Anthology*. H. Coombes, ed. Harmondsworth: Penguin Books Inc. 94–6.

Moore, Harry T. [1954]. 1962. *The Intelligent Heart*. New York: Viking Press. Reprint. New York: Grove Press, Inc.

Nehls, Edward, ed. 1958. *D.H. Lawrence: A Composite Biography. Volume Two, 1919–1925*. Madison: University of Wisconsin Press.

Newman, Frances. [1924] 1925. *The Short Story's Mutations*. New York: B.W. Huebsch, Inc. Reprint. Same.

Powell, Lawrence Clark. 1937. *The Manuscripts of D.H. Lawrence: A Descriptive Catalogue*. Los Angeles Public Library.

Ross, Donald. 1976. "Who's Talking? How Characters Become Narrators in Fiction." *Modern Language Notes* 91: 1222–42.

Sagar, Keith. 1979. *D.H. Lawrence: A Calendar of His Works with a Checklist of the Manuscripts of D.H. Lawrence by Lindeth Vasey*. Austin: University of Texas Press.

Sale, Roger. [1973] 1975. *Modern Heroism*. Berkeley: University of California Press. Reprint. Same.

Seidl, Frances. 1973. "Lawrence's 'The Shadow in the Rose Garden.'" *Explicator* 32: Item 9.

Tedlock, E.W. 1963. *D.H. Lawrence: Artist and Rebel*. Albuquerque: University of New Mexico Press.

———. 1948. *The Frieda Lawrence Collection of D.H. Lawrence Manuscripts: A Descriptive Bibliography*. Albuquerque: University of New Mexico Press.

Thornton, Weldon. 1985. "D. H. Lawrence." *The English Short Story: 1880–1945*. Boston: Twayne. 39–56.

Van Spanckeren, Kathryn. 1986. "Lawrence and the Uses of Story." *The D.H. Lawrence Review* 18.2–3: 291–301.

Worthen, John. 1991. *D.H. Lawrence: The Early Years 1885–1912*. Cambridge: Cambridge University Press.

———, ed. 1983. *The Prussian Officer and Other Stories*. Cambridge: Cambridge University Press.

III

"Daughters of the Vicar"

PUBLICATION HISTORY

D.H. Lawrence entitled the first version of "Daughters of the Vicar," written in 1911, the year following Lawrence's mother's death, "Two Marriages." In a letter to Louie Burrows dated July 15, 1911, Lawrence described spending all the day and until ten o'clock that evening writing thirty-eight pages of a lengthy short story. The following day he wrote his fiancée to announce that he had finished the tale he called "Two Marriages" (Boulton 1979, 287–88).

Although Lawrence would not meet Edward Garnett face to face until early October of 1911, the agent wrote Lawrence the previous August to request some short fiction for possible publication in the American magazine *The Century*, which he represented, and toward the end of September, two weeks after his twenty-sixth birthday, Lawrence sent Garnett "Two Marriages." The representative thought it publishable, given some revision (Cushman 1978, 81), and during their October meeting Garnett made helpful suggestions to that end (Worthen 1989, 17).

In the course of his revisions, Lawrence divided the story into three parts and tried to restrict its length to between twelve and fifteen thousand words. He returned the manuscript to Garnett in November only to be rejected by *The Century* in December, a decision that confirmed for Lawrence a want of intelligence among American publishers (Worthen 1983, xli). Responding defensively to this latest rejection, Lawrence wrote to Garnett on December 30, 1911, that "the Americans are just as stupid as we expected" (Boulton 1979, 343).

In this early version of the tale, Lawrence contrasted the marriages of Mary Lindley and Louisa Lindley so as to form a kind of resolution to the recurring question posed in his fiction: should a "superior" woman marry equal to or lower than her social station? Mary's husband—the tiny, deformed, abstract Massey—disgusts Louisa who, in turning away from the cold religious hypocrisy and class consciousness of her family, turns toward the physical closeness of the working class. In this early version, Louisa fails to analyze her own attraction to the working class, and her decision to marry Alfred is more the result of keeping a promise made in response to Mrs. Durant's death-bed request and her rebellion against Massey and his world view, than a reflection of personal desire (Delavenay 1972, 110).

The conclusion of this early version—with Louisa and Alfred marrying, having several children, and living "happily ever after,"— follows a fairy-tale formula (Finney 1975, 330). Ultimately, the focus of this 1911 variant falls upon the description of the community and the working lives of its members (Kalnins 1976, 39). Never published in Lawrence's lifetime, "Two Marriages" first appeared in the March 24, 1934, edition of *Time and Tide*.

A year and a half later, during the summer of 1913, Lawrence once again turned his attention to this story. In letters to his agent, Edward Garnett, and his typist, Douglas Clayton, Lawrence told the former that he was having this freshly rewritten tale retyped and had renamed it "Daughters of the Vicar." He asked the latter to send him the page proofs after retyping the revision. At this time, Lawrence was busily sending short stories out to such magazines as the *North American Review*, the *New Statesman*, and the *English Review*. He was "sick of messing with these short things," but he wanted to complete as many projects as he could and perhaps earn some money before he and Frieda returned to Germany in early August (Boulton 1981, 44–5).

The 1913 variant of the tale was "less juvenile" and displays a control of subject, structure, and language quite remarkable for this early in his career (Hobsbaum 1980, 115). In 1911, only Louisa has to choose between dependence and independence, but in 1913, both protagonists make choices. Still, the ending is too tidy: Louisa and

Alfred marry and live a vital life together in an England suddenly oblivious of class (Finney 1975, 330–31).

Still, the superiority of this version over those of 1911 must be affirmed. Alfred Durant's character develops. It now becomes clear that the young man's mother caused his sense of inadequateness with women. Smothering his sensitive nature, she had transferred to herself his need for approval and affection. Until he experiences Louisa's kiss, he is unable to relinquish his self-consciousness (Delavenay 1972, 187–88).

In an August 24, 1913, letter to Garnett, Lawrence enclosed a letter from the Northern Newspaper Syndicate reflecting an interest in his work. Lawrence thought the syndicate might buy "Daughters of the Vicar" and divide it into a three-part serial. He wanted the typescript, which he believed to be in James Pinker's possession, sent to the Northern Syndicate so as to ensure that Garnett, not Pinker, received the ten-percent commission. In a subsequent letter of September 4, 1913, however, Lawrence is more pessimistic; he directed that the manuscript be sent to the Northern Syndicate people "who will [however] refuse it" (Boulton 1981, 65–7).

He was right. Unable to place "Daughters of the Vicar" with the Northern Syndicate, Lawrence tried again in the latter part of 1913. His other agent, James Pinker, submitted the story to the American periodical *Smart Set*, which rejected it on March 12, 1914 (Boulton 1981, 197).

"Daughters of the Vicar," in fact, never appeared in a magazine during Lawrence's lifetime. A near-novella, its length probably accounted for the resistance. As critic Kathryn Van Spanckeren (1986) noted, contemporary magazine editors expected manuscripts of twenty or fewer pages since a long and unpopular story hindered sales. Also, editors liked to keep their stories short to include as many authors as possible, for reasons of both fairness and audience interest. The budget was another consideration; generally, it "could not sustain lengthy numbers" (295).

"Daughters of the Vicar" underwent a major revision in 1914. In preparation for the soon-to-be published collection of short stories Garnett had arranged with Duckworth Publishing, Lawrence reworked the tale in July and sent it, now expanded to 19,000 words, to Garnett on July 14 along with ten other stories. In October, Lawrence made some 250 alterations to the page proofs (Worthen 1983, xxxii), and by the time the story finally reached print with the November publication of *The Prussian Officer and Other Stories*, it approached 21,000 words. (With regard to the first American edition and the 1983 Cambridge Edition of this short story collection, consult the Publication History section in Chapter One.)

Among the major differences between early versions of "Daughters of the Vicar" and its published final form, the former were much shorter and relied heavily on plot, while the latter contains fewer factual details and events and exchanges sentimentality for authentic emotion (Finney 1975, 322). In addition, in its final form the tale presents setting and scene more insightfully, renders more psychologically complex characters, is more accomplished in technique, and uses language and style more innovatively (Kalnins 1976, 32).

More precisely, in the final version of "Daughters of the Vicar," Lawrence both muted his antipathy to Christianity (and consequently his clergy caricatures) and reduced somewhat his satirical presentation of Eastwood and its citizens. Mary appears in 1914 as more complexly human, for the reader can now see the generosity of her motives and her sincere sympathy for Massey's moral merit, those "qualities" that account for her marrying the man despite his physical repugnance. Less a caricature by 1914, Massey remains a powerful portrait of an unfeeling "theoretical form of Christianity" (Delavenay 1972, 204).

Louisa's changes reflect a consistent development that resulted in a much more intelligible and human character. In 1914, she no longer marries at the behest of Mrs. Durant. An independent woman, she bases her decision on both instinct and reason: she is drawn physically and spiritually to Alfred, while her reason informs her of the horror of Mary's sacrifice (Delavenay 1972, 205). Lawrence also improved his tale by muting the earlier didacticism and depicting more action in his characters (188).

A January 23, 1915, book review of *The Prussian Officer and Other Stories* referred to the prose in "Daughters of the Vicar" as "sensuous." But, the reviewer then went on to criticize the work for the stark contrast it establishes between humanity's primitive side and the loveliness of nature (*Athenaeum*, 68).

CIRCUMSTANCES OF COMPOSITION, SOURCES, AND INFLUENCES

Lawrence completed "Two Marriages" in that time of his life when his mother had died, he had broken off with Jessie Chambers, he had become engaged to Louie Burrows in an increasingly frustrating arrangement, and he still felt the loss of Jessie's support in his creative endeavors (Delavenay 1972, 82). In response to Martin Secker's June, 1911, request for a book of short fiction, Lawrence wrote "The Old Adam," the long short story "Love Among the Haystacks," and "Two Marriages," the first version of "Daughters of the Vicar" (Worthen 1989, 16).

In July of 1911, while writing "Two Marriages," Lawrence resided at 12 Colworth Road, Croydon, a suburb of London. (A full account of Lawrence's 1911 itinerary appears in the Circumstances of Composition section in Chapter One.)

The reflection of Lawrence's fiancée, Louie Burrows, in the Louisa character seems almost palpable. Lawrence, his sister Ada, and Louie spent a two-week holiday together at Prestatyn, Wales, in late July and early August of 1911. Also at this time, Lawrence passed frequent weekends at the Quorn, the Burrows home (Sagar 1979, 18).

As intimated above, Lawrence met Edward Garnett for the first time in early October of 1911, their conference resulting from Garnett's August letter requesting some short fiction for possible publication in the American magazine *The Century*. Lawrence first sent Garnett "Two Marriages" on September 25, describing it as a first draft with some good later segments compensating for the initial tediousness. Lawrence said that he had tried to infuse the story with adequate emotion and morality, and that he had tried to make the story "American" (Boulton 1979, 307). Garnett returned the tale to him on October 2. He thought it publishable, but that first it needed revisions. Lawrence then divided the story into three parts and tried to limit its length to between twelve and fifteen thousand words (Boulton 1979, 308).

Lawrence sent the manuscript to a typist during the first week of October but had difficulty getting it back. In an October 11 letter to Garnett, Lawrence referred to Arthur Stanley Corke as "the wretched type writer" who would not return his story (Boulton 1979, 311, 323). A month later, Lawrence learned that after having received his advance payment, the typist had gone on a drinking binge, leaving the typing to a friend. It would be November 21 before "Two Marriages" finally reached Garnett. By that time, Lawrence was so ill with pneumonia that his landlady had to write the accompanying note to Garnett while Lawrence dictated.

Recovering in late December of 1911, Lawrence learned from Garnett on the thirtieth that *The Century* had rejected his story. Although the precise reason for the rejection has never come to light, Lawrence called the decision "comical" and noted that *The Century*'s eyes were "holy" (Boulton 1979, 343, 345), implying that the American magazine objected to his frank treatment of sexuality .

Having accompanied his future wife, then Mrs. Frieda Weekley, to Germany in May of 1912, Lawrence returned with her to England in June of 1913 intending to revise and sell as many of his "pre-Frieda" short stories as possible. He had recently published *Sons and Lovers* and was progressing nicely on what would become *The Rainbow*. Maturing artistically, Lawrence found himself full of new ideas to introduce into 1913's summer revisions. Residing at The Cearne, Edward Garnett's home in Kent, from June 19 to July 9, he rewrote "Two Marriages," retitled it "Daughters of the Vicar," and on July 20 sent it to Douglas Clayton to be typed. The direction the tale took in its 1914 final form began in the 1913 reworking (Cushman 1978, 83).

Lawrence and Frieda returned to Germany in August and remained on the continent until the following summer. On June 24, 1914, they returned to England and established quarters at 9 Selwood Terrace, South Kensington, London. (A detailed account of Lawrence's activities during the second half of 1914 appears in the Circumstances of Composition section in Chapter Two.) He was introduced to poet Rupert Brooke on June 27, and stayed at The Cearne for several days in the first week of July. Then on July 14, the day following his wedding to Frieda, he posted a newly revised "Daughters of the Vicar" to Garnett.

Lawrence revised the tale once again in October and November while he and Frieda lived near Chesham, at The Triangle. These late modifications revealed some new attitudes toward his art (Cushman 1978, 83). Then, at long last, "Daughters of the Vicar" appeared in print on November 26, 1914, in Duckworth's edition of *The Prussian Officer and Other Stories*.

A major influence on "Daughters of the Vicar" appears to have been the interest in realism expressed by such magazine editors as Ford Madox Ford. But the story offers more than just the requisite impressions of working-class life and love. Lawrence raises such fiction to the level of art with the transfusion of his own perceptions of sexual ceremony, rebirth, and vitalism (Harris 1984, 56).

Starting from the premise that he might develop the relationships of his two couples, Lawrence produced his first published work that focused on the configuration of two sisters. In addition, the 1913 and the 1914 versions displayed, by means of metaphysical language and a splendidly patterned comparison and contrast between the major characters, a new visionary technique that reproduced Lawrence's own changing world view since Frieda (Harris 1984, 109). But much of the story, from first version to last, relies on Lawrence's experiences of his own family and the two young women he had loved before he met Frieda.

Lawrence's early writing always reflects to one degree or another his own experience, and "Daughters of the Vicar" looks back to Lawrence's beginnings (Cushman 1978, 78). Prior to this story, his work seems focused on either family relationships or thwarted youthful love. But in "Two Marriages," the two preoccupations appear together for the first time (Harris 1984, 59). For example, Lawrence's paternal grandparents are portrayed in "Daughters of the Vicar," albeit briefly (Worthen 1991b, 24), and as we have already noted, Louie Burrows appears as the female protagonist, Louisa.

Lawrence had known Louisa (Louie) Burrows for some time before the break up with his longtime sweetheart and literary companion, Jessie Chambers. More candid and less exacting than Jessie, Louie was cordial and vivacious. Lawrence's engagement to her shortly before his mother's death (Lydia fully approved of Louie as fit for her son) appears to presage Alfred's newfound love for Louisa coming, in the tale, soon after his mother's death (Worthen 1985, 11). Similarly, the intense grief Lawrence felt on his mother's death, an agony that seemed an extension of her own, probably intensified the description of Alfred Durant's torment as he awaited his mother's death (Worthen 1991b, 293). Then, too, Durant's haste to marry Louisa paralleled Lawrence's sudden, unexpected proposal to Louie.

Furthermore, both Louisas had thick luxurious hair, equanimity, and the unhappy task of informing vexed parents of their choice in husbands.

In fact, Alfred's sexual inhibitions may have been Lawrence's own in 1911. Like Paul in *Sons and Lovers* and Aaron Sisson in *Aaron's Rod*, Alfred's music and Lawrence's art helped sustain them during the difficult time of sexual adjustment, both apparently suffering the ignominy of an overlong chastity followed by headlong indulgence. Both Alfred and Lawrence, too, returned to their work to escape their painful situations (Schneider 1986, 36–7). Another influence upon the story may have been the accord Lawrence felt with his mother and with Louie, which exactly parallels Alfred's situation in the tale (Worthen 1991b, 319).

The idea that sex might plunge one into some dark oblivion where the self momentarily dies and enters life eternal appears in the 1914 revisions of "Daughters of the Vicar," and Frieda certainly presented Lawrence with this experience (Delavenay 1972, 155). Despite Lawrence's attempts to reconcile his feelings for his mother in *Sons and Lovers*, he came to these terms only tentatively. But having lived with Frieda for a year before the 1913 revisions, he found it easy to manifest this reconciliation. Alfred's vital love for Louisa helped him to confront his love for his mother just as Lawrence's liaison with Frieda helped him exchange an excruciating mother love for a "tender and radiant" love (Cushman 1978, 97). In effect, Alfred's Oedipal torment yields to a "celebration of the mysterious otherness of his new beloved and of the powerful energies radiating through the universe" (Cushman 1978, 98).

Lawrence's work in 1912 and 1913, his first two years with Frieda, broke new ground. New assertive feminine types like Louisa Lindley begin to appear and a great deal of material focuses on moral questions and sexual problems in particular. Finally synthesized in *The Rainbow*, these new facets of Lawrence's work play a large though incipient role in "Daughters of the Vicar" (Delavenay 1972, 205).

Decamping with Frieda to Germany in 1912, Lawrence's maturity as man and artist developed rapidly. By 1913 he had abandoned heavy superficial plotting and clever dialogue and had begun to dig down into unconscious emotions. Internal feelings superseded plotted events, as psychological realism replaced sentimentality. Likewise, narrative objectivity supplanted intrusive autobiographical material. After 1912, what had been explicit in Lawrence's writing became implicit (Finney 1975, 331–32).

Meanwhile, Graham Hough (1957) was the first critic to observe that the characters of Mary Lindley and Reverend Massey appear to be modeled on Dorothea and Casaubon in George Eliot's *Middlemarch*, just as Lawrence's "patent objectivity" in the tale parallels Eliot's style (170). Much later, Cushman (1978), too, discussed the Massey-Casaubon connection and further noted that Eliot's character is the less flat and abstract (108). Another critic, David Holbrook (1992), agreed with the earlier two but suggested that an author less famous than Eliot also may have served as a source for the Mary-Massey relationship: Elizabeth Gaskell (136). Holbrook named no characters or work; however, Ruth Hilton and the Reverend Benson of Gaskell's 1853 novel, *Ruth*, are likely candidates.

Emile Delavenay (1972) perceived other influences upon this tale. First, he believed that Massey's character and the marriage of Mary Lindley's parents owed a debt to Samuel Butler's *The Way of All Flesh*. Next, he noted that Butler and Nietzsche helped focus Lawrence's abhorrence of a cold, unvital family life and the sense of moral superiority he found implicit in middle-class families like the Lindleys. Depicting this "good" family and drawing his portrait of Massey, Lawrence leveled an attack upon the morality of self-sacrifice (110).

John Worthen (1983) advanced the interesting view that the Reverend Ernest Lindley was based upon The Reverend Percival Page, fourth vicar of Brinsley between 1881 and 1918. Page had five children, three daughters and two sons; and the eldest girl, Mabel Elsie, married The Reverend Albert Hooper in 1906. Another daughter, Margaret Page, also married a minister. Although neither husband was named Massey, in 1911 a minister by the name of The Reverend Canon J. C. Massey, M.A., was serving as the vicar of Risley, a village some eight miles south of Eastwood (252–55).

Moreover, Miss Louisa's name seems significant. One is reminded that when drafting "Daughters of the Vicar" in 1911 Lawrence was engaged to Louisa (Louie) Burrows. In addition, Lawrence's paternal grandmother was named Louisa Parsons (Worthen 1983, 252).

Worthen also noted that the story's setting, the town of Aldecross, closely resembled Brinsley near Lawrence's native Eastwood. He called it Aldecar in "Two Marriages," and a village with this very name was located two miles southwest of Brinsley (1983, 252). Lawrence's sister Ada's reminiscences help inform Worthen's geography. She recalled that Brinsley, like Aldecross, consisted of "a straggling row of cottages" from the Brinsley Crossings down to the Nethergreen railway bridge. She also described her grandfather Lawrence's house in Brinsley as being situated in a deep hollow and surrounded by a large garden, a setting rather like the Durant's cottage (Nehls 1957, 17).

Worthen (1983) speculated that the church at Greymeed, spelled Greymede in "Two Marriages" and in *The White Peacock*, is based on St. Mary's Church in Greasley, a town near Eastwood (252).

As for the surname Durant, Lawrence might have found it even closer to home. C.N. Wright's *Directory: Twelve Miles Round Nottingham* listed a contractor and undertaker named William Durant who lived on Albert Street in Eastwood when Lawrence was a lad (Aldington 1961, 150).

THE RELATIONSHIP OF "DAUGHTERS OF THE VICAR" TO OTHER LAWRENCE WORKS

Set in the Nottinghamshire and Derbyshire area, "Daughters of the Vicar" shared this locale with Lawrence's first and third novels, *The White Peacock* and *Sons and Lovers*. In fact, he used the same setting in seven other tales from *The Prussian Officer and Other Stories*: "Goose Fair," "A Sick Collier," "Strike Pay," "The Christening," "Odour of Chrysanthemums," "Second Best," and "The Shades of Spring."

Beside the setting, other parallels exist between "Daughters of the Vicar" and *Sons and Lovers*. Several critics have connected the death of Mrs. Durant in this tale with Mrs. Morel's demise in Lawrence's third novel. Frank O'Connor (1962) considered Mrs. Durant's death one of Lawrence's most moving pieces, and he thought it belonged properly in *Sons and Lovers*, where Paul Morel's absorption in Nottingham and in Clara blunted the emotional edge of his mother's death (147).

E.W. Tedlock (1963), too, noted that Alfred's mother's malignant tumor and his feelings toward her resembled Mrs. Morel's fatal illness and her son's emotional response. Like Paul after his mother's death, Alfred also drifted toward death, until Louisa's embrace restored him (32–3).

Michael Black's (1986) examination of what he termed a "masterpiece" noted several parallels between "Daughters of the Vicar" and "Odour of Chrysanthemums." Since Lawrence completed both stories after *Sons and Lovers* appeared, Black regarded them as later comments on the marriage of the Morels and on Paul's future. Elizabeth and Walter Bates of "Chrysanthemums" seem clearly to be based on Gertrude and Walter Morel, right down to the wife's disdain and sense of superiority and the husband's occupation and first name (188).

In "Daughters," Mrs. Durant is strong minded and efficient, while her bearded husband, coarser than she, appears to be in moral and physical decline. Alfred, the Paul figure, likewise survives a temporary sense of disintegration when his mother dies, but his progress toward self-realization begins when a lover's affection replaces a mother's (188).

Critic Daniel Schneider (1986) also found autobiographical links among Lawrence, Alfred Durant, and several other Lawrence characters. Compelled to escape his strict, moral upbringing that had produced sexual inhibition, Lawrence revealed his compulsion in correspondence dating in 1910 and 1911, as well as in such stories as "Daughters of the Vicar," "The Old Adam," "The Witch a la Mode," and "A Modern Lover." In each of these tales the protagonist is physically attracted to a woman, but his bashfulness and self consciousness restrain him from approaching her, producing a sense of inadequacy. One can thus see the women in these tales as surrogates for Mrs. Jones, Lawrence's appealing Croydon landlady; Helen Corke, his colleague and a romantic interest in Croydon; Louie Burrows; and Jessie Chambers (350).

The figure of Alfred Durant has fascinated many critics, some of whom find similarities between him and other Lawrence characters. Frank O'Connor (1962), for example, saw the gamekeeper, Oliver Mellors, of *Lady Chatterley's Lover* as Alfred Durant, "with the whole sense of actuality omitted" (154). Emile Delavenay (1972) believed that Alfred Durant, like Tom Brangwen of *The Rainbow* and Rupert Birkin of *Women in Love*, resembled Lawrence himself in his preference for the "idea of women" to actual women (153). Keith Cushman (1978) noted that Alfred's "masculine modesty" as presented in the early versions of the tale was like that of Cyril Beardsall in *The White Peacock*, of Cyril Mersham in "A Modern Lover," of Edward Severn in "The Old Adam," and of Bernard Coutts in "The Witch a la Mode"— all fastidious protagonists in Lawrence's early work (98).

Janice Harris (1984), even more specific, noted that Alfred, like Geoffrey in "Love Among the Haystacks" and Severn in "The Old Adam," found himself unable to enter into an adult sexual relationship. Alfred and Geoffrey overcame their hesitancy, but only after overcoming earlier non-threatening dependencies—Alfred on his mother, Geoffrey on his brother (51).

Harris pointed out other parallels between "Daughters of the Vicar" and "Love among the Haystacks." In fact, the two stories follow identical patterns: each explores the personal lives of two siblings of the same sex; in each, the reticent, recalcitrant sibling observes, estimates, and inevitably attains a genuine love for herself or himself; in each, class restrictions are disregarded as the two protagonists choose partners beneath them socially (70). This identification carries over into *Sons and Lovers* and "Odour of Chrysanthemums," although the marriages of the Morels and the Bateses prove unhappy because, unlike Alfred and Louisa, the partners deny one another their true selves (Worthen 1991b, 300–01).

Several critics have noted striking parallels between Alfred and *The Rainbow*'s Tom Brangwen. Mara Kalnins (1976) observed that Lawrence's complex analysis of Alfred's sexual inhibitions in this tale came so close to Brangwen's dilemma in the novel's opening chapter that the phrasing at times seems identical (44). John Worthen (1983), in fact, cited a paragraph from one of the last revisions of the story Lawrence inserted in the corrected page proofs; he next noted that the passage brought to mind Tom Brangwen's description in the first chapter of the 1915 variant of *The Rainbow* (1983, 257).

Another theme connects "Daughters of the Vicar" with *Sons and Lovers*, *The Rainbow*, and *Women in Love*. In each work, upon the loss of a parent a male character turns to a woman attempting to find solace through passion. Paul Morel goes to Clara, Will Brangwen to his wife, and Gerald Crich to Gudrun, just as Alfred is drawn to Louisa following his mother's death (Worthen 1991b, 290–91).

Regarding the Canadian connection, Worthen (1983) also suggested that Alfred and Louisa's intention to marry, then emigrate to Canada, reflected Lawrence's fascination with North America, an interest also evident in *The White Peacock*, as illustrated through the Saxton's interest; in "The Fox," where Henry and March emigrate to Canada; and in Hadrian's Canadian experience as recounted in "You Touched Me" (257).

Philip Hobsbaum (1980) viewed Canada as Alfred and Louisa's sanctuary away from the deadness of English class consciousness; he added that Henry and March go there as well and that Mellors and Connie Chatterley also planned to emigrate to Canada in early versions of *Lady Chatterley's Lover* (115).

George Orwell (1945) considered "Daughters of the Vicar" a remarkably effective tale that shares with *Lady Chatterley's Lover* an implicit condemnation of class consciousness. Unlike her older sister, the young girl, Louisa, refuses to allow her vitality to be destroyed by snobbishness (32–33). A later critic, Marko Modiano (1987), also saw community and social discord coming under intense scrutiny in this tale as in an earlier short story, "The Christening" (63).

Critics generally noticed in "Daughters of the Vicar" Lawrence's well-known antipathy to the military, a stance also prominent in *Sons and Lovers*, "The Prussian Officer," and "The Thorn in the Flesh." Alfred joins the navy to the horror of his mother, and in each of these other works the type of discipline one associates with the military takes its toll upon some character's sense of selfhood. As Delavenay (1972) pointed out, such a socially mechanistic force Lawrence saw as death to self-realization (204).

Expressing an associated idea in a more specific context, John Vickery (1973) categorized Lawrence's fiction within a mythic pattern. He placed "Daughters of the Vicar" alongside *Sons and Lovers*, *Women in Love*, *Lady Chatterley's Lover*, "The Thorn in the Flesh," *The Virgin and the Gipsy*, "England, My England," "None of That," "The Captain's Doll," "St. Mawr," and "The Princess" as tales centered on combat or a series of struggles between characters and ways of life. Usually the clashes occur between a character who desires or attains a more fulfilling way of life than one typically finds in the world, and an antagonist oblivious of life's and society's repressive nature (324–25).

Brian Finney (1975) also noticed the struggle motif in "Daughters of the Vicar." He observed that internal and external forms of authority collided there as they do in the last two tales written for *The Prussian Officer and Other Stories*: "The Thorn in the Flesh" and "The Prussian Officer." Finney surmised that Lawrence and Frieda, living in exile at the time, had become acutely aware of this conflict and had made their choice in favor of the internal forms (331).

Widmer's (1962) early study adduced in much of Lawrence's work only incidental "class conflict"; the real theme concerned "erotic doom." Thus, in "Daughters of the Vicar," as in *The Rainbow*, *Women in Love*, *The Virgin and the Gipsy*, and *Lady Chatterley's Lover*, the reader finds passion in conflict with intellect, as well as destructive middle-class morality (unvital and intellectual) versus a virile outsider (126).

A somewhat subtler examination of conflict by Gerald Doherty (1984) found commonality among "Daughters," "The White Stocking," *The Fox*, and *The Virgin and the Gipsy*. By means of the love relationships depicted in these works, Lawrence displays a "trinitarian schemata" wherein the Epoch of Law (female) and the Epoch of Love (male), now obsolete, are frustrated as they struggle toward a third epoch, the nature of which remains unknown, unimagined, and unconsummated. This metaphysical crisis confronts humanity in the form of inhibited desire or unfulfilling relationships. Thus, the four respective courtships, each of which involves three meetings of a would-be couple, demonstrate this eschatological construct, wherein the third epoch fails to materialize (135, 138–9).

Louisa Lindley, then, has attracted her full complement of critical attention. She shares with such other Lawrence protagonists as Ursula Brangwen of *Women in Love* and Connie Chatterley of *Lady Chatterley's Lover* what Stephen Potter (1930) called the traits of the Lawrence heroine. She is fallible, slightly unwilling "to abandon herself," incompletely independent, and she eventually will be as completely fulfilled by means of sexual experience as the hero is (26–27).

Similarly, John Worthen (1991a) pointed out that Lawrence in his early years wrote more than a few short stories that depicted women whose self-discovery evolved through their love relationships with men. Examples include Louisa in "Daughters of the Vicar," Emilie in "The Thorn in the Flesh," Elsie in "The White Stocking," and Paula in "New Eve and Old Adam" (34).

Then, too, we find comparisons between "Daughters of the Vicar" and *Women in Love*, which Lawrence was writing even as he made final revisions in his first short story collection. Janice Harris (1984) perceived "Daughters" as a kind of miniature *Women in Love* for it, too, followed the wooing and wedlock of two quite different sisters (55).

Yet another major thematic pattern, the Sleeping Beauty motif, connects "Daughters" with such later works as *The Virgin and the Gipsy* and *Lady Chatterley's Lover*. Herein, however, characters' roles are reversed; Louisa, a rescuing princess, approaches and "saves" the "slumbering" Alfred, who has yet to awaken into life on his own (Harris 1984, 59). The horse-dealers's daughter, too, plays this role.

Two critics drew parallels between "Daughters" and *The Virgin and the Gipsy*. Keith Cushman (1978) noted that the short story's structure and theme, as well as a commonality of incidents, anticipated Lawrence's 1926 novella (77). Philip Hobsbaum (1980) observed that the struggle between refined virginity and the physicality of natural man in "Daughters of the Vicar" foreshadows both *The Virgin and the Gipsy* and *Lady Chatterley's Lover* (115).

Much earlier, Mark Spilka (1955) examined thoroughly this facet of physicality in Lawrence's work. He noted that Lawrence's stress upon the sensory and emotional life of the body, as opposed to the rationalization of physicality and thus the subversion of its honesty, appears throughout "Daughters of the Vicar" in the juxtaposition of the Reverend Massey's "unthinkable" body and crippled psyche, on the one hand, and Alfred Durant's vital body, on the other. The same contrast appears in Mary's acceptance of the little minister and Louisa's subsequent horror and disgust. Thus, the Reverend Massey, with his infirmity and limited range of human emotions, presages Clifford Chatterley, a character similarly deficient in human compassion. The reverend's union to the spiritual Mary dramatizes the tension between mind and body, for the spouse of this chiefly cerebral creature is subsequently "degraded in the body" (203).

F.R. Leavis (1956) observed that this identical idea emerges much later in Lawrence's essay "A Propos of *Lady Chatterley's Lover*." In both "Daughters" and the novel, the body is spontaneous and vital. While the conscious mind could thwart it, the mind could not control or supplant it (85, 102, 105). Indeed, as Emile Delavenay (1972) observed, such cerebral facets as willfulness, self consciousness, or ulterior motive would, in Lawrence's view, doom love (155).

Delavenay was, in fact, one of the first critics to examine the "psychology" of sex Lawrence employed. The prospect of characters plunging into oblivion by means of sex so that their selves die and enter life eternal appears in the 1914 short-story revisions of such works as "Daughters of the Vicar" and "Second Best" (155).

Similarly, Keith Cushman (1978) discerned in the 1913 and 1914 revisions of "Daughters of the Vicar" an important role assumed by what would become typical Lawrentian language regarding sexual attraction. This language appears in the expanded back-washing scene of Section X, a scene Cushman referred to as "the emotional culmination" of a passage that parallels in its climactic importance and narrative tension the corpse-washing scene in "Odour of Chrysanthemums" (100–102). Again, in both "Daughters" and "Chrysanthemums," the insight the two female protagonists gain into "impersonal maleness" and the mysterious unknown results from each having established a vital connection with life by means of her contact with "a beautiful male body" (103).

Cushman noticed, too, a relation between Louisa's experience and Paul Morel's in *Sons and Lovers* where Paul and Miriam examine the white roses. In both scenes, an apprehension of another living thing's otherness—its separate and individual self—reaches the consciousness of the two life-seeking characters. Similarly, Lawrence's language in this bathing scene echoes descriptions of Tom Brangwen's passionate courtship in the 1914 version of *The Rainbow*. In both instances, self-consciousness and will are temporarily obliterated as desire increases. New life rises from oblivion's slumber (1978, 103, 105).

Cushman also discerned that Lawrence's descriptive language and the experience of the young lovers in "Daughters of the Vicar" foreshadow the language and experience of the lovers in "The Horse Dealer's Daughter," Jack Fergusson and Mabel Pervin. In both stories, the lovers are "drawn together by an irresistible force in a scene of intense, mysterious passion." Likewise, in "The Thorn in the Flesh," Bachmann connects by means of his lover with the eternal, and becomes a more complete human being. Again, Lawrence's use of language to describe both transfigurations is remarkably consistent (1978, 105–6).

In *The Rainbow*, Tom Brangwen and Lydia Lensky's courtship bears a remarkable resemblance to Alfred and Louisa's in "Daughters of the Vicar." As Cushman (1975) observed, when the lovers embrace they experience the presence of "the great impersonal." Through passion, Tom and Lydia's and Alfred and Louisa's alliances transcend personality as their essential selves connect. In both instances, their elemental meeting is distressing and demanding. In both works, the motif is one of departing into new being (189).

Despite such scenes of connection between men and women, Cushman pointed out that isolation appears far more frequently in *The Rainbow* and *The Prussian Officer and Other Stories* than communion. The bridge between two people is always flimsy, and one must avoid the violation of another's otherness (1975, 190).

In basic agreement with Cushman, Gordon Hirsch (1977) found in many of Lawrence's short stories fear of separateness and isolation, as well as the need to love and be loved. Hirsch cited "The Rocking-Horse Winner" as a case in point. Yet, a fear of engagement and the threat of the humiliation that might ensue are also present. To cope with this danger, which Hirsch considered maternal in origin, Lawrence used masculine "doubles": either a weak sensitive, intellectual male like Philip Farquhar in "The Border Line" and Egbert in "England, My England," or the vital blood-conscious male like Maurice Pervin in "The Blind Man" and the mine electrician in "The Shadow in the Rose Garden." These versions of Lawrence's own split nature and his severe criticism of both male roles may indicate self-loathing. Neither type, noted Hirsch, could protect itself completely from menacing women. Thus, in "The Man Who Loved Islands," Cathcart retreats from society, marriage, and family into himself, and self-destruction results from his fear of human connection. Accordingly, in such tales as "The Horse Dealer's Daughter" and "Daughters of the Vicar," the woman who actively pursues a vital relationship finds realization despite the male's passivity. One also finds relationships where a reluctance to participate results in violence, as in "Tickets, Please" and "None of That," both of which illustrate the danger of real intimacy and the brittle nature of self-identity. Regardless of which role the Lawrentian male accepts, he remains vulnerable. Thus, for Lawrence, all variants of the self are unsatisfactory and insecure (Hirsch 1977, 270–77).

Perhaps this evident insecurity in Lawrence prompted another critic, John Vickery (1973), to group "Daughters of the Vicar" with "Second Best," "The Horse Dealer's Daughter," and parts of *The Rainbow*. Each of these works presents marriage and love as inherently dangerous. Yet, Vickery also noted that Lawrence made great use of rituals, some rather unusual, others occurring in everyday activity. For example, the miner washes up before the hearth after his day in pit, a ritual that appears in "Daughters," *Sons and Lovers*, *The Rainbow*, "A Sick Collier" and "Jimmy and the Desperate Woman." In "Daughters of the Vicar," Lawrence stressed Alfred's rote, unconscious movement involved in the laving, the subsequent arousal of awe and trepidation in Louisa, and the basic "phallic core of object and attitude" (313, 316). This arousal in response to ritual reappeared years later in Lawrence's work when Connie Chatterley happens upon the bathing Mellors, who is unaware he is being observed and that his ritual bathing is deeply affecting the lady.

CRITICAL STUDIES

From the earliest reviews of "Daughters of the Vicar," much of the critical attention focused on the tautly wrought tension in the story between a person's emotional being and society's strictures. In 1914, Monkhouse remarked that this long tale has the scope of a novel. Louisa perceives her sister's cold marriage as a warning, and the last scene, where she and Alfred bear the condescension of her parents, is depicted strongly and beautifully, Lawrence's skill as a dramatist coming to the fore. Only a powerful writer, observed the critic, could "be so moderate" (94–5). In 1916, Lawrence's editor and advisor, Edward Garnett, noted the way this tale analyzed the oft-occurring clash between nature's morality, as manifested in the sexuality and worldly conduct it depicts (380).

Lawrence's death in 1930 occasioned much critical assessment of the writer's talent, much of the negative commentary exemplified by Joseph Wood Krutch's surprisingly hostile remarks in *The Nation*.

Beginning with the wrong date of death (March 3) and the incorrect age of the deceased (45), Krutch seemed to be striving for objectivity. Then he reported that Lawrence had been born "in a miner's cottage in Derbyshire" (320). Neither cot nor shire was correct. Repulsed by Lawrence's *Lady Chatterly* [sic] novel, Krutch refused to admit Lawrence into the first rank of novelists. Whether or not his biographical errors came from carelessness, his dismissal of Lawrence's talent seems rancorous. It does seem safe to say, however, that Krutch's opinion contained a bias perhaps social at its root. If so, his charge that Lawrence's work did not concern society appears in its utter wrong-headedness marvelously ironic (346).

In a subsequent article, Lionel Trilling (1930) differed with Krutch on this very point and argued that Lawrence's work struck "square into the middle of the cause of all misery—the social order" (363).

Trilling's critical position received strong reinforcement in F.R. Leavis's 1956 study *D.H. Lawrence: Novelist*. (The second chapter, entitled "Lawrence and Class," had first appeared two years earlier in *Sewanee Review* under the same title.) Leavis focused specifically on "Daughters of the Vicar" because it serves so well to rebut T.S. Eliot's charges that Lawrence was class conscious to the point of being a snob, and that Lawrence's characters, with their absence of moral or social sense, are unrecognizable as human beings (78–9). In point of fact, Leavis and Eliot had been sparring on this issue since 1934.

As to Eliot's first charge, Leavis illustrated how the tale's theme took up the triumph of life over class consciousness by means of Louisa's marriage to Alfred Durant, the miner, and by the coercion of Mary—both by her parents and her own ideal of "goodness"—into marrying Reverend Massey. As for the second charge, Leavis noted how Lawrence's depiction of working-class life remains unsentimental and realistic, a practice rare among his contemporaries (1956, 79).

Moreover, Leavis argued, Lawrence methodically developed his characters so as to illustrate that the emotional Louisa and Alfred are much closer to the warmth of life than the materialistic, unfeeling, class-conscious, willful, and maladjusted vicar, his wife, their daughter Mary, and the "little abortion," Massey—all of whom sacrifice true facets of humanity to an idea, an ideal, and a subsequent death-in-life existence. Indeed, argued Leavis, Lawrence's tale exhibits splendidly the greatest aspect of his art: life is to be approached reverently and with "a certain tenderness" (1956, 81). Having scuttled T.S. Eliot's argument, Leavis devoted the rest of his chapter to a vigorous thematic analysis of Lawrence's vitalistic expression.

Leavis carefully illustrated how "Daughters" ministered to life and established a true moral sense. After all, Mary bases her decision to marry the diminutive Massey on (1) the urging of her social-conscious parents, and (2) her willful decision to betray her own instincts and emotions by embracing the little Oxfordian, who is totally unconnected with life, as a representative of ideal "goodness." Mary's decision to sacrifice herself to the unvital, to class-consciousness and to hypocritical middle-class morality contrasts starkly with Louisa's decision to take a coal miner for a mate. Ultimately, Louisa's judgments manifest "a moral sense that [speaks] out of a fulness of life" (1956, 91). Louisa's courage is both heroic and moral. Consequently, we see expressed in this tale, in the form of "radical anti-snobbery," Lawrence's awareness of class distinction (89–95).

Ultimately, Louisa's resolution to have the man she desires expresses her vital quality, an attribute Leavis believed her deep-gold hair emblemizes. She thus refuses to allow their class differences to become an issue between them, helping him overcome his sense of inferiority by, in effect, proposing marriage to him. This climactic scene, asserted Leavis, "affect[s] us as a heroic triumph of life" (1956, 106).

Graham Hough's (1957) study did not focus solely upon "Daughters of the Vicar," but what he stated largely concurred with Leavis. Noting that the story's extended length and "elaborateness of pattern" rendered it a more ambitious work than "Odour of Chrysanthemums," Hough asserted that "Daughters" initiates Lawrence's familiar criticism of English class-consciousness. Also, the deadening influence of social consciousness and middle-class morality upon the vitality of a well-bred woman who turns for love to a socially inferior man, noted Hough, would become a signature Lawrentian theme (170).

Kingsley Widmer (1962) noted that "Daughters of the Vicar" contains many facets of social realism, primarily to show the moribund nature of the class-conscious clergy. Thus, he argued, the vicar and his wife encourage their "frigid" daughter to marry the repulsive Reverend Massey, which, convinced that his benevolence makes him truly good, she dutifully does. This sacrifice, Widmer asserted, illustrates Lawrence's belief that altruistic love is nihilistic (128).

The real subject of "Daughters" is not, Widmer concluded, social satire; rather, it is the dual nature of Eros. As Louisa washes Alfred's back, she experiences both a personal tenderness and an impersonal passion for the declassed, sensitive miner. With the return to the vicar's class-consciousness at the tales's conclusion—a condition the couple will escape by emigrating—we observe Lawrence's "usual moral": Eros simultaneously obliterates and transcends the social (1962, 130).

Frank O'Connor (1962) seemed to pick up where T.S. Eliot had left off. He was certain that Louisa's choice of a common working man for her husband manifests Lawrence's desire to attack the hierarchical society in which he was raised. Thus, O'Connor perceived in "Daughters of the Vicar" a sexual "ritual defilement" of the socially superior young lady by the miner (147).

Less controversial, E.W. Tedlock (1963) deemed this short story the most complicated of the tales appearing in *The Prussian Officer and Other Stories*. He considered it a revolutionary examination of the conflict between the colliers' natures and lives and their "cultural supervisors'" spiritual and virtuous contemplation (30). Accordingly, Tedlock argued that Mary and Louisa are suppressed into refinement and respectability, are encouraged to be ambitious, and are weighted down with duty. Indignant over the nature of Mary's marriage, Louisa's connection with Alfred combines physical attraction and love's reality. Saved from an ideal love, Louisa's vital connection with Alfred is awakened by the intimate physical act of washing the pit dirt from his back. Tedlock examined this scene closely, noting how Lawrence anticipated here his later method of repeating key words to establish "the qualitative differences" in Louisa's emotions, which linked sexual attraction with a humorous human response (30—32).

The next year, Ronald Draper's (1964) study of "Daughters" praised the accuracy with which Lawrence illustrated by means of Mr. and Mrs. Lindley a snobbishness peculiar to the lower-middle classes in rural England at the turn of the century. He found strength in the true-to-life rendering of the two sisters' feelings toward what each considered "good." Mary places principle before instinct; Louisa places instinct first. Mary sacrifices a vital life for devotion to an "abstract goodness." Louisa's attraction and eventual marriage to Alfred comes from her fidelity to "the blood." Obviously, Lawrence sided with Louisa, and Mary comes to share Massey's stigma. Yet, noted Draper, Lawrence was able to lend sympathy to Mary, for her marriage to Massey is encouraged by her parents, whose financial situation improves significantly as a result of the match (122–23).

Tony Slade's 1969 controversial analysis of "Daughters of the Vicar" took at least a fresh approach. Slade wondered if the story's acclaim was perhaps attributable more to its social comment than to its literary quality. He thought the story meritorious, but he considered the opposition established in the tale between vital working-class life and the sterile middle-class world of the vicar's family naive. He contended that Lawrence intimated, but failed to develop, how the working-class values of the Durants are so meaningful as to offer Louisa fulfillment through her marriage to Alfred. Such values, noted Slade, could not have been imparted to Louisa merely by her scrubbing a coal miner's back. Another weakness lay in Lawrence's failure to develop the important theme of Alfred's reticence and apparent impotence. Since Louisa presumably is to be Alfred's salvation, as he is to be hers, this theme needs more definition. Yet another flaw in the tale, as Slade saw it, is how Lawrence "stack[ed] the deck" against the Reverend Massey. Clearly Lawrence wanted the reader to deem Durant superior to the minister, but his intensely negative portrayal became a caricature. Unlike Casaubon in George Eliot's *Middlemarch*, to whom critics compared Massey, Slade found Lawrence's creation unconvincing. Despite these weaknesses, Slade considered the tale a powerfully effective assault upon the pride of class consciousness (101–03).

A study by R.E. Pritchard (1971) likewise criticized Lawrence's portrayal of society in "Daughters." Specifically, Pritchard faulted Lawrence's "uncertain" handling of the middle class. For example, he thought it unlikely that a vicar's wife of this period would think of Massey in terms of an abortion. Similarly, he deemed Louisa's independence and freedom of action "improbable." But the tale's excellent development of the two sisters and its thematic development transcended these weaknesses (61).

The following year, 1972, marked the publication of Delavenay's landmark study of Lawrence and his work, in which he noted that after 1912 Lawrence's concept and depiction of physical love changed. The greatest change appeared in the presentation of women as sexual beings. Their reactions became more believable, especially the sufferings of sexually unsatisfied women. They also displayed more audacity. No longer simply passive, Louisa Lindley, in her invitation to Alfred to marry her, becomes the first of Lawrence's female characters to take an active role in a matter of the heart. In their mutual commitment, instinct is victorious. Yet each has something to overcome. For Alfred it is his inhibitions with women and his sense of social inferiority. For Louisa it is the social prejudice of her class and society's condemnation of aggressive women. For them, as with all other of Lawrence's would-be lovers, the "artificial self" that denies the instinctive life must be obliterated. To experience sensual bliss and to awaken to cosmic interrelatedness, the old self existing on the levels of social and individual concepts must die, as it does in "Daughters of the Vicar" (200–03).

Anthony Piccolo's (1979) sociological examination addressed the question of whether Lawrence's short fiction possessed formal structure. Noting that Lawrence's work mostly concerned emotional elements and the evolution of relationships, Piccolo argued that Lawrence's short stories contained specific patterns of myth and ritual that formulated formal constructs. Consequently, in Lawrence's tales, one finds a logical and progressive "realistic narrative" countered by the process of a "submerged ritual strategy" that by means of its "inevitability" promotes a non-traditional scale of norms (88).

In "Daughters of the Vicar," Piccolo saw the "codified gentility" of Louisa's family as a device that distanced actual intimacy. In Lawrence's fiction it served to juxtapose the artificiality of modern English life with the vitality of much earlier societies. Similarly, noted Piccolo, such rituals of incorporation in middle-class codes of behavior illustrate to what extent the ancient rites had deteriorated (1979, 93).

In the following year, George Becker's (1980) study noted the way "Daughters" broached how class consciousness promotes the view of marriage as a kind of safety net. Thus, Mary weds Massey for financial security, but loses her life in the process, while Louisa throws caution and snobbery to the winds by marrying the miner, Alfred Durant, to whom she is attracted physically (116).

Marko Modiano (1987) also focused on the class-conflict theme in "Daughters of the Vicar." Industrialization had ruptured the intimate connection between men and women now replaced by the kind of rationality in the Reverend and Mrs. Lindley's lifeless marriage. Portraying the working class as possessed of a basic dignity and contrasting Alfred with Louisa's prim parents, Lawrence presented the working class as superior to other classes. Thus, condemning class repression, the tale lauded the human spirit, illustrating that a happy marriage could cut across class lines (64–68).

Three years elapsed before a critic again addressed the picture of society "Daughters" presented. Robert Kiely (1990) took a marxist-feminist approach in arguing that the class system in England both dehumanized workers and distanced the middle and upper classes from the vital earth itself, and from those who worked close to it. Consequently, in "Daughters," Louisa's loss of class consciousness when she washes the dirt from Alfred's back signals a victory of actual gender differences over the artificial difference in class. Her exclusion from vital earthly contact resulted less from a gender deficiency than from class-oriented constraints. By expressing her female sexuality, Louisa destroys a class barrier and determines herself, like Durant, to be of the earth rather than a possessor of it. Once class distinction is obliterated and she accepts her sex, Kiely argued, both she and her male lover can blossom in their new-found "common ground" (97–99).

David Holbrook's (1992) post-feminist examination of this story posited a more traditional love relationship. Unlike *The Virgin and the Gipsy*, where Yvette's desire stems more from her libido than from a need to discover a sense of meaning in her lover's uniqueness, the love relationship between Alfred and Louisa is of the latter type. In the face of their mortality and an irrelevant morality, their love lends their lives meaning, for it leads outward toward community, a vital family relationship, work, and responsibility. In other words, as Holbrook saw it, marriage is the end, and love is the means to that end (136).

The very fact that the most recent discussion of the way society is presented in "Daughters"—Graham Martin's (1992) materialist criticism steeped in the British Marxist humanism tradition—attempted to refute the much earlier F.R. Leavis illustrates the abiding importance of Leavis's work. Martin acknowledged the centrality of "class" in Lawrence's works but took issue with Leavis's reading. Whereas Leavis believed that the class-consciousness presented in this tale is defeated by "life" in the form of the two lovers' determination to marry despite class differences, Martin qualified the triumphant nature of their newly discovered "classless truth." The victory occurs at the personal level from Lawrence's authorial stance; however, Martin argued, the narrative surpassed authorial apprehension. Despite the Lindleys' loss of esteem in the reader's eyes, their ability to urge emigration upon the couple leaves the family's position in the community intact and confirms their social power. Thus, Martin concluded, the Lindleys prevail. Alfred and Louisa will flee the country, leaving its class system as firmly entrenched as ever (1992, 35–37).

The first study of Lawrence's work to apply facets of psychology to "Daughters of the Vicar" appeared in 1916 and was produced by Lawrence's own editor (of the *Prussian Officer* stories), Edward Garnett. Obviously familiar with Lawrence's short fiction, Garnett gave readers a rare glimpse into how those "in the know" received this young writer's art. Garnett asserted that in Lawrence's work "passion" is akin to its original meaning of "suffering"; his lovers experience a mixture of pain and pleasure stemming from the roots of their sexual lives that complements the dichotomy of senses and soul in the flux and flow of "surging emotion." Alfred and Louisa suffer in turn, but to them is granted a subsequent revelation concerning what is significant in their lives. Not merely a gratification of their senses, these lovers' experiences are also spiritual (380–81).

The next study to utilize psychology, Lionel Trilling's (1930) examination, consulted Lawrence's *Fantasia of the Unconscious* and noted how social and educational pressure develops the upper level of consciousness while it denigrates the lower level, or the unconscious, resulting in "the messy sterility of modern life" (366). As a result, man lives from only half his being. Lawrence's hope for mankind lay in the resurgence of blood knowledge in modern man.

More than thirty years passed before anyone approached "Daughters of the Vicar" again from the perspective of psychology. John Bayley (1962) set up a problem central to Lawrence's work, as he saw it: the brain receives romantic messages; thus, the romantic vision is paradoxical in its focus upon "dark and mysterious places of human desire and experience" even though the messages appear to illuminate that darkness in that one apprehends and appreciates them cerebrally (230). Bayley was obviously troubled by Lawrence's use of two levels of consciousness—mental and phallic. He interpreted them as denoting egoistic individuality and universal connection, respectively. Thus, by means of a love relationship, Lawrence universalized his characters, which removed their human wholeness leaving only "mind and will." But in a few short stories, notably "Daughters," the generalized figures (of Louisa and Alfred) do seem convincingly real (34, 122).

Daniel Weiss's (1962) examination of the tale emphasized its strong autobiographical aspects paralleling those in *Sons and Lovers*. For example, Mrs. Durant dies from a tumor identical to that of Gertrude Morel, and her relationship with her son is close enough to Gertrude's with Paul that Weiss considered the sons "interchangeable" (89). This view was curious when one contemplated the loathing that Mrs. Durant sometimes feels for her son. But Weiss argued that in "Daughters" Alfred's marriage to Louisa Lindley mirrors the marriage of Lawrence's parents, except that the son figure in the story assumes the father's rightful role by means of a mechanical transposition. Weiss saw the situation here as "counter-Oedipal," in that what might be seen as the son's submission to the father figure was, in fact, the expression of the son's desire to be like his father, spontaneous and direct in his manner of attaining satisfaction (91).

Kingsley Widmer's (1962) study of "Daughters" also focused on Alfred's Oedipal nature. Widmer asserted that the son's mother-love manifested itself for years as sex-in-the-head, an erotic dysfunction. With his mother's death, Alfred's old "narcissistic, incestuous, self-conscious and false freedom of restraint" disintegrated, his intense grief eventually leading him to "great chaos" and a splendid emancipation (129).

In 1971, R.E. Pritchard made some interesting assertions about the psychological makeup and portent of the vicar's two daughters and of Alfred. Mary's nature is "masochistic-idealistic" (61). As for the world of the mine as Alfred experiences it, Pritchard viewed it as less diabolic than amoral, representing "a force for integrative life" (61). The crucial scene where Louisa and Alfred commit completely to one another results from a timeless moment wherein, their inhibitions momentarily destroyed, they experience "a new simple truth" (62).

Emile Delavenay's (1972) study of "Daughters" discussed earlier in the sociological section placed "Daughters" within the psychological literature of the twentieth century, a fact we should note here (188).

In a 1975 essay on Lawrence's short fiction, Shirley Rose noted that Alfred Durant is quite susceptible to pain and suffers much during his mother's final agony. She then noted significance in the fact that Alfred finds solace and then optimism in the sudden revelation that his heart is still intact (1975, 78).

Gordon Hirsch's (1977) study found Lawrence incorporating into much of his literature "male doubles" (the weak sensitive male versus the virile blood-conscious man), and Hirsch perceived these roles as the two major facets of Lawrence's own nature. Believing that this dichotomy stemmed from Lawrence's ambivalent feelings about women in general and about his mother in particular, Hirsch discerned its formation as Lawrence's subconscious effort to protect himself from threats that might come from that quarter. Accordingly, Alfred Durant became the embodiment of Lawrence's own personality. As a miner, a reader of books, and a piccolo player, Alfred represents Lawrence's own split desire for manliness, as well as his largely passive nature. Like Alfred, he had to be rescued by an active woman who would awaken his virility, for Hirsch believed Lawrence's masculine identity to be "tenuous and fragile" (275).

Keith Cushman's (1980) study of the short fiction merged the psychological with the mythical by means of his observation that in

"Daughters" Louisa's awakening into a vital, alive courtship constituted a rewriting of the Sleeping Beauty *Märchen* (33).

The most recent work of criticism to approach "Daughters" from a psychological perspective came from Michael Black in 1986. He focused largely on the way Lawrence referred to Christianity in an endeavor to return to an earlier period. Thus, Reverend Lindley, Reverend Massey, and Mary Lindley-Massey appear as "an ascending order of limited Christian beings" (193).

All three express negative kinds of will and diverse types of faith. The vicar, a failure both as a man and as a man of the cloth, wills himself to be regarded as the social and moral head of the community, sacrificing Mary to that "social faith." Reverend Massey, against whom Lawrence "stacked the deck" further weakening a weakling characterization, represents reason, the life of the upper level of consciousness, the social persona, and "religion as a system of observances." Significantly, Massey is devoted to ministering to—and seeing to it that others serve—the Higher Will, the exact nature of which he seems to have an insider's knowledge. Mary Lindley's deference to Massey, wherein she willfully denies her body so as to embrace "the good" she deems present in Massey, Black perceived as a parallel to Mary, the Mother of Christ, while one might view Massey as "an awful parody of the Holy Ghost" as apprehended by "social" Christians (1986, 193–97).

In fact, Mary's determination to become a kind of handmaiden to the Highest Will is the exact opposite of Louisa's willful goal: to love someone enough to marry *him*, rather than merely what he *represents*. Black inferred from this difference that Lawrence did not condemn all forms of will; rather, one might appraise will by its type and its effect upon oneself and others (1986, 194).

Focusing upon the crucial scene where Louisa washes the pit dirt from Alfred's back, Black saw an allusion to Luke I: 26–38 that presents the Annunciation. Just as Mary willingly becomes handmaiden of the Lord, so too, by means of the ritual washing of Alfred's back (reminiscent of Mary Magdalene washing Christ's feet and of Christ washing his disciples' feet and which leads to Louisa's almost visionary experience), she feels love for and ministers to this man for whom she will soon relinquish her social position and even her native land. Far different from her sister's will to serve the will of another,

Louisa undergoes her own Annunciation and, consequently, quickens with new life which she then brings forth as "the next stage of herself" (190–92). In Black's words, "in ministering to him as a miner's wife naturally would, she receives her Annunciation, which is true where Mary's was false" (1986, 199).

When Alfred subsequently gazed down upon the nape of Louisa's neck and her golden hair, he too lost himself in the sudden revelation of her "otherness." Black astutely and ingeniously noted how Lawrence achieved this effect with language that involves neither reflection nor rationalization. Alfred's experience is visionary, and he is unable to capture it in words. Still, Louisa and he have yet actually to bridge the gulf that separates them. They are moved strongly to do so, not on the conscious level but rather on the unconscious plane of "internal process" (1986, 190–91).

The union between the lovers occurs near the story's end in a powerful scene that parallels the earlier bathing scene. In plain words and spontaneous gestures, they convey their love to one another. Louisa asks Alfred if he wants her, and he responds silently, extending his hand to her. Black viewed this passage as vital, as subtle, and as moving as the washing scene. When they embrace, each is reborn, and significantly, this act precedes yet another ritualistic washing, as Louisa tells Alfred, still in his dirty pit clothes, to make himself clean. Louisa's courage thus initiates the lovers' movement past their former self-conscious selves to their true selves in an act of transcendence that takes them beyond egoism (1986, 198–202).

The open-ended nature of the tale implies its theme: neither marriage partner could wholly know the other; for either to try to possess the other would doom the love. Each had to respect the integrity of the partner's "otherness" if they would both grow (Black 1986, 209).

Walter Nash (1982) published the first linguistic study to focus on "Daughters of the Vicar." Having adduced the significance of distinctive linguistic features in "Odour of Chrysanthemums" like deixis, article changes, and specific verb-types, Nash turned to "Daughters of the Vicar" to illustrate his point. He presented the long passage where Reverend Lindley visits the Durants, and then posed questions designed to guide a linguistic analysis and to illuminate a complex exemplar of "the language of narrative" (116–20).

Two years later, Gerald Doherty's (1984) linguistic study combined Lawrence's metaphysics with the narrative process in the tale, and related them both to Louisa and Alfred's courtship. Doherty posited an apocalyptic typology as the basis for Lawrence's eschatological model where a first epoch (law-female-metonymy) and a second epoch (love-male-irony) are in the process of being superseded by a projected third unspecified epoch, precipitating a crisis characterized by inhibited desire and unhappy relationships (1984, 135). Thus, Lawrence presented Louisa's initial romantic apprehension of Alfred as an ideal lover in a "rhetoric of representation"—an image—that subsequently became metaphor when she washes his back. The hope that they might move toward future contentment, as expressed at the conclusion of the second scene is, however, frustrated during their third meeting where the "transgression of social codes" capped by constrained verbalization results in the replacement of imaginative metaphors by trite patterns of usage. Lawrence's depiction of his lovers' moment of crisis dramatizes the demise of "figural language." This obstruction scenario both ended one "narrative epoch" and extended into an indeterminate future dynamic of desire and frustration, as evinced in the couple's new restraints that compel their emigration (141–42).

A good deal of critical attention has focused upon the text of "Daughters of the Vicar." A December 1914 book review of *The Prussian Officer and Other Stories* singled out "Daughters of the Vicar" for specific praise. The anonymous reviewer called this tale (and, in fairness, all the other eleven in the volume) "brilliant." The characters' passions are at times "volcanic," but unlike the stories where emotions are extreme, the tone of "Daughters" is temperate (*Outlook* (London), 796).

In 1924, Eliseo Vivas's thorough formalist study of Lawrence's fiction included an examination of "Daughters of the Vicar" and divided Lawrence's work in half. Vivas deemed everything after *Women in Love* mere manipulation of language, for he failed to see it dealing with the reality "and phenomenology of pure experience" as honestly or adeptly as the two great early novels *The Rainbow* and *Women in Love*. Vivas condemned the late novella "St. Mawr" as drawing upon stock situations and characters. Questionable, certainly, in the context of his thesis was Vivas's castigation of "Daughters of the Vicar" on these very grounds (123).

A critical work from 1930, Rebecca West's *D.H. Lawrence*, recognized that Lawrence's work did "justice to the seriousness of life," for (according to West) Lawrence had been granted deeper insight into the nature of life's seriousness than most (37).

By 1950 the reputation of "Daughters" had grown, so that critic Anthony West comfortably proclaimed it as "without limitation," and surely among "the best short stories in the English language" (105).

A 1966 article presenting a thorough textual analysis of this story showed just how wrong Vivas's appraisal had been. J.F.C. Littlewood examined earlier versions of "Daughters of the Vicar," using them to show F.R. Leavis's error in ascribing this tale and others in *The Prussian Officer and Other Stories* to Lawrence's astounding artistic maturity in the very early phase of his career when he wrote *The White Peacock* and *Sons and Lovers* (107–24).

Littlewood showed how the final version of "Daughters" as published in the collection could not have been written before 1913 when Lawrence began the first version of *The Rainbow*, following the November 1912 completion of *Sons and Lovers*. Littlewood developed his argument by comparing all variants of "Daughters of the Vicar" and certain passages in the second and the third versions of *The Rainbow* written in 1914—passages that reveal a new insight into "otherness" through Lawrence's living, responsive characters who are in tune with their essential selves (1966, 124). This artistic breakthrough resolved a problem concerning personal integration present in his earlier writing, and Littlewood attributed it to Lawrence's several rewrites of *The Rainbow* and having "come through" with Frieda's help (112). Littlewood's study also presented excerpts from some of Lawrence's letters to Edward Garnett and fiancée Louie Burrows between 1911 and 1914, serving to associate the various aspects of the critical argument.

A subsequent textual study of the "Daughters" variants resembled Littlewood's. In it, Brian Finney (1975) asserted that Lawrence's masterful short stories in *The Prussian Officer and Other Stories* were not further evidence of a style already present in *Sons and Lovers*. Rather, none of the pre–1912 tales revealed any more maturity than that found in his first two novels, 1911's *The White Peacock* and 1912's *The Trespasser* (321).

By collating the different versions of "Daughters of the Vicar," Finney noted major differences between early variants and the final. First, the earlier ones were much shorter. Second, the final contains fewer factual details and events. Third, the earlier variants rely heavily upon plot. Fourth, the last version replaces the earlier sentimentality with real emotion (1975, 322).

Finney also traced Lawrence's maturation as revealed in these several texts, and he decided that the 1911 variant, "Two Marriages," like the early version of "The Shadow in the Rose Garden," documented unresolved personal problems, for in each, a possessive woman seems to hold a male protagonist in thrall. In "Daughters," Alfred's mother offers to leave her son to Louisa so that he will not go wrong after her death. This sentimentality disappears from the two later versions, as did the *Märchen*-like ending where Alfred and Louisa are wed, have several children, and live happily ever after (1975, 330).

In the 1913 version, much closer to that of 1914, both protagonists must choose between dependence and independence; only Louisa does so in 1911. Again, however, the ending is too tidy: the two marry and share a vital life together in a suddenly class-unconscious England (Finney 1975, 330).

"Daughters of the Vicar" underwent a major transformation in 1914. Louisa's parents and England's class-consciousness force Louisa and Alfred outside the circle. Marrying against society's stricture, the couple must emigrate to Canada—the price for placing personal satisfaction above social convention (Finney 1975, 300–331).

Mara Kalnins' (1976) textual analysis of "Daughters" furthered the work of Littlewood and Finney. Her examination of its final form in relation to its original embodiment as "Two Marriages" effectively illustrated the advances Lawrence made in his art between 1911 and 1914. During this period, Lawrence reshaped the tale so as to: (1) present a more discerning story line, (2) display a deeper psychological understanding of the characters, (3) reveal a more accomplished technique, and (4) experiment effectively with language and style (32–34).

Beyond his new awareness of class consciousness in "Daughters of the Vicar," Lawrence developed an ability to depict with equal deftness states of mind and states of being. Using Mary's resignation in reaction to her misshapen husband, Kalnins illustrated how Lawrence delved beyond Mary's "verbal consciousness" to communicate both her emotions and her unspoken thoughts, giving a reader the sense of being in direct contact with Mary's psyche. To achieve this feat, Lawrence united his narrative with "free indirect speech"—partially formulated thoughts presented in the third-person and the past tense. Such a merger clarified both the narrative and the character's thoughts (1976, 34–38).

As another stylistic innovation in "Daughters of the Vicar," Lawrence adopted unusual grammatical and semantical constructions to convey experiences as yet undenoted by a settled vocabulary (Kalnins 1976, 44). For example, he would exchange the language of vision for that of hearing. Sometimes linguistic confusion, like Alfred's apprehension of reality following his mother's death, parallels the confusion in a character's mind (45). Another example appears in Lawrence's use of "lexical and semantic repetition," subordinate clauses, and many conjunctions and connecting adverbs, reminiscent of Biblical language, a strategy that suggests Lawrence's belief in the religion of instinctive blood-consciousness (44–47).

Thematic differences between the two variants also exist. While both versions promote the primacy of deep instinctive powers over the superficiality of class consciousness, the latter broaches the mystery of sexual attraction and presents a way to describe this mystery. Only in the "Daughters of the Vicar" version does Lawrence's idea of "otherness" appear and, subsequently, the paradox that the more intimate two people become, the greater their sense of being separate. Also in this later rendition, Louisa recognizes the mystery of her attraction to Alfred and the human body's "living reality." She is drawn to Alfred on more than merely the sexual level: to Louisa he represents spontaneity, vitality, and the integrity of being (Kalnins 1976, 39–42).

Another significant difference between the early and late versions concerns Lawrence's use of "will." Kalnins pointed out that in "Daughters of the Vicar" Louisa, Alfred, and Mary are all involved in an effort to emerge into conscious being. In so presenting them,

Lawrence illustrated right and wrong "will." Mary's willed rejection of her body—abstract and mental in nature—is negative. Louisa's will to love the man she marries is positive, for it is a conscious decision to embrace a "right moral judgment," which, in turn, determines the positive character of her fate. Mary's fate, however, reflects her wrong "will." Also in "Daughters of the Vicar" but not in "Two Marriages," the germ of an idea appears that would be developed fully in *The Rainbow*: fulfillment has a religious nature, for it goes beyond individual passion and personality, striving to connect with what is both beyond and superior to man (Kalnins 1976, 42–45).

Keith Cushman's (1978) study *D.H. Lawrence at Work: The Emergence of "The Prussian Officer" Stories* presents the most thorough textual analysis of "Daughters of the Vicar." Building upon the earlier studies, Cushman examined all five early variants of the tale and showed how they provided "new theoretical insights into human personality (and the language expressing these insights)" (78). These five early forms follow: (1) a July 15, 1911, 23-page holograph rough draft fragment entitled "Two Marriages" beginning after Louisa washed Alfred Durant's back and concluding at the finished story's end; (2) the first part of the October 1911 revision Lawrence had typed and then tried unsuccessfully to sell (a fragment of this variant was sold by Curtis Brown for Frieda after Lawrence's death and appeared as "Two Marriages" in the journal *Time and Tide* and both of these fragments ended suddenly after the backwashing scene); (3) a holograph revision and a subsequent holograph fair copy of the 1911 typescript made the summer of 1913—a major revision that included a new title, "Daughters of the Vicar"; (4) the July 14, 1914, revision which became galley sheets; and (5) the October 1914 revision of these proof pages (78–80). Although Cushman discussed each of these early versions, his analysis focused mainly on the October 1911 revision of "Two Marriages" and the tale's final form as published in *The Prussian Officer* collection.

Cushman adduced four primary patterns of revision that best reflect the progress Lawrence, the artist, was making. The first pattern concerned the picturing of class distinctions. Only in the 1914 revision of the 1911 and 1913 variants did Lawrence come to terms with his fears that Louisa, like his own mother, marries beneath herself. In the earlier versions, he presented Louisa's husband as her intellectual and social inferior, which she attempts to make more bearable by concentrating on the vitality he brings to their relationship. As Cushman noted, their happy marriage seems a fairy tale variant of Lawrence's parents' marriage. Finally, in the 1914 revisions, Lawrence removed class consciousness as a threat to the marriage by allowing them to leave for Canada, where society will not deprecate a love based on a foundation other than class identity. As the final versions of the backwashing scene and Alfred's request for Louisa's hand make clear, "a world of class awareness had been replaced by a world of transfiguration" (1978, 87–91).

The second pattern of revision involved the Oedipal facets of the mother-son relationship. As it did *Sons and Lovers*, this aspect infuses both "Two Marriages" and "Daughters of the Vicar." In the earlier variant, however, Alfred never comes to terms with his mother-love: after Mrs. Durant dies, he marries Louisa, seeing in her a surrogate mother. But in the 1913 and 1914 revisions, Alfred frees himself from maternal bonds by a marriage wherein "the dark mystery of the body" saves him. The mother-love so evident in the 1911 versions yields to a vital man-woman relationship; no Oedipal overtones remain in the Alfred-Louisa relationship of "Daughters of the Vicar," for their deep, lasting love is of a vital nature (Cushman 1978, 99–100).

The fact that Lawrence took greater pains to control the Oedipal elements in the later versions of the tale illustrated two important points: (1) Alfred's passage from a "death-in-life" existence to a vital one seems all the more victorious, and (2) Lawrence considered his own sons-and-lovers problem resolved. He had finished *Sons and Lovers* the November before the 1913 revision of "Daughters." While he had attempted to reconcile his feeling for his mother in *Sons and Lovers*, such a coming to terms must have been tentative at best. But having lived with Frieda for a year before the 1913 revisions, he evidently achieved and could then depict this reconciliation. Significantly, too, the revisions illustrate the exchange of Alfred's Oedipal torment for a "celebration of the mysterious otherness of his new beloved and of the powerful energies radiating through the universe." Thus, Cushman ascertained that whereas "Daughters of the Vicar" celebrates the possibility of a vital man-woman relationship, "Two Marriages" seems instead a lesson in "the primacy and persistence of mother love" (1978, 97–99).

The third revision pattern Cushman focused upon involved increases in the characteristic Lawrentian intensity, especially in his description of sexual passion. In the 1913 and 1914 revisions, what would become typical Lawrentian language regarding sexual attraction begins to assume prominence. This language is very much in evidence in the greatly expanded backwashing scene in Section X, what Cushman called "the emotional culmination of "Daughters of the Vicar" (1978, 101). In the 1914 revision, in fact, the scene becomes central to the story. In the revised passage, Louisa's awareness of Alfred begins on the social level, progresses on to a human awareness, and then proceeds beyond, as she ascends the stairs feeling somewhat strange and quick with life (102–03).

Another passage revised in 1914 and indicative of Lawrence's newly bold descriptions of sexual passion shows Louisa and Alfred embracing for the first time. Their mutually strong ardor replaces what in the earlier versions had been Louisa's maternal response to a "grieving son." In 1914, self-consciousness and will give way to desire and new life (Cushman 1978, 104–105).

The final focus of Cushman's textual study concerned the central polarity—the body and human connection versus the psyche and abstraction—that became more clearly defined and stated in the 1914 revisions of "Daughters of the Vicar", wherein the metaphysics and theoretical idiom appeared prominently. Calling "Daughters" a splendid work for illustrating how Lawrence merged metaphysic and art, Cushman took Emile Delavenay to task for missing the metaphysic in this tale—seeing only that Alfred's character was more developed as a real person, as shown by his sensitivity and human potential, and overlooking Lawrence's development of the miner by going beyond his "old stable ego" (1978, 107).

A most important facet of Lawrence's metaphysic at the time pertained to the negative nature of "will," or willfulness. Cushman observed that the language of will is ubiquitous in "Daughters of the Vicar," especially in connection with the Reverend Massey's marriage to Mary. In the 1911 typescript, Mary bases her decision to wed upon economics, but in the 1914 versions, the will predominates. Likewise, in the two daughters' marriages one finds the heart of the matter: the polarity between a vital relationship based upon human contact and a death-in-life existence emanating from "abstract goodness." The

Masseys' marriage becomes a battle of wills; the Durants' becomes one of spontaneity and fleshly contact. This dichotomy is so well developed and firmly established in the final version as to make parts of it schematic. Yet, one result of Lawrence's metaphysic visible in the 1914 versions is the addition of the impersonal passion that would become a mainstay device throughout his career (1978, 109–110).

Cushman concluded his study with a discussion of the important theme of human isolation so pervasive in the final versions of "Daughters of the Vicar." While the early variants showed the class-conscious Louisa's efforts to see more in Alfred than his social class, the 1914 versions show her seeking beyond "personality" to the miner's essential self. While "Two Marriages" was based firmly upon social criticism, "Daughters of the Vicar" is far more concerned with the vitality of Alfred and Louisa's love, "based on the dark mystery residing in the flesh [and of coming] together in the presence of the mysterious nonhuman source of life" (1978, 112–115).

Thus, Cushman resolved that the essential polarities in the tale—"mind versus body, abstract virtue versus human contact, religion versus life"—appear clearer in "Daughters of the Vicar" than in the earlier versions because of "the emergence and crystallization of many of Lawrence's ideas" in 1914 when he was close to finishing *The Rainbow* and revising *The Prussian Officer* stories. Thus, "Daughters of the Vicar" is a more "doctrinaire" story than its earlier variants, which served to make it at once more abstract and, paradoxically, more infused with life through the development of Alfred and Louisa's love (1978, 114).

Janice Harris's 1984 study observed that the 1913 revision where "Two Marriages" became "Daughters of the Vicar" presents a new artistic style: realism is still employed, but in deference to a new visionary quality (49). Of all the stories Lawrence wrote at Croydon, only "Two Marriages" focused on the great happiness a successful love could bring two people. This detailed attention to the two protagonists' bliss marked Lawrence's inevitable departure from the school of realism (54). In fact, Harris noted, the tale's focus upon two sisters and their suitors multiplied the possible affiliations, options, and confrontations, all of which illustrate Lawrence's movement "toward a new mode of short story" (1984, 57).

Harris, focused on Lawrence's language, also noted that by 1913 and 1914, he had abandoned "the language of pure, referential realism" that characterized his early writing in favor of a more penetrating visionary style she heralded as "a true linguistic breakthrough" (1984, 55 & 60).

This discussion of the "Daughters of the Vicar" criticism concludes with John Worthen's (1991b) study, the latest to focus upon textual variations. In comparing a passage from "Two Marriages" with its 1911 revision, Worthen observed that Lawrence originally had Louisa confide in Alfred that his mother had asked her to accept him. This news makes the young man feel reconciled to the two women in his life, even though his mother has died. In the revision, Louisa informs Alfred simply that his mother had told her he would ask her to marry, and Alfred subsequently feels in harmony with life. The difference, concluded Worthen, suggests that in July of 1911, Lawrence had derived solace from his loyalty to his dead mother's wishes effected by his engagement to Louie Burrows, of whom his mother had approved (318–19).

One might also conclude, however, that the textual emendation made just months later in 1911 reflected the waning of both his sense of obligation to his mother and the amount of comfort that it afforded him.

Begun after the 1914 revisions of *The Prussian Officer* tales, *The Rainbow* in its fourth and final form contained a dual vision: the view that man's being relates to the eternal rhythms of the cosmos, on the one hand, and this ethereal vision of radiance arising from the common workaday world, on the other. This same dual vision appears in the best stories of *The Prussian Officer*, including the title story. Keith Cushman (1978) asserted that Lawrence's ability to present these two aspects of his imagination so harmoniously is unequalled in any of his later work, including *The Rainbow* (44).

The initial difficulty Lawrence experienced in seeing "Daughters of the Vicar" into print belied the short story's masterful craftsmanship. Once it appeared in 1914's *The Prussian Officer and Other Stories*, however, praise came quickly. The critical appreciation of this story held steady over the years, and it is still recognized as one of Lawrence's great early achievements.

WORKS CITED

Aldington, Richard. [1959] 1961. "The Composite Biography as Biography." Harry T. Moore, Ed. *A D.H. Lawrence Miscellany.* Carbondale: Southern Illinois University Press. London: Heinemann Ltd. 143–152.

Athenaeum. 1915. "Fiction," No. 4552 (January 23): 68.

Bayley, John. [1960] 1962. *The Character of Love: A Study in the Literature of Personality.* New York: Basic Books. Reprint. London: Constable and Co. Ltd.

Becker, George. 1980. *D.H.Lawrence.* New York: Frederick Ungar Publishing Co.

Black, Michael. 1986. *D.H. Lawrence: The Early Fiction.* Cambridge: Cambridge University Press.

Boulton, James T., ed. 1979. *The Letters of D.H. Lawrence.* Vol.1. Cambridge: Cambridge University Press.

———. 1981. *The Letters of D.H. Lawrence.* Vol.2. Cambridge: Cambridge University Press.

Cushman, Keith. 1980. "The Achievement of *England, My England and Other Stories.*" *D.H. Lawrence: The Man Who Lived.* H.T. Moore and R.B. Partlow, eds. Carbondale: Southern Illinois University Press. 27–38.

———. 1978. *D.H. Lawrence at Work: The Emergence of The Prussian Officer Stories.* Charlottesville: University of Virginia Press.

———. 1975. "'I am going through a transition stage.'" *The D.H. Lawrence Review* 8: 176–97.

Delavenay, Emile. 1972. *D.H. Lawrence: The Man and His Work.* Carbondale, Illinois: Southern Illinois University Press.

Doherty, Gerald. 1984. "The Third Encounter: Paradigms of Courtship in D.H. Lawrence's Shorter Fiction." *The D.H. Lawrence Review* 17.1: 135–51.

Draper, Ronald. 1964. *D.H. Lawrence.* Boston: Twayne Publishers.

Eliot, T.S. 1933. *After Strange Gods: A Primer of Modern Heresy.* London: Jonathan Cape.

———. 1951. "Foreword." *D.H. Lawrence and Human Existence.* Father William Tiverton [pseudonym of Martin Jarrett- Kerr]. London: Philosophical Library. vii–viii.

Finncy, Brian. 1975. "D.H. Lawrence's Progress to Maturity: From Holograph Manuscript to Final Publication of *The Prussian Officer and Other Stories.*" *Studies in Bibliography*: 321–32.

Garnett, Edward. 1916. "Art and Moralists: Mr. D.H. Lawrence's Work." *The Dial* 61(November 16): 377–81.

Harris, Janice. 1984. *The Short Fiction of D.H. Lawrence.* New Brunswick, New Jersey: Rutgers University Press.

Hirsch, Gordon D. 1977. "The Lawrentian Double: Images of D.H. Lawrence in the Stories." *The D.H. Lawrence Review* 10.3 (Fall): 270–77.

Hobsbaum, Philip. 1980. *A Reader's Guide to D.H. Lawrence.* London: Thames & Hudson.

Holbrook, David. 1992. *Where Lawrence Was Wrong About Women.* Lewisburg: Bucknell University Press.

Kalnins, Mara. 1976. "D.H. Lawrence's 'Two Marriages' and 'Daughters of the Vicar.'" *Ariel* 7: 32–49.

Kiely, Robert. 1990. "Out on Strike: The Language and Power of the Working Class in Lawrence's Fiction." *The Challenge of D.H. Lawrence.* Michael Squires and Keith Cushman, eds. Madison: University of Wisconsin Press. 89–102.

Krutch, Joseph Wood. 1930. "D.H. Lawrence." *The Nation* 130(March): 320, 346.

Lawrence, D.H. 1934. "Two Marriages." *Time and Tide* (March 24): 394–99.

Leavis, F.R. [1956] 1979. *D.H. Lawrence: Novelist.* New York: Alfred A. Knopf. Reprint. Chicago: University of Chicago Press.

Littlewood, J.F.C. 1966. "D.H. Lawrence's Early Tales." *The Cambridge Quarterly* 1: 107–124.

Martin, Graham. 1992. "D.H. Lawrence and Class." *D.H. Lawrence.* Peter Widowson, ed. New York: Longman Publishing. 83–97.

Modiano, Marko. 1987. *Domestic Disharmony and Industrialization in D.H. Lawrence's Early Fiction.* Sweden: Uppsala.

Monkhouse, Allan (A.N.M.). [1914] 1973. "Review of *The Prussian Officer and Other Stories.*" *Manchester Guardian* Dec. 17. Reprint. *D.H. Lawrence: A Critical Anthology.* H. Coombes, ed. Harmondsworth: Penguin Books Inc. 94–6.

Nash, Walter. 1982. "On a Passage from Lawrence's 'Odour of Chrysanthemums.'" *Language and Literature: An Introductory Reader in Stylistics.* Ronald Carter, ed. London: George Allen & Unwin. 101–23.

Nehls, Edward, ed. 1957. *D.H. Lawrence: A Composite Biography. Volume One, 1885–1919.* Madison: University of Wisconsin Press.

O'Connor, Frank. 1962 [1963]. *The Lonely Voice: A Study of the Short Story.* Cleveland: The World Publishing Co. Reprint. Same publisher.

Orwell, George. 1945 [1968]. [*The Prussian Officer and Other Stories.*] *London Tribune.* November 16. Reprint. *The Collected Essays, Journalism and Letters of George Orwell, Vol. 4: In Front of Your Nose, 1945–1950.* Sonia Orwell, ed. New York: Harcourt, Brace. 31–33.

Outlook (London). 1914. "Novels," 24(Dec. 19): 795–96. Reprint. 1970. *D.H.Lawrence: The Critical Heritage.* R.P. Draper, ed. London: Routledge & Kegan Paul; New York: Barnes & Noble. 81–3.

Piccolo, Anthony. 1979. "Ritual Strategy: Concealed Form in the Short Stories of D.H. Lawrence." *Mid-Hudson Language Studies* 2: 88–99.

Potter, Stephen. 1930. *D.H.Lawrence: A First Study*. London: Garden City Press Ltd.

Pritchard, R.E. 1971. *D.H. Lawrence: Body of Darkness.* Pittsburgh: University of Pittsburgh Press.

Rose, Shirley. 1975. "Physical Trauma in D.H. Lawrence's Short Fiction." *Contemporary Literature* 16: 73–83.

Sagar, Keith. 1979. *D.H. Lawrence: A Calendar of His Works with a Checklist of the Manuscripts of D.H. Lawrence by Lindeth Vasey.* Austin: University of Texas Press.

Saturday Review (London). 1915. [*The Prussian Officer and Other Stories*] 9 January: 42–43.

Schneider, Daniel J. 1986. *The Consciousness of D.H. Lawrence: An Intellectual Biography.* Lawrence: University Press of Kansas.

Slade, Tony. 1969. *D.H. Lawrence.* New York: Arco Publishing Co., Inc.

Spilka, Mark. 1955. *The Love Ethic of D.H. Lawrence.* Bloomington: Indiana University Press.

Tedlock, E.W. 1963. *D.H. Lawrence: Artist and Rebel.* Albuquerque: University of New Mexico Press.

Trilling, Lionel. 1930. "D.H. Lawrence: A Neglected Aspect." *Symposium* I(July): 361–70.

Van Spanckeren, Kathryn. 1986. "Lawrence and the Uses of Story." *The D.H. Lawrence Review* 18.2–3: 291–301.

Vickery, John. 1973. *The Literary Impact of 'The Golden Bough.'* Princeton, N.J.: Princeton University Press.

Vivas, Eliseo. 1960. *D.H. Lawrence: The Failure and the Triumph of Art.* Evanston: Northwestern University Press.

Weiss, Daniel. 1962. *Oedipus in Nottingham: D.H. Lawrence.* Seattle: University of Washington Press.

West, Anthony. [1950] 1977. *D.H. Lawrence.* Denver: Alan Swallow. Reprint. Norwood Editions.

West, Rebecca. [1930] 1969. *D.H. Lawrence.* London: Martin Secker. Reprint. Folcroft, PA: The Folcroft Press, Inc.

Widmer, Kingsley. 1962. *The Art of Perversity: D.H. Lawrence's Shorter Fiction.* Seattle: University of Washington Press.

Worthen, John. 1991a. *D.H. Lawrence.* London: Edward Arnold.

———. 1991b. *D.H. Lawrence: The Early Years 1885–1912.* Cambridge: Cambridge University Press.

———. 1989. *D.H. Lawrence: A Literary Life.* New York: St. Martin's Press.

Worthen, John, ed. 1983. *The Prussian Officer and Other Stories.* Cambridge: Cambridge University Press.

IV
"The Prussian Officer"

PUBLICATION HISTORY

In early June of 1913, having finished the initial draft of "The Sisters," which would eventually become the two novels *The Rainbow* and *Women in Love*, Lawrence turned again to writing short fiction. The immediate results were: "Honour and Arms," eventually retitled "The Prussian Officer"; "Vin Ordinaire," retitled later "The Thorn in the Flesh"; and "Eve and Old Adam," which would become "New Eve and Old Adam" (Worthen 1983, xii). Lawrence composed his renowned story about a German officer and his orderly at one sitting while in Germany (Delavenay 1972, 196). In a June 10 letter posted from Irschenhausen, Oberbayern, to Edward Garnett, his literary advisor, Lawrence excitedly referred to "the best short story I have ever done" (Boulton 1981, 21).

In a June 21 letter to Garnett from Garnett's own residence, The Cearne, in Kent, Lawrence asked if he should send Ezra Pound, agent for the magazine *Smart Set*, the three "good short stories" composed immediately prior to his and Frieda's recent return from Germany (Boulton 1981, 26 & n. 5). But before he sent them anywhere, Lawrence wanted to rework them.

The July revision of "Honour and Arms," however, required no reconceptualization of the tale, for the original holograph had been brilliantly structured by Lawrence's metaphysic, which had guided an ingenious integration of art and philosophy. So pleased was Lawrence with his newfound metaphysic that he revised the remaining tales infusing them with his new idea of man as phenomenon or as representing some transcendent will (Cushman 1978, 40, 173). Although Lawrence amended a number of words and expressions in

"Honour and Arms" that July, he retained the force of the tale. This variant proved close to the one that would reach print in a magazine the following year, except for some unauthorized cuts made by the journal's editors (211–12).

On July 20, Lawrence sent Garnett "Honour and Arms" and "Vin Ordinaire" with instructions to send them to either the *English Review* or the literary agent J.B. Pinker, whichever Garnett considered the wiser course (Boulton 1981, 44–45, n. 9). Garnett chose the former for "Vin Ordinaire" and the latter for "Honour and Arms." In his cover letter of July 23 to Pinker, Garnett called the tale "very fine" and compared its psychological genius to the work of Stephen Crane and Joseph Conrad. Garnett also promised Pinker that if he sold the tale, more from Lawrence would be forthcoming. Pinker accepted the challenge, sending the tale to the *English Review* and the American magazine *Metropolitan* (Boulton 1981, 6).

Before the *English Review* had the two German military tales long in its possession, however, its editor, Austin Harrison, wrote to Lawrence on October 3, 1913, with a proposition. If Lawrence could provide one or two additional such tales, the *English Review* would pay Lawrence fifteen pounds apiece for the four stories, advertise them prominently, and do all it could to promote their author. Lawrence was thrilled with Harrison's offer (Boulton 1981, 81–2). Unfortunately, Pinker had been sent "Honour and Arms," and the *English Review* doubted he would settle for fifteen pounds. Thus, Lawrence resolved to retrieve the story from Pinker.

In his letter of October 6, 1913, Lawrence asked Garnett to get the story back for him. He had two tales, "Once" and "The Mortal Coil," he thought would meet the *English Review*'s offer. Evidently receiving no satisfaction through Garnett, Lawrence himself wrote Pinker on October 19, informed him of Harrison's four-story proposition, and asked him to give "Honour and Arms" to the *English Review* for fifteen pounds. Then on October 26, Lawrence wrote Arthur McLeod, telling him, too, of the *English Review*'s offer to publish three or four soldier stories as a series, after which Lawrence might put them out in book form (Boulton 1981, 90).

By December, however, the winds had shifted. Despite telling Garnett in a December 21 letter that Harrison—now described as a "vague and common" man of "cheap suggestions"—would soon publish the four military tales, Lawrence never saw the proposed series in print (Boulton 1981, 127). No record explains why the idea died, but Lawrence's castigation of Harrison's character in the December letter presaged ill for the project.

By mid-July of 1914, Lawrence had sent Garnett several recently revised stories to be published by Duckworth in what would become the first collection of Lawrence's short fiction. Listing the twelve tales in the order that he wanted to see them, he placed "Honour and Arms" last, after "Vin Ordinaire." The other two soldier stories were not included. Lawrence also estimated the length of "Honour and Arms" at 9,600 words (Boulton 1981, 196–97).

By return post, Garnett asked him to open the volume with "Vin Ordinaire," and Lawrence responded that Garnett should first read the latest revision Lawrence had just finished, for, as he said, "we don't want them to sneeze at the first whiff." In fact, Garnett would place this tale, now called "The Thorn in the Flesh," second in the collection, right after "Honour and Arms," the story Garnett himself eventually retitled "The Prussian Officer" (Boulton 1981, 198–99).

Meanwhile, Pinker had sold "Honour and Arms" to the *English Review* for fifteen pounds (Worthen 1989, 40). Accepted in October of 1913, it appeared in print for the first time in the *English Review* 18 (August, 1914). Then on September 15, 1914, Lawrence wrote to Pinker complaining of how the *English Review* had abridged "Honour and Arms" (Boulton 1981, 216). The magazine had, in fact, deleted large chunks to squeeze the story to a length that accommodated its policy at that time (Worthen 1983, xxxviii).

Blame for these deletions fell upon editor Norman Douglas, who would eventually become an outspoken adversary of Lawrence. His cuts produced a tale some 1500 words shorter than the one eventually published as "The Prussian Officer" in the Duckworth collection (Cushman 1978, 212–13). Lawrence also informed Pinker in this same letter that his sister, Ada, would send the agent a typescript of the complete tale, and that he was glad to hear Pinker had placed the story in an American magazine ((216).

The next month, Lawrence told Garnett that Pinker had sent him twenty-five pounds for "Honour and Arms" and that it would appear in the November 1914 issue of the American journal *Metropolitan* with illustrations by Harry E. Townsend (Boulton 1981, 222, 197, n. 2). But any hopes Lawrence had that *Metropolitan* would print the tale intact disappeared when the story appeared with the same deletions the *English Review* had made (Worthen 1983, xxxviii).

The various commercial abridgements failed to erase the tale's coherence or dramatic force. Rather, the omission of entire paragraphs or the arguably redundant sections resulted only in a less fully developed story (Harris 1984, 271 n. 14). Of the fifteen paragraphs cut by the *English Review*, however, readers acquainted with the story would note the absence of two: the scene where the orderly knocks over a bottle of wine while serving the officer, and the disarming description of the squirrels (Cushman 1978, 212).

In July of 1914, Lawrence suggested to Duckworth a tentative title for his forthcoming collection of short stories: *Goose Fair*, then a few days later, *The Thorn in the Flesh*, and finally, in October, *The Fighting Line* (Worthen 1983, xiii). This latter title, Lawrence's final suggestion, reflected his awareness that the stories challenged commonly held beliefs and forms of perception. (Cushman 1978, 46). He also had firm ideas about the arrangement of the tales in the volume, placing "Honour and Arms" last to achieve a favorable impression of the overall volume at its conclusion. To his dismay, Edward Garnett differed with him on both the title and the arrangement.

As his next task, Lawrence began to examine the Duckworth page proofs during October of 1914. Although he declined to correct the "Honour and Arms" page proofs extensively, some of the changes are interesting (Worthen 1983, xxxix). For example, in earlier manuscript form the orderly shows much more respect for the officer's body: the corpse was "laid" and "put" rather than "pushed" away, and is often thought of as "him" (250). Generally speaking, however, the October revisions were slight.

In a letter of October 16, 1914, to Amy Lowell, Lawrence mentioned his imminent short-story collection from Duckworth entitled *The Prussian Officer and Other Stories*, which would open with the title tale earlier called "Honour and Arms." He also told her that if the American publishing firm of Houghton Mifflin were interested in this collection, they could contact Duckworth (Boulton 1981, 222–23). (When the collection finally appeared in America in 1916, Huebsch was its publisher.)

On November 26, 1914, *The Prussian Officer and Other Stories* came out of Duckworth in two slightly different forms. At the end of the book one publisher's catalogue ran to sixteen pages, the other to twenty pages. It is impossible to determine which is the earlier, and both books are first editions (McDonald, 1925, 34–6). The selling price was six shillings (*Athenaeum* 1915, 68).

In a letter to J.B. Pinker on December 5, 1914, Lawrence castigated Garnett for titling his book *The Prussian Officer*. He called Garnett "a devil" and asked, "What Prussian Officer?" (Boulton 1981, 240–41). Lawrence had neither called his story "The Prussian Officer," nor had the retitled "Honour and Arms" concerned the Prussian Army, but the Bavarian, which prior to World War I was not part of the Prussian Army (Worthen 1983, 249).

Edward Garnett's audacious decisions to change the titles of Lawrence's story and book and to rearrange the tales appear to have been attempts at both topicality and commercialism, the First World War having begun only the previous August (Worthen 1989, 38). On the other hand, Duckworth may have resented Lawrence giving his latest novel, *The Rainbow*, to another publisher, Methuen, the summer before.

Nevertheless, it appears that Duckworth did what was necessary to issue a successful book; the author's preferences bore little weight at this juncture (Worthen 1983, xxxi). Lawrence's indignation over these unsolicited changes, however, ended his association with Garnett. (The significance of the short story collection as Lawrence planned it is pondered in the "Introduction.")

Two weeks later he wrote Amy Lowell again, told her that his collection of stories was out, said it was doing poorly, and observed that the critics hated him, as "they ought" (Boulton 1981, 242–43). On January 3, 1915, he responded to Lady Ottoline Morrell's letter praising his short fiction. He told her that he enjoyed "the appreciation of the few" (253–54). In a letter to Arthur McLeod of January 5, 1915, Lawrence again mentioned the slow sales of his collection and described as typical of his work that it should struggle in the marketplace (254).

On January 7, 1915, Lawrence wrote to thank Pinker for an additional five pounds from *Metropolitan* and speculate on why they had sent it so unexpectedly. He thought the money might have come from the sale of "Honour and Arms" the previous year and represented additional payment. In this same letter he asked Pinker if he had contacted America yet concerning the short story collection (Boulton 1981, 256, n. 3).

In a January 13, 1915, letter to Garnett, Lawrence quipped that Boots—the chain of chemist shops with lending libraries had allegedly refused to stock *The Prussian Officer and Other Stories* because of its shocking nature—had "booted" him out of his place as a popular writer of fiction. He went on to ask about the volume's sales by stating that he *wouldn't* ask about them for fear that the news might sadden him (Boulton 1981, 257–58).

Lawrence wrote his old friend William Hopkin on January 18, 1915, to promise him a set of duplicate page proofs from Duckworth in lieu of a copy of the published volume. He urged Hopkin to accept the proofs instead of "a proper book," for the corrected proofs might be valuable some day, containing as they did many differences from the stories as published (Boulton 1981, 258–59). These "Hopkin Proofs" were dated October, 1914, and consisted of the galleys of the stories Lawrence revised in June and July. They contained corrections and revisions in Lawrence's hand, and they now reside at the Nottinghamshire County Library in Nottingham.

On February 1, 1915, Lawrence yet again asked Pinker if he had written to America concerning the book of short fiction (Boulton 1918, 270–71). But the fact that Lawrence seldom mentioned this first collection of his short fiction in letters after February of 1915 suggests the intensity with which he was approaching his work in progress, *The Rainbow*, and his keen disappointment in the reception of his latest offering. In fact, the general lack of success of *The Prussian Officer and Other Stories* seems to have altered Lawrence's view of his reading public and his art.

Perhaps this change in perception contributed later to his adamant refusal to change *The Rainbow* to suit a more middle-brow, less avant-garde taste (Worthen 1983, xxx). He would not suffer gladly opposition from dogs, asses, and apes, as he perceived so many editors, publishers, critics, and readers to be. News from E.M. Forster in February 1915 that police might intervene and halt the sale of *The Prussian Officer and Other Stories* no doubt encouraged such a contentious view. As inane as the explanation now may seem, the reason for the official hostility to the collection lay with two stories in particular, "The Prussian Officer" and "The Thorn in the Flesh," neither of which served to raise military morale while England was fighting a World War (Delavenay 1972, 232).

Although actual censorship never occurred and thus never influenced the sales directly, the mere possibility alerted the young writer to what would come with the publication of *The Rainbow*.

Over a year later, in late May of 1916, Lawrence wrote Amy Lowell that the George H. Doran Publishing Company of New York City had agreed to publish his travel book *Twilight in Italy* and his volume of verse *Amores*. In fact, Doran would transfer the publishing contract, which also included *The Prussian Officer*, to B.W. Huebsch Publishing as shown in a letter from Doran to Lawrence's agent, Pinker, dated July 14, 1916 (Boulton 1981, 610–11, n. 4).

Thus, *The Prussian Officer and Other Stories* first appeared in America from Huebsch in 1916, but it was reprinted in November of 1924 by Thomas Seltzer, Lawrence's American publisher from June 5, 1920 to March 9, 1925 (Worthen 1989, 127). The title story would eventually find its way into many short story anthologies, one of the first being *Great English Short Stories*, edited by Lewis Melville and published in New York by Viking Press in 1930 (McDonald 1969, 86). "The Prussian Officer" in somewhat different form also appeared in 1983 in Cambridge University Press's "corrected" textual edition of *The Prussian Officer and Other Stories*.

CIRCUMSTANCES OF COMPOSITION, SOURCES, AND INFLUENCES

Lawrence composed "The Prussian Officer," initially titled "Honour and Arms," in early June of 1913 when he and Frieda were living at Irschenhausen, Oberbayern, Germany. Returning to England that same month, Lawrence revised and then tried to place such stories as "Daughters of the Vicar" and "The Shadow in the Rose Garden." He may have been attempting to tie up such loose ends as earlier unpublished works so as to shore up his finances as he set out on the difficult path of life he had chosen for himself (Cushman 1978, 32). (Chapter Three provides a complete account of Lawrence's activities during the remainder of 1913, and through 1914.)

A letter of January 5, 1915, speaks volumes about the Lawrence's financial circumstances. He tells his friend Arthur McLeod that he would have sent a copy of *The Prussian Officer and Other Stories* but various "thieves" disguised as friends had carried off copies they might easily have purchased. Lawrence also noted that he was "badly off" financially and was liable to remain so through the duration of the war (Boulton 1981, 254–55).

An important source for "The Prussian Officer" appears to be Friedrich von Richthofen, Frieda's father. As an officer during the Franco-Prussian War, he participated in the siege of Strasbourg in the summer and fall of 1870 (Moore [1954] 1962, 156). The young officer once whipped an artillery officer with his sabre. Apparently, the future baron also beat his servant once for getting drunk (Cushman 1978, 209).

Moreover, an actual incident may have informed the brutality in "The Prussian Officer." In 1912, a sensational trial took place in Austria wherein a captain stood accused of kicking his orderly to death. (The officer was acquitted because it was "only the second time" that he had beaten an orderly.) Lawrence, who had been traveling through Austria in 1912, might well have heard of the incident (Delavenay 1972, 196).

Another possible source for "The Prussian Officer" appears in mythology. A parallel exists between the scene of the orderly killing his superior officer and the life-and-death struggle between a warrior-priest and a runaway slave in a grove at Nemi. Both conflicts involved ritual combat in a wood, and in both instances, the victor momentarily enters "a new and unfamiliar life that leads to a final defeat" (Vickery 1973, 309–10). Similarly, Lawrence often associated a setting with ancient fertility gods, complemented by images of vegetative fecundity. The woman, the ripe wheat, and the green corn present in "The Prussian Officer" might thus be associated with Sir James Frazer's presentation of the Corn Goddess (318).

Meanwhile, the tale's original title, "Honour and Arms," alludes to Händel's oratorio *Samson*, where a giant taunts sightless Samson:

Honour and arms scorn such a foe,
>   Though I could end thee at a blow,
>   Poor victory, to conquer thee,

> Or glory in thy overthrow!
> Vanquish a slave that is half slain!
> So mean a triumph I disdain. (Cushman 1978, 209)

Critics often associate "The Prussian Officer" with Herman Melville's *Billy Budd* as having remarkably parallel themes and treatments (Amon 1953, 226). The fact that Melville's novella first appeared in 1924, however, renders the similarities more curious than causal.

Far more certain, Lawrence's wanderings in Europe between 1912 and 1914 had a strong influence upon this story (Hobsbaum 1980, 41). As critic Mark Schorer (1956) noted, the settings of Lawrence's works "follow upon the march of his feet" (3). Germany provided Lawrence with a natural backdrop. More specifically, the Loisach and Isar valleys form the models for the landscape in "The Prussian Officer" (Worthen 1983, 250).

But as several of Lawrence's own essays aver, the German landscape gave him more than mere scenery. During his German travels in 1912, his perceptions of the icy blue mountains and dark firs contributed to what Schorer called the story's "extraordinary destructive atmosphere" (1956, 8). Moreover, Lawrence observed the soldiers of the Bavarian and Imperial armies in 1912–13 while visiting Metz, Trier, and the area near Munich (Black 1986, 211). Thus, the intimidating terrain combined with the ubiquitous military presence seemed to invest the surroundings with menace.

Critic Harry T. Moore ([1954] 1962) suggested that "The Prussian Officer" addressed directly a kind of militarism fraught with class consciousness and a desire for conquest (194–95). A 1913 murder of a crippled cobbler by an irate German officer in Zabern typified this kind of militarism. Having clearly struck down the tradesman with his sword, the officer was nevertheless found innocent of murder after his successful if tenuous plea of self-defense. The infamous "Zabern Affair" outraged much of Germany, and Lawrence certainly knew of it. The implicit homosexuality in the tale also projects, according to Moore, a particular type of cruelty. In a letter to Edward Garnett concerning Garnett's play *Jeanne d'Arc*, Lawrence connected cruelty with unnatural sex. Preceding "The Prussian Officer" by several months, the letter may have anticipated "the underlying impulse" of the story (194–95).

Nor can one overestimate the importance his mother's death and his subsequent cohabitation with Frieda played in the development of Lawrence's world view in 1913 and 1914 (Cushman 1978, 6–7). Cushman attributed this new vision of Lawrence's to the deep personal fulfillment and the assurance of his manhood he found with Frieda (44). This assurance, in fact, appeared in a letter to A.W. McLeod in early June of 1914. Lawrence wrote, "I think the only re-sourcing of art, re-vivifying it, is to make it more the joint work of man and woman" (Boulton 1981, 181). From these feelings of fulfillment and surety unfolded the "radiant affirmation" that characterizes many of the stories, including the title tale, in *The Prussian Officer and Other Stories* (Cushman 1978, 45). If, indeed, the processes of art and life are inseparable, it stands to reason that Lawrence's personal change translated immediately into artistic change. Thus, such tales as "The Prussian Officer," revised in 1914, possess an "artistic integrity" attributable largely to Lawrence's better self-understanding, which accompanied his aesthetic and intellectual development (191). Lawrence's art, in fact, changed dramatically in this period. As Cushman pointed out, he was to abandon "traditional notions of form and conventional representations of scene, character, and story" (15).

Near the time of the June 1914 revision of "Honour and Arms," Lawrence wrote Edward Garnett to say that the theme of his fiction was not diamond, not coal, not soot, but carbon. He told Garnett, subsequently, that he was not interested in the way a character felt; rather, he was concerned with what she was "as a phenomenon or as representing some greater, inhuman will" (Boulton 1981, 183). To Janice Harris (1984), this carbon metaphor denoted the elemental in humanity, that human component in human beings that necessarily joins universal and cultural rhythms that extend beyond one's own person or understanding (93). Keith Cushman (1978) saw implicit in Lawrence's letter Lawrence's desire for his fictional character to be understood "in terms of the elemental laws of matter and energy that govern the universe." By means of this new perspective, man could be seen to exist in a world of animate and inanimate matter as one of the various phenomena, and in 1914, the successful rendering of this vision into his art was Lawrence's major concern (37).

Cushman recalled here that Lawrence's authorial discoveries were personal and aesthetic, as one can see in the final revisions of "The Prussian Officer" (1978, 194). His new artistic perception of 1914 led to a focus on "the larger ordering beyond the flux of time"—that is to say "the larger meaning beyond the everyday" (198). Consequently, the tales that initially combined symbolism with realism eventually assumed visionary qualities, to which Lawrence added "abstract and idiosyncratic speculation embodied in the metaphysic" (199). "The Prussian Officer" thus became a perfect blend of art and metaphysic: they formed a "seamless whole wherein art and idea became indistinguishable" (200).

THE RELATIONSHIP OF "THE PRUSSIAN OFFICER" TO OTHER LAWRENCE WORKS

Critic Keith Cushman (1978) argued convincingly that Lawrence's key years of authorial development came between 1912 and 1915, and 1914 was his "annus mirabilis," the time when he realized what he was about with *The Rainbow*, when he first formulated his philosophy in his *Study of Thomas Hardy*, and when he revised the tales for *The Prussian Officer and Other Stories* (9). Lawrence's quest at that time to discover the great impersonal source—an eternal stillness that underlies all movement, all change, all life—was no less than "an attempt to create an art capable of discovering the deepest reality" (35). Examples of "the great impersonal" in Lawrence's short fiction include the officer's murder in "The Prussian Officer," Louisa bathing Alfred in "Daughters of the Vicar," Elsie's dance with Sam Adams in "The White Stocking," Mrs. Bates's meditation over her dead husband in "Odour of Chrysanthemums," and the vital passion of Bachmann and Emilie in "The Thorn in the Flesh" (35). Lawrence's "Odour of Chrysanthemums," "Daughters of the Vicar," "Shades of Spring," and "The Prussian Officer" in their 1914 formats all show evidence of his newly found insight, and they illustrate his attempt to create an artistic fiction that also embodies deeply held beliefs (26).

An interesting study conducted in 1957 by Philip Appleman linked Lawrence's technique employed in "The Prussian Officer" and other works with Shakespeare's as examined in Thomas De Quincey's essay

"On the Knocking at the Gate in *Macbeth*." Lawrence introduces an "intrusive knock" into "The Prussian Officer," "The Rocking-Horse Winner," *The Trespasser* and *The First Lady Chatterley*. By means of this intruding-knock device, Lawrence reveals a character's sudden realization that an unbridgeable abyss exists between the 'normal' world he had known and a nightmare world that has replaced it (328).

Thomas McCabe's (1972) analysis of Lawrence's use of form in his fiction noted the way in which scenes within specific works are repeated or echoed so as internally to reinforce an overall rhythm. "The White Stocking," "The Shadow in the Rose Garden," and "The Prussian Officer" exemplify works where these iterations appear. In the case of "The Prussian Officer," Lawrence used balanced and opposed characters to the same effect. "Daughters of the Vicar" is also unified rhythmically in this way (65).

Much has been written about Lawrence's realism, and a general discussion of the influence the school of realism exerted upon Lawrence's fiction is found in Chapter One. With regard to "The Prussian Officer," critic Emile Delavenay (1972) felt that the description of the officer's brutal murder takes realism to an extreme and reminded him of Siegmund's suicide, also graphically detailed, in *The Trespasser* (197). The realism in Lawrence's work intensifies with the violent death of Evelyn Daughtry in the 1915 version of "England, My England," (432). Noting the graphic nature of the Prussian officer's death, as well as the fact that no fewer than eleven paragraphs in the final form of "England, My England" describe the protagonists's death, Kingsley Widmer (1962) suspected that death agony held a special fascination for Lawrence (20). Similarly, Janice Harris (1984) observed that the language Lawrence used to recount the violence in "The Prussian Officer" and in "The White Stocking" involved, in each instance, the blood lust of one person bent upon killing another (111).

Stylistically, Kingsley Widmer noted "The Prussian Officer" closely resembles the final section of "The Man Who Loved Islands," for it metamorphoses "psychological realism" into a surreal exaggeration of detail to achieve "obsessive emotions" (1962, 14).

Emile Delavenay (1972) placed "The Prussian Officer," "The Thorn in the Flesh," and "The Mortal Coil" in what he called

Lawrence's "German Cycle" (430). James Scott (1977) associated "The Prussian Officer" with all of Lawrence's other short fiction set in or near Germany—namely "The Thorn in the Flesh," "The Ladybird," "The Captain's Doll," and "The Border Line" (142). Closely reading Lawrence's "A Letter from Germany" and *Twilight in Italy* in conjunction with these five works, Scott found ethnic and racial assumptions leading to historical and regional flexibility Lawrence used to explain the social condition of Germany between 1914 and 1924 (142–64).

Frank Amon (1953) noted that the theme of this tale, the conflict between the flesh and the spirit, appears in many of Lawrence's works, just as he used the same symbolic valley-mountain imagery in such works as *Women in Love*, *The Lost Girl*, the poem "Meeting in the Mountains," and the early pages of *Twilight in Italy* (230).

Kingsley Widmer (1962) also noticed Lawrence's use of mountainous terrain, observing that in "The Prussian Officer" the snow-capped mountains represent the essence of the cold death Lawrence connected with Christian and northern European ideals and conscience. The same image serves the identical function in *Women in Love*, "The Captain's Doll," "The Princess," "The Woman Who Rode Away," and "St. Mawr" (8–9).

This juxtaposition of valleys with mountains, heat with cold, life with death, and the conscious with the unconscious illustrates Lawrence's dualistic vision he first used successfully in "The Prussian Officer" (Cushman 1978, 170). Lawrence's great concern with doctrine first became manifest with the 1914 variants of *The Rainbow* and the final revisions of *The Prussian Officer* stories, providing all these works with a central coherence. Despite occasion-ally radical public pronouncements, all of Lawrence's art after 1914 seeks to explore facets of his dualistic doctrine. He believed that the lives and visions of mankind resonated with a gradual burgeoning and withering perception preceded by and evinced as a dynamic concept or metaphysic. This premonition subsequently unfolded into life and art, and each of Lawrence's works following and during this period, as it succeeded its immediate ancestor, endeavored "to explore and annex new territory (22–3). He discussed this metaphysic of duality explicitly in such lengthy essays as *Study of Thomas Hardy* and *Fantasia of the Unconscious*.

The short stories as revised in 1914 contain three major themes destined to become integral facets of Lawrence's mature artistic vision: (1) the alienation of man from his fellow man; (2) the salvific nature of "human contact"; and (3)"the celebration of the powerful dark forces in the universe" (Cushman 1978, 205). The remainder of this section illustrates these themes at work in Lawrence's fiction.

Both "The Prussian Officer" and "The Thorn in the Flesh" con-cerned young men pressed into the lowest ranks of military service who take flight following their attack upon a superior (Moore [1954] 1962, 195). In both of these tales, too, Lawrence contrasted the beauty of nature with the bare barrack's "vitalistic deformity" (Tedlock 1963, 81).

This tale parallels the "The Rocking-Horse Winner" in the description of the Prussian officer's eyes as containing a cold blue fire, for Paul's eyes in "Rocking-Horse" are analogous. In each story, cold eyes are symptomatic of repression and perversity (Ford 1965, 79).

Lawrence's archetypal scene involving the mortal combat between the orderly and the officer appears in similar form in some of his other works, as well. Two men do their best to destroy each other in "The Old Adam," *Sons and Lovers*, and *Women in Love* (Cushman 1978, 16). Furthermore, Black (1986) associated the officer and the orderly with the male rivals in five other Lawrence stories: "A Modern Lover," *Sons and Lovers*, "Love Among the Haystacks," "The Shades of Spring," and "The Old Adam." The absence in "The Prussian Officer" of the woman who typically served in the other works as the focus of contention serves to develop and transform the feelings of the officer and orderly into a fatal love-hate (214). As for Schöner's girlfriend, who influences the formation of the officer's feelings for her beau, her depiction as the faithful lover seems a direct parallel to the portrayal of Emilie in "The Thorn in the Flesh," who unconditionally supports her soldier sweetheart (269).

As regards the officer's feelings for his orderly, elements of covert and overt homosexuality represent to some critics like Widmer (1962) a major component of Lawrence's fiction (223). The relationship between the officer and his orderly certainly anticipates that between Birkin and Crich in *Women in Love*, which might or might not be homosexual (Niven 1980, 83). In addition, Harris (1984) suggested that Lawrence meant the link between violence and sex in this short story, unlike that in "The White Stocking," to be seen as a perversion. The forced, suffocating closeness of a military without women could lead to a "cul de sac," as Lawrence showed in both "The Prussian Officer" and "The Thorn in the Flesh" (112, 119).

The orderly's abstract state of mind following the murder is hardly unique in Lawrence's fiction. His sense of being somewhere between life and death reminds one of the protagonist's condition at the beginning of "The Man Who Died" (Tedlock 1963, 80). And as Jack Stewart (1986) noted, Schöner's final reflections oscillate between "waking and dream consciousness," as do the thoughts of the mortally wounded protagonist in "England, My England" (284). Also, both "The Prussian Officer" and "The Escaped Cock" (the earliest form of "The Man Who Died") focus upon the main character's "preternaturally intensified" response to nature's "otherness," even though Schöner loses connection with this "otherness" while the man who died eventually finds it (275).

The utter intact separation from life the orderly feels after the killing might well illustrate Lawrence's beliefs about man's essential loneliness and how people can be driven as outcasts from a conformist society to perish from exposure and isolation in the wilderness. First treated in Lawrence's early tale "A Fragment of Stained Glass," these themes are rendered brilliantly in "The Prussian Officer" (Ford 1965, 75). Moreover, this tale and "The Thorn in the Flesh" embody the trepidation and imminent demise of the individual who flees his community for a fervent relationship that is, in the final analysis, sexual (Harris 1984, 7). Similarly, these same two stories both focus on how the self can be lost and then either augmented or diminished (86).

CRITICAL STUDIES

Initial evaluations of "The Prussian Officer" were mixed. In November of 1914, Alfred Kuttner cited "Honour and Arms" as evidence that Lawrence labored "under terrible sexual morbidities" (Boulton 1981, 246, n.1). A reviewer for the *Manchester Guardian*, Allan Monkhouse, said in December 1914 of the officer and orderly that Lawrence's characters generally seem oblivious of right and wrong. Despite their occasional humane impulses, they are uninterested in the rules.

Sufficient to Lawrence were their perceptions, which he presented poetically (94).

A December 19, 1914, review in *Outlook* noted the power of "The Prussian Officer" but went on to condemn the emotions presented there as extreme. Additionally, the reviewer described Lawrence's characters as abnormal, almost as if they were from another planet (81–3). Similarly the *New Statesman*'s review of December 26, 1914, referred to the story's power; however, the reviewer disapproved of what he saw as Lawrence's fondness for focusing upon life's "queer dark corners" (Worthen 1983, xxxiv).

Conversely, the January 9, 1915, review in *The Saturday Review* praised highly "The Prussian Officer," deeming it one of the two most powerful and poignant stories in the collection, the other being "The Thorn in the Flesh." The reviewer noted that Lawrence's two greatest assets included a great vitality and an intense earnestness. Also, he credited Lawrence with a "singular ability" to convey a sense of the soul's complete isolation (43–4). Less impressed, the January 16, 1915, reviewer in *Academy* referred to "The Prussian Officer" as morbid (Worthen 1983, xxxiv). But then *Athenaeum*'s January 1915 review of the story found it an impressive if not convincing study in psychology that dealt with how instinctive revenge is the natural reaction to instinctive brutality (68).

Edward Garnett undertook to enlighten the reviewers and the public by means of an article in *The Dial* printed in November of 1916. "The Prussian Officer," asserted Garnett, reveals passion's triumph over "the material of life," as the former rises from darkness into light. Thus in both the officer's enduring "lust of cruelty" and the servant's revenge, the merging of pleasure and pain that at its most fundamental involves sexuality is presented as a combination of sense and spirit (380).

A 1917 review by the American H.W. Boynton criticized Lawrence's fiction as protesting that "literary respectability" embodied in the adjective "Victorian." Although "The Prussian Officer" focused upon the human soul's isolation, Boynton saw in Lawrence's work insufficient power to excuse its grim pictures of reality (646). Yet another review in 1917, this one in *The Nation*, noted how Lawrence focused on the complete isolation of man's soul and its "desperate loneliness" as it struggled "toward death as an end if not a solution."

Thus, one might see the orderly and officer as victims of a force much greater than they (314).

Henry B. Fuller's March 1917 review of *The Prussian Officer* short stories approached hysteria. He took Lawrence to task for writing literature lacking in reticence and delicacy. It made Fuller uncomfortable, like an eavesdropper. In an effort to characterize Lawrence's indulgence "in an intensive, horrific study of the nexus which unites flesh and blood," Fuller depicted Lawrence as a mucker, a haruspex, and a medical student preoccupied by the remains of dissection. Fuller found everything in this collection to be "surcharged" and "over-manipulated" (237). As for the title story, Fuller attributed Schöner's death to a combination of ire, extreme physical discomfort, humiliation, and most threatening of all, the soldier's inability to coordinate the sudden surge of "mental processes" (238).

This uneven early critical response to what became a universally acknowledged masterpiece marvelously illustrates how essential the passage of time is to the evaluation of art. Later studies of "The Prussian Officer," benefitting from the objectivity lent by the years, have been far more appreciative.

Many critics of Lawrence's 1914 work, including the early commentators, focused upon the author as stylist. *The Nation*'s March 1917 anonymous review of *The Prussian Officer* stories began by quoting a note by Henry James who grouped Lawrence with the likes of Compton Mackenzie and Hugh Walpole as leading practitioners of "the new novel," which eschewed the sentimentalism of the 19th century English novel and embraced the realism of the 19th century continental novels. Equating realism with naturalism, the reviewer saw Lawrence as a "minor prophet" whose "polished naturalistic detail" revealed the foreignness of his style to the point that his authorial voice was much less John Bull than that of an expatriate (314).

Facets of expressionism, as well as the realism, gained attention. Horace Shipp noted in 1927 that "The Prussian Officer" was outstanding for its intensity of vision of the natural world "coloured by the passion or emotion of the moment" (xiii). George Orwell (1945), impressed deeply by the tale, singled out Lawrence's understanding of military discipline and his ability to project himself into such an atmosphere despite never having been a soldier (31).

Conscious of Lawrence's antagonism to class consciousness, his working-class background, and his condemnation of people who live primarily from their intellect, Virginia Woolf (1947) was less than generous in her comments on the author and his art. She saw him as a "remarkable" writer whose words came to him "fast and direct" like splashed beads of water resulting from a flying stone. But, she found his literature to be of no tradition, nor did she believe him to be interested in "literature as literature," as revealed by his spontaneous word choice. Woolf thought Lawrence's literature utilitarian, but with more use than meaning. "The Prussian Officer," itself, left her with the lingering impression "of starting [sic] muscles and forced obscenity" (79, 81). One senses envy in a novelist, who at times forced herself to stand at a podium while writing, over the ready manner in which vibrant language came to Lawrence.

John Bayley's (1962) assessment was less subjective. He noted Lawrence's unity and intensity of intelligence; however, he found this same intelligence rendering the world of love more strangely and purely abstract than had any other great author (24).

The first thorough stylistic examination of "The Prussian Officer" appeared in Kingsley Widmer's 1962 study of the short fiction. Widmer praised the tale's skillful "fusion of theme and form." As Widmer perceived it, the story examines the theme of authority and innocence by means of intensified images of nature produced by naive Schöner's death wish. The lush sensual descriptions complement the theme of innocence: they form the tip of the iceberg, so to speak. For what Lawrence was actually depicting here, and in other works of fiction, was a character's simultaneous yearning for "the extremity of experience" and, unconsciously, for the destruction with which it would culminate (16). (Widmer's psychological analysis of this story follows shortly.)

Keith Cushman's accomplished 1978 study noted that despite Lawrence's famous 1914 letter to Garnett where he refused to develop characters in traditional ways, Lawrence's art did not become "rather abstract and remote from human experience" as some critics had charged. In fact, the characters in *The Prussian Officer* stories and in *The Rainbow* are recognizably human and do "relate to one another in traditional fictional ways." Moreover, the tales combine tradition and experiment wherein "ordinary human experience" is subsumed by "the impersonal reality" (197–98).

Alistair Niven (1980) observed that the story possesses a unique "violent imagination" (83). Janice Harris's analysis of four years later thoroughly discussed this violence, astutely noting that in "The Prussian Officer" Lawrence successfully integrated for the first time realism and religious exemplars. Concerned with the soul's journey, the tale offers a kind of map by means of "a dynamic balance between mimesis and exemplum." The result is a visionary tale about two possible directions the protagonist may take: toward death, or toward life. The journey becomes believable primarily by means of the language Lawrence selected. But the style is more compressed and intricate than one generally finds in realistic tales, which by comparison seem translucent. Lengthy, convoluted sentences and paragraphs appear, as do biblical images and language rhythms. Place offers more than a mere backdrop for the action; place contains the basic polarities of life and death, of creation and annihilation. In the course of the visionary plot, no longer purely a history of an individual but more of a "central cultural rite," Lawrence presents characters with the opportunity to choose, in almost sacramental fashion, life over death (1984, 89–93).

In 1985, Weldon Thornton used "The Prussian Officer" to illustrate Lawrence's "psychic texture," which Weldon judged the result of and the vehicle for Lawrence's sense of personality being connected with physical surroundings. The tale's opening paragraph, with its vivid description of sun and shade, valley and mountains, and crops and snow, creates energy and straining dualities that form an appropriate "psychic backdrop" (52–3). (Lawrence's use of place in "The Prussian Officer" receives more attention in the discussion of symbolism to follow.)

In his 1986 examination of "The Prussian Officer," Jack Stewart concluded that although facets of realism appear, it presents primarily "an expressionist vision of disintegration." As such, the tale's conflict is intensified, polarized, and universalized in the manner associated with expressionism. Rather than revelling in what some critics saw as his obsessions, Lawrence created an expressionistic masterpiece while working ingeniously within the scope of this visionary approach—an approach characterized by a hyperintensification of experience, a

fragmentation of traditional format, and the reorganization of the shards
so as to present distinctively thought and sensory experience (Stewart
1986, 275–76, 287).

Fusing locus and emotion in the story's opening scene, Stewart
continued, Lawrence brilliantly captured Schöner's bruised psyche. By
means of polarizing the foreground and background planes, Lawrence
implied a "dynamic continuity" of a divided self and a cleft nature.
Such a breakdown between self and the outside world is intrinsic also
in the expressionistic art of Vincent Van Gogh (277).

Similarly (still drawing upon Stewart), Part II of "The Prussian
Officer" starts with a facet of expressionism associated with Franz
Marc: intensified apprehension suggested by a distortion of physical
surrounding. Merging images of spatial movement with Schöner's
fragmented consciousness, Lawrence's prose advances into the realm of
visual art (277–78).

Lawrence juxtaposed such fluid images with "freeze-frame
cameos," reminiscent of Erich Heckel's woodcuts and Ernst Ludwig
Kirchner's paintings. The officer's penetrating glare at the hapless
orderly who had just spilled a bottle of wine, and the two dead bodies
side by side in the mortuary, are two such powerful scenes, the former
stressing opposition, and the latter achieving a kind of balance (278,
283).

This opposition between the two soldiers is existential in nature
and, thus, could be connected to the vision of expressionism.
Consciousness, for Sartrean existentialists, must maintain itself by
means of perception, or deteriorate "into an agonizing void." The
officer had seized, held, and ravished the orderly's essence, and
Schöner could only reclaim it by obliterating the officer. Resolved on
the level of blood consciousness, the orderly's focus upon the
annihilation of his superior renders him the stronger of the two. After
the officer's murder, the interior existential tension is depicted as
increasingly expressionistic. For example, Lawrence's use of fractured
visual images and terse, abrupt sentences, as well as phrases that often
overlap, to illustrate Schöner's alienation following the murder, are
reminiscent of Van Gogh's "hectic brushwork." Moreover, the
apocalyptic countryside where Schöner's longing to fuse with the
distant mountains reflects his desire for annihilation, recalls Kirchner's
"sweeping mountain forms." Viewed in this light, the orderly's desire

for transcendence is suicidal; the never-to-be-gained mountains represent "an abstract unity" that surpasses "alienated consciousness" (Stewart 1986, 283–84, 287).

Psychological studies of "The Prussian Officer" have, as one might expect, been numerous. Perhaps less expected are the widely diverse psychological views of "The Prussian Officer" that critics have expressed over the years. In the first study to take this approach, Seligmann (1924) saw the tale as "a study of sadism" (33).

Anthony West's ([1950] 1977) subjective examination of the tale posited the sudden onset of violence as a manifestation of a peculiarly German type of hysteria, such venting of cruelty resulting from intolerable angst. West considered "The Prussian Officer" and "The Thorn in the Flesh," important case studies of the German psyche and, as such, indicators of how and why Germany had fomented and lost two world wars (97–99).

Robert Davis's (1953) discussion of "The Prussian Officer" noted the power with which it treated the result of unspoken or unacknowledged passion (306). Approaching the psychological facet of the story on a more allegorical level, Graham Hough (1957) observed that Lawrence's loss of interest in conventional characterization resulted in characters who represented certain states of mind. Thus, in this tale, attention falls on the psyches of the officer and his orderly (171).

Philip Appleman's (1957–1958) examination of this tale noted how Lawrence uses, much as De Quincey's essay "On the Knocking at the Gate in *Macbeth*" described, the device of "the intrusive knock" wherewith the gulf between the "normal" and the nightmare world is suddenly revealed. In "The Prussian Officer," Schöner is roused from feverish slumber by a small bird's loud pecking, which plunges him nightmarishly into a now-remote natural world. Despite attempts to re-establish consciousness and justify the murder, the orderly is overcome by horror before he again collapses. Only in death does Schöner again become "one with nature" (328–29).

Taking this idea further in 1962, Kingsley Widmer noted Lawrence's emphasis upon Schöner's subjective shift as the orderly loses connection with everything that had once held meaning for him: home, friends, sweetheart, and duty. After he murders the officer and retires this symbol of authority, a full quarter of the narrative remains to examine the psyche of the once innocent orderly. The servant's craving to rebel against this hateful authority takes him out of himself—that is, away from his conventional innocent self "to his deepest self of passion and violence and ecstacy and death." This savaged innocent longs to leave behind life's agony and passion and find pure nothingness. Thus, argued Widmer, the orderly finds himself outside the realm of pure existence in an intense and ultimately fatal "state of subjectivity and awareness" (6–11).

Another psychological excursion through "The Prussian Officer" conducted that same year took a decidedly Freudian approach. Daniel Weiss (1962) perceived a continuation of elements first presented in *Sons and Lovers*. Thus, just as the Morels served as symbolic representatives of Lydia, Arthur, and D.H. Lawrence himself, and just as Baxter Dawes was yet another father figure, so do the Prussian officer and his orderly represent Lawrence and his father. In this tale, however, Weiss observed a more mature working through of the Oedipal problem. Lawrence had realigned father-son identities so that the orderly represented both the son, as illustrated by the lad's youth and subordination, and the father presented in all of his ideal goodness. But this son figure also became the brutal father in the form of the Prussian officer, who conversely embodied the weaknesses Lawrence despised in himself, like his hypersensitivity and his overly cerebral nature. Thus, each character had become a hybrid: the orderly combined all of the father and son's good aspects, the officer all the negative attributes of father and son. Therefore, for Weiss, "hero and antihero" stood face-to-face. The "good" father-son figures, consolidated in the orderly, retaliate against the brutal side of the father-officer and lay him to rest, along with such "unmanly" traits as the mother fixation. Thus, in this complex, even schizoid manner, Lawrence reconciled his past with his parents (95).

Ann Englander's (1963) analysis of "The Prussian Officer" introduced an aspect of Lawrence's own theory of the dual nature of man's psyche. She believed that the infusion of Lawrence's "theory" into his story served more to obfuscate than to illuminate human behavior. Asserting that Lawrence had forced his captain into the role of the Conscious half of the psyche, and his orderly into the role of the Unconscious half, Englander noted that while this deployment created real tension, it also generated confusion, for the double function of the characters as human beings and as symbols "condemned them to incoherence." She found the tale ultimately flawed, for if the men were viewed as flesh and blood, the significance of their human battle was impenetrable. On the other hand, if they are symbols of Lawrence's concept of man's two-part psyche, they become no more than "diagrams with pretensions to human status" (605–07, 619).

In 1964, Tedlock published Frieda Lawrence's letter written in 1953 to a critic concerning what she thought a misreading of this tale by Anthony West. She took West to task for speaking "like the Lord–so absolute" in his assessment of "The Prussian Officer" (Tedlock 1964, 357). Frieda thought West a snob–a man who judged "on the old social level" (357). Contrary to his conclusion that Lawrence wrote poorly of subjects that extended beyond his personal experience, she argued that Lawrence always wrote about only subjects with which he had formed a personal connection. Furthermore, West's view of "The Prussian Officer" as a statement about race Frieda found to be superficial, the human conflict within the tale being profound and universal (357).

In response to criticism of Germany in general and of her father in particular, Frieda acknowledged that her father had once slapped his young orderly but certainly never beat him. Acknowledging, as well, the cruelty implicit in the story, she suggested that such cruelty, while associated with some Germans, appears in all other nationalities. Her father, meanwhile, had been a lovely parent who had written poems for her when she was a child (Tedlock 1964, 463).

Another interesting psychological analysis of "The Prussian Officer" used one of Frieda's ideas. George Ford (1965) asserted that, typical in Lawrence, this story focused on a human relationship as it followed the interaction of two individuals, and despite all its violence and brutality, which rendered the tale repulsive and unwholesome to some, it was simply too well done to damn on those grounds. In fact, Ford argued, no critics had yet addressed the subtle theme of the tale, and he deferred to Frieda in the first phase of his analysis. Frieda believed that the two soldiers, the officer and his servant, one conscious and one unconscious (close to his emotions and instincts), represented the same facets of Lawrence's divided soul. Ford thought that this insight helped explain Lawrence's solicitousness to both in the story: he described the captain's suffering in detail; he described the orderly's suffering the same way. In the role reversal after the climactic beating, the officer used alcohol to obliterate his memory of the deed—a facet of conscious thought—whereas, the orderly awakened painfully "not into full consciousness but out of innocence." This way, according to Ford, Lawrence traced the development of this isolated pair before Schöner's end in total isolation (Ford 1965, 76, 79).

Ford concluded his engaging examination of "The Prussian Officer" with Lawrence's observation that most neuroses stemmed from man's internal sense of isolation, which developed as man became less animalistic and more rational, less unconscious and more conscious. The subsequent sense of aloneness experienced by the formerly "unconscious" orderly receives a remarkably sympathetic treatment in this powerful work (1965, 80).

R.E. Pritchard's (1971) study of the story took a different tack than Ford's, asserting that the officer directs his hostility toward his orderly's natural completeness and lack of self consciousness. Thus, the assault upon Schöner is as psychological as it is physical, for the officer attempts to possess the young orderly himself by forcing the lad to express his feelings for his girl. His unselfconsciousness destroyed, Schöner's retaliation casts him into a frightful new reality. Citing an image from Lawrence's travel book *Twilight in Italy*, Pritchard saw Schöner's experience akin to the crucifixion of the powerful manly life defeated by physical violence wherein forbidden passion results in a new perception of reality. Thus, Schöner ultimately finds himself utterly alone in a nightmarish reality (64–5).

Emile Delavenay's (1972) analysis took yet another psychoanalytical path. Delavenay noted that the behavior of the two central characters appears to stem from "the realm of dreams": their unconscious and conscious selves are kept from acknowledging their bodies' acts. In the mechanical role of order-giver, the captain must repress any personal feelings toward his men. Consequently, when he discerns the person behind his orderly, he reacts violently, which leads to his death. One could thus say that the officer is the victim of his repression (197).

Shirley Rose's (1975) examination of "The Prussian Officer" took issue with critics who believed Lawrence obsessed with suffering to the point of sado-masochism. She argued instead that Lawrence condemned physical pain, and that far from leading to enlightenment, he believed that pain reduced one's "range of humanness," containing a person within that single sensation so as to obliterate everything else. Accordingly, Lawrence advocated the avoidance of pain. "The Prussian Officer" displays that viciousness arouses viciousness and that unabated physical anguish begins and ends with monomania (Rose 1975, 73–83).

The thorough 1984 examination of "The Prussian Officer" by Janice Harris focused on the kinds of consciousness, perception, and wisdom Lawrence believed people required. She perceived both the officer and orderly as lacking consciousness, hence their metaphorical imprisonment in a valley depicted as "a flatland of insufficient consciousness" lying beneath cool mountains of integration. Making contact with another for the first time in his struggle-to-the-death with the officer, Schöner nevertheless quelled the knowledge of himself that came from confronting and clasping the other man. Finally experiencing his autonomous being and his separation from the world, he died. Lawrence's point, asserted Harris, was that just as knowledge issues from isolation, anguish, and dissolution, so could the kind of knowledge Schöner gains arrive in isolation, anguish, and dissolution. Lawrence illustrated that kinds of knowledge vary, as do "ways of losing the self" (97–8).

A year later, Walter Anderson's (1985) examination of Lawrence's story elaborated upon several of the earlier psychological studies. Anderson concluded that with the destruction of Schöner—an "Old-Adam" figure—by the captain, himself a willful death-in-life figure representing Adam after the fall, Lawrence presented an allegory of man's descent from a life of instinct, unconsciousness, and spontaneity into a mechanized, conscious life controlled by will. Citing apposite passages from Lawrence's essays—on Hawthorne's *The Scarlet Letter*, "The Individual Consciousness vs. The Social Consciousness," and on Trigant Burrow's *The Social Basis of Consciousness*—Anderson illustrated how "the advent of consciousness in human development" had subverted man's unconscious spontaneous approach to life, which resulted in self-consciousness: the awareness that one was separate from a vital continuum of all other living things. Anderson also noted that Lawrence understood the basic reason for modern man's neurosis (contrary to Freud's theory about incest) as Burrow's "inward sense of separateness" which arose out of man's fall into self consciousness (Anderson 1985, 216).

In "The Prussian Officer," Anderson argued, Schöner provides an emblem of unfallen man—completely unconscious of himself—until the self-conscious officer, who resents the orderly's autonomy, forces him into self-consciousness by means of hate and violence. The result of Schöner's new awareness is a sense of alienation: he no longer feels in sympathy with nature or the life around him. He has come to know but ceased to be, and he undergoes physical and spiritual disintegration. In this way, Lawrence presented his vision of modern man's divided self, born in that moment of evolution when man's consciousness became cognitive (217–20).

John Haegert's (1988) study of "The Prussian Officer" posited the story as a thematic archetype found in much of Lawrence's fiction. Haegert discerned a "pattern of collusion and complicity" in the tale that undermined the story's more noticeable divisions. Thus, at times in the tale, each of the soldiers adopts the traits, like self-consciousness or "unconsciousness," he had found so objectionable in the other. Each penetrates the other's psyche, then embraces the other's traits. Consequently, rather than individual differences being established between the two, the tale stresses "interpenetration." In this way, Lawrence illustrated the impossibility of determining "*any* definitive view of human nature"; thus, the process of selfhood and the concept of otherness are "inseparably linked" (3).

The theme of homosexuality in "The Prussian Officer" received so much critical attention since the 1950's that despite the abundance of psychological discussion in the studies, homosexuality became a discrete category.

Frank Amon's (1953) study initiated the trend. He broached there the psychological complexities in the (perhaps) latent sexual attraction the orderly held for the officer. Amon went on to picture a tale of a courtship wherein the captain, despite himself, succumbs to the allure of his orderly, while the latter, sensing the advances, rejects the officer. After the kicking incident, the captain becomes aware of Schöner's heterosexual nature, tacitly acknowledges the futility of his lust, dismisses the lad from his presence, and denies the whole affair to himself. But Schöner remembers. His emotion and his person have been violated, which moves him to kill the officer in an act of purgation that temporarily restores him to himself. But the sense of triumph is short-lived, argued Amon, for in killing the captain Schöner has surrendered to him, capitulating to the coercion the officer had represented (Amon 1953, 229–30).

Two years later, Mark Spilka (1955) took a different view. Spilka argued with Amon's assertion that homosexuality lay at the root of the relationship between the captain and his servant. Rather, Spilka found in "The Prussian Officer" the obverse of *Blütbrüdershaft* (Blood brother affinity)—the "fixed, rigid, inorganic" officer strongly resents the orderly's completeness (172).

Another 1955 study added yet a new twist: sado-masochism. Mary Freeman focused on Lawrence's interest in "the obscure relations between the aggressor and the victim." Brutality being its subject, Freeman perceived "The Prussian Officer" as depicting "a forbidden kind of understanding" wherein the satisfactions of pain are delineated, for violence, given or taken, provides satisfaction (71–2).

Kingsley Widmer's (1962) study picked up where Amon's had left off, finding homosexual underpinnings in the officer-orderly relationship. Discerning a great deal of much "covert homosexuality" in Lawrence's fiction, Widmer found the captain's homosexuality overt. Beating his servant, argued Widmer, the captain feels a thrilling new emotion, and a sense of alienation from person and place results from his entrapment in the chaos of that new sensation (6–11).

Gary Adelman's (1963) astute analysis of "The Prussian Officer" took a cultural-psychological approach to the captain and Schöner's relationship. The symbolic modern man, cold and detached from life, the captain has a sudden awakening to emotion that both shames and controls him, and this new awareness becomes the driving force of the story. The aristocratic captain's death-in-life nature is, after all, the product of a society that for twenty-five centuries has denied and evaded life (12).

Identifying Schöner with the officer's horse (the captain has "mounted" and kicked both; thus, both are connected with him) Adelman went on to develop a clever theory in which the once-unconscious orderly willingly participates in the perverse love relationship. The "murder described as sexual act" consequently fulfills the captain's desire to instill in Schöner passion and leaves the orderly as unconnected with life and as aware of his degradation as the captain, his tragic lover, has been. In effect, Schöner is raped into an awareness of the modern world's deathward direction (Adelman 1963, 12–15). Ultimately, the tale concerns the captain and orderly's want of honor, a lacking that may well extend to include the modern human condition— "honor" being Lawrence's term denoting one's "faithful observance of the individual life" that "*by nature*" gives one identity (8–9).

A 1964 examination of the tale by Ronald Draper assimilated both Amon's and Freeman's insights and added new ones. Noting the sadistic militarism in the work, Draper argued that a military caste system served to block the homosexual attraction the officer feels for his orderly, but the tension continues to build, which Lawrence conveyed with a sensitive immediacy. The orderly's beating is the result of "a violent perversion of natural vitality," which leads to the demise of both soldiers. Contrary to Lawrence's own statements about the effect of the military upon heterosexuality, the tale illustrated to Draper Lawrence's awareness that one's refusal to acknowledge "certain laws of life" that violate society's patterns and to indulge desires outside these laws might bring catastrophe (123–24).

Nine years elapsed before Roger Sale's ([1973] 1975) examination of "The Prussian Officer" again took up the homosexual theme. Sale noted that like a spring 1913 version of Paul Morel and Baxter Dawes, the relationship between the orderly and the officer, with no woman intervening, certainly approaches homosexuality. Sale suggested that the Prussian officer's homosexual passion was Lawrence's own and that the captain's need to dominate other men was Lawrence's need, too, for the officer's harsh and violent gestures serve to repress his acknowledgment of his true feelings for the physically and emotionally strong orderly, who was Lawrence's idealized male cast in the mold of his father (45–6).

Just as the soldiers in the tale come "consummately together in an act of mutual self destruction," Sale continued, so did Lawrence's feelings when they became increasingly conscious to him become destructive. Yet Lawrence's willful domination of others, including his attempts to control Frieda, bespoke more an evaded ideal heterosexuality than homosexuality. Living with Frieda, herself willful, Lawrence sensed the threat to ideal love posed by impulses toward domination and independence. Indeed, he may have been tempted and endangered by his sense that the obverse of the need to dominate and punish included "consummation and death" (Sale [1973] 1975, 45–6).

Roger Sale concluded his study with the observation that the closer Lawrence came to "realizing the implications of Love Triumphant," the closer he approached its opposite and antithesis: the passionate desire to impose his will upon others. Lawrence's heroism was evinced in his dogged approach to the light while fully aware of his simultaneous approach to the darkness ([1973] 1975, 47).

Keith Cushman's (1978) examination of "The Prussian Officer" noted the homosexual approach several critics had taken, but he speculated that the homosexual elements of the story were "purposive." He saw far more to the tale in that it contained the fully realized Lawrence metaphysic of dualistic vision. Consequently, it was in actuality a story of counterpoints and contracomplementation: the captain and the orderly, valleys and mountains, heat and cold, life and death (170).

George Becker's (1980) study of Lawrence merely noted that "The Prussian Officer" was "antimilitary" and that it explored physical and psychological violence. From a tension between orderly and officer homosexual in origin, observed Becker, a duel occurs (117).

In an interesting later study of "The Prussian Officer," Michael Black (1986) appraised the story a masterpiece under-appreciated because its nightmarish and hallucinatory elements focused on— indeed, compelled a reader to experience almost directly—downright frightening ideas and images (211).

Next, Black examined the relationship between the officer and the orderly, seeing in the officer's fascination for Schöner a perverted love overwhelming the captain with a compulsion to nullify the orderly's "otherness," which he envied. Suggesting that the officer's jealousy sprung from habitual failure with women, Black hastened to concede that the officer's feelings were too complex to be labeled merely as jealousy or repressed homosexuality. In fact, Black noted, Lawrence had used deflective language to discourage such an oversimplification. For example, the consistent references to animals in connection with Schöner removed the reader "from the world of social humanity" rendering the orderly and the officer "less schematic and more mysterious" (Black 1986, 213, 215).

Expanding on this idea, Black saw the officer's overwhelming will to power (which kept "his inner chaos" in check) occurring on the level of "social reaction" rather than thought. Schöner's unselfconsciousness and vitality contrasted so greatly with his own repressed nature that it evoked envy, desire, and resentment. Their roles in the military provided an opportunity for the officer to prey upon this superior-seeming inferior (1986, 215–16).

Black next charted the process that led to the orderly's humiliation and the subsequent demise of both men. First one sees the officer's vague irritation, which becomes more intense after Schöner spills the wine. From the captain's irate glare, the orderly suddenly and inexplicably senses his own vulnerability: the protective wall of unselfconsciousness has been breached. The pitiless process continues until the captain kicks his servant. The tale then returns to the opening scene, the field exercise, and one finds the orderly in a kind of "suspended consciousness" resulting from the combination of physical pain, mortification, and a sense of having been violated. As he sees the mounted officer watching him, the orderly feels blank, nullified. But this feeling of disintegration soon gives way to a sense of invulnerable selfhood that helps transform him from prey to predator. Watching the captain drink his beer, Schöner sees in him what Black called the "polar opposite" of what Louisa Lindley had perceived in the bathing of Alfred. Instinctively, he seeks his chance and strikes when it arrives. After the murder (Black found Schöner's enjoyment of the murder disconcerting), the orderly wanders off, sensing a great distance between himself and the world caused by his passage from what he had understood into "a place without known features or boundaries" (1986, 219, 222).

Black concluded that "The Prussian Officer" conveys much more than Lawrence's earlier statement in 1912 that sexual perversion could stem from cruelty, and that fermenting sexual lust could trigger atrocity. Black saw a bond created between the two men, unwilled or self-willed, perhaps, but illustrated in the final scene wherein the two corpses lie side-by-side in "parody of marriage," the unequal nature of which is evident in many other Lawrentian married couples (1986, 213–23).

James Cowan's (1990) analysis of "The Prussian Officer" focused upon the importance of the sense of touch in Lawrence's work, and noted how touch could be destructive as well as constructive. In this tale, the orderly's innocent and impersonal rubdowns awaken in the captain his latent homosexuality. While the officer has no wish to be roused into life by means of his servant's touch, he finds it increasingly difficult to regard him impersonally. Consequently, the captain unleashes his pent-up emotions in his sadistic attack on the lad that leads directly to his death. Thus, Schöner's innocence is destructive, his touch having effected not only the officer's ruin, but also his own: his instinctive strangling of his master having separated him forever from all he had loved. The sense of wholeness he enjoyed before his beating is lost forever (149–52).

A discerning study by John Worthen (1991) took issue with critics who viewed this story as concerned mainly with homosexuality or sadism. The officer's primary emotional response to his orderly is far from sexual, insisted Worthen. The officer is, in fact, overwhelmed by his envy of the servant's simple, unselfconscious nature he once possessed himself but has since irretrievably lost. Envy becomes hatred, hence the beating. The tale focuses upon what becomes of someone so mistreated, as Lawrence presented the "psychological and personal disintegration" of the orderly after his instinctive desire to kill the officer becomes an act of "willed volition." A smashed vessel, the orderly's desires are fragmented, his selves now mere shards, his instinctive, integral self now exploded and splintered (45–6).

After 1957, when Graham Hough first noted the compelling presentation of the society in which the brutal murders of the tale could occur (171), several critics have approached "The Prussian Officer" from the cultural standpoint.

E.W. Tedlock's (1963) study of the tale asserted that its high reputation derives from the vital, psychological-ethical struggle presented within the plot with strong emotion and "wholeness." Although the antagonism between the officer and his servant has a psychological basis, Tedlock noted that Lawrence took pains to establish cultural causes for their conflict. The arrogant aristocrat does not want to be brought into life by means of his orderly's touch. Lawrence established the officer's willfulness in his skill as an equestrian, which requires a conscious display of power over something natural and vital. His subsequent attack upon his orderly's vital wholeness stems from his "abstract socially-sanctioned authority" (Tedlock 1963, 79– 81).

Deranged following the murder of his superior officer, the orderly finds himself consumed by a fever Tedlock interpreted to be the physical manifestation of the rebellion in Schöner's manhood. Tedlock argued that the serene and intact white-capped mountains in the distance, the last thing seen by Schöner before his death, contrast dramatically with the orderly's destroyed integration with the natural world (1963, 80).

Fourteen years passed before another critic, this one James Scott (1977), examined "The Prussian Officer" culturally. A tale of "cultural aggression," as Scott perceived it, the story illustrates what happens when the unyielding willful nature of northern Germany confronts the more easy-going instinctive life of Bavaria and Alsace. The captain serves as the Prussian-aristocrat figure who would destroy the orderly, who lives on an instinctive level typical of Bavaria. Through the captain's life-denying authoritarianism directed against Schöner's warm flow of life and the officer's metaphorical military glove thrown into the orderly's face, the story illustrates "Prussia's ineradicable will to power." Paradoxically, the orderly who so loves life is also enamored of death, as the cool mountains hovering mysteriously and out of reach suggest. For Scott, Schöner's acceptance of his own nullification fulfills "a racial destiny," for, as in "The Thorn in the Flesh," the tale examines the effect of Prussian domination on German culture and shows that such forced unification had frustrated chances for assimilation (146–51).

Philip Hobsbaum (1980) found "The Prussian Officer" disturbing for two reasons: (1) homosexuality was implicit therein, and (2) the socially superior character is granted a "psychological ascendancy" that results in a relationship based on the common man's humiliation, for the orderly had depended emotionally upon his officer (32–3).

James Boulton (1981) noted that when Edward Garnett changed the title from "Honour and Arms" to "The Prussian Officer," he shifted the focus of the work from a critical examination of militarism in general to specific criticism of German militarism (5–6).

Several critics found elements of mythology in "The Prussian Officer." Frank Amon (1957) asserted that it was "one of the world's masterpieces of short fiction" and argued that Lawrence masterfully incorporated there myth, psychology, and imagery so that they operated simultaneously to develop the theme of conflict between flesh and spirit. On the mythic level, Lawrence reenacted the Fall of Man: the natural unconscious man, Schöner, being the Adam figure against the officer's "Aryan Mephistopheles" character, who possessed an innate hatred for innocence and good. As in the biblical account of Adam, Eve, and Satan, man succumbs to evil temptation, thus losing his innocence and possibly his salvation (Amon 1957, 226–30).

John Humma (1974) explored Amon's insights further. As Amon had noted earlier, striking parallels exist between Melville's presentation of the conflict between Billy and Claggart in *Billy Budd* and Lawrence's pattern of opposition between the captain and his orderly in "The Prussian Officer" (Amon 1953, 226). Even though *Billy Budd* first appeared in 1924, approximately ten years after Lawrence's tale first broke into print, Humma traced close parallels in characterization and theme (1974, 83). He deemed Schöner and Budd figures representative of Adam before the Fall as the instinctive unselfconscious man; whereas, the Prussian officer and Claggart suffer from the illness of mechanical consciousness responsible for their desire to obliterate their former selves in the persons of their underlings. Thus, the orderly and Budd became figures of the fallen Adam who unwittingly accepted the role of his own corruptor, Satan, in their complicit destruction of innocence. The instinctive retaliations of the young men may have been self-destructive, but they did not lead to ultimate defeat. In both instances, the implication of a rebirth or resurrection follows the scenes of the protagonists' deaths (87–8).

As precursors to Melville and Lawrence's view that self-consciousness is a curse, Humma cited Dostoyevsky, Nietzsche, and William Blake. He saw in Blake's Urizen, yet another figure of mythic proportions, a prototype for the Prussian officer and the master-at-arms (1974, 86).

Janice Harris's (1984) examination of "The Prussian Officer" story pointed out that "Biblical imagery and sentence rhythms" permeate the story and heighten its whole linguistic expression (92).

Although many critics have remarked upon Lawrence's presentation of the valley-mountain opposition in "The Prussian Officer," three in particular examined this landscape from the critical perspective of symbolism. Frank Amon's (1953) study focused in part upon the emotional significance of the valley-garden-mountain imagery Lawrence wove throughout the tale. Lawrence established the tension between "the life of the earth" and "the heaven of the spirit" by means of Schöner's torment in the hellishly hot valley and his longing for the cool distant mountains (229–30).

In 1978, Keith Cushman observed that Lawrence identified the vale in the story with Schöner—both having been warm, unconscious, and vital. He equated the mountains with the officer and his cold, unquickened conscious nature. In the course of the story, the orderly is corrupted, losing his identification with the valley in the process as he ultimately relates to the mountains (170–71).

Two years later, Judith Wilt (1980) explained the tale in terms of "the crisis of placement in the modern displaced world." The actual fulfillment of that placement, she argued, is unbearable, necessitating one's dissolution "on the very threshold of completion." Thus, Lawrence developed his tale largely through sun and shadow images. The captain and the orderly compete for association with the sun, with the officer as the primary sun figure intent upon keeping the orderly in his shadow. But meeting in the wood, where the light is scattered randomly within the darkness beneath the trees, they fought man to man. Following their passionate, deadly "bodily oneness," they endure "an equal diminution to shadow" (280, 282).

Janice Harris's (1984) study expanded upon Cushman (1978), but she interpreted the mountains quite differently than the earlier critic had. To Harris, they symbolized an "ideal of integration" that illustrate what each man lacks: consciousness of a vital connection with another that contributes to the establishment of selfhood (95–6).

Finally, Rosemary Davies's (1984) analysis of "The Prussian Officer" enumerated its many references to what she characterized as "emotional explosions," "heat of the day depictions," and instances of "radiant light." As the tale progresses, the references to the day's heat give way to words connoting radiance and light, so as to prepare a reader for the death of the once warm and vital orderly. As the heat of the day contrasts with the radiant light reflecting off of the icy mountaintops, the orderly dies with an overwhelming sense of loss. The mountains—silent, still, icily rigid—symbolize "the ultimate death of the body" (270–71).

This chapter's length attests to the greatness of "The Prussian Officer." Numerous critics and scholars have been drawn to the challenging story with a subtle fascination clearly displayed in their varied investigations. Lawrence's great sense of accomplishment upon composing this story in 1913 was warranted, certainly, for today it is recognized as one of his finest achievements.

WORKS CITED

Adelman, Gary. 1963. "Beyond the Pleasure Principle: An Analysis of D.H. Lawrence's 'The Prussian Officer.'" *Studies in Short Fiction* 1: 8–15.

Amon, Frank. 1953. "D.H. Lawrence and the Short Story." *The Achievement of D.H. Lawrence*. F.J. Hoffman and H.T. Moore, eds. Norman: University of Oklahoma Press. 222–34.

Anderson, Walter. 1985. "'The Prussian Officer': Lawrence's Version of the Fall of Man Legend." *Essays in Literature* 12.2 (Fall): 215–23.

Appleman, Philip. 1957–1958. "D.H. Lawrence and the Intrusive Knock." *Modern Fiction Studies* 3: 328–32.

Athenaeum. 1915. ["Fiction,"] No. 4552 (January 23): 68.

Bayley, John. [1960] 1962. *The Character of Love: A Study in the Literature of Personality.* New York: Basic Books. Reprint. London: Constable and Co. Ltd.

Becker, George. 1980. *D.H. Lawrence.* New York: Frederick Ungar Publishing Co.

Black, Michael. 1986. *D.H. Lawrence: The Early Fiction.* Cambridge: Cambridge University Press.

Boulton, James T., ed. 1981. *The Letters of D.H. Lawrence.* Vol. 2. Cambridge: Cambridge University Press.

Boynton, H.W. 1917. [*The Prussian Officer and Other Stories.*] *Bookman* (February): 645–46.

Cowan, James. 1990. *D.H. Lawrence and the Trembling Balance.* University Park: The Pennsylvania State University Press.

Cushman, Keith. 1978. *D.H. Lawrence at Work: The Emergence of the Prussian Officer Stories.* Charlottesville: University of Virginia Press.

Davies, Rosemary. 1984. "From Heat to Radiance: D.H. Lawrence's 'The Prussian Officer.'" *Studies in Short Fiction* 21: 269–71.

Davis, Robert, ed. 1953. "D.H. Lawrence." *Ten Modern Masters: An Anthology of the Short Story.* New York: Harcourt, Brace & World, Inc. 305–07.

Delavenay, Emile. 1972. *D.H. Lawrence: The Man and His Work.* Carbondale, Illinois: Southern Illinois University Press.

Englander, Ann. 1963. "'The Prussian Officer': The Self Divided." *Sewanee Review* 71: 605–19.

Ford, George. 1965. *Double Measure: A Study of the Novels and Stories of D.H. Lawrence.* New York: Holt, Rinehart, and Winston.

Freeman, Mary. 1955. *D.H. Lawrence: A Basic Study of His Ideas.* Gainesville: University of Florida Press.

Fuller, Henry B. 1917. "Embracing the Realities." *The Dial* 62(March 22): 237–38.

Garnett, Edward. 1916. "Art and Moralists: Mr. D.H. Lawrence's Work." *The Dial* 61(November 16): 377–81.

Haegert, John. 1991. "D.H. Lawrence and the Aesthetics of Transgression." *Modern Philology* 88: 2–25.

Händel, G.F. n.d. *Samson: An Oratorio in Vocal Score.* New York: Novello's Original Octavo Edition.

Harris, Janice. 1984. *The Short Fiction of D.H. Lawrence.* New Brunswick, New Jersey: Rutgers University Press.

Hobsbaum, Philip. 1980. *A Reader's Guide to D.H. Lawrence.* London: Thames & Hudson.

Hough, Graham. 1957. *Dark Sun: A Study of D.H. Lawrence.* New York: The Macmillan Company.

Humma, John B. 1974. "Melville's *Billy Budd* and Lawrence's 'The Prussian Officer': Old Adams and New." *Essays in Literature* 1: 83–8.

Lawrence, D.H. 1913. "Honour and Arms." *English Review* 18(August): 24–43.
———. 1914. "Honour and Arms." *Metropolitan* 40(November): 12–14, 61–3.

McDonald, Edward. [1931] 1969. *The Writings of D.H. Lawrence 1925–1930.* Philadelphia: Centaur Book Shop. Reprint. New York: Kraus Publishing.

Monkhouse, Allan (A.N.M.). [1914] 1973. "Review of *The Prussian Officer and Other Stories. Manchester Guardian* Dec. 17. Reprint. *D.H. Lawrence: A Critical Anthology.* H. Coombes, ed. Harmondsworth: Penguin Books Inc. 94–6.

Moore, Harry T. [1954] 1962. *The Intelligent Heart.* New York: Viking Press. Reprint. New York: Grove Press.

The Nation. 1917. ["D.H. Lawrence,"] 104(March 15): 313–14.

Niven, Alistair. 1980. *D.H. Lawrence: The Writer and His Work.* New York: Charles Scribner's Sons.

Orwell, George. 1945. [1968.] *[The Prussian Officer and Other Stories,] London Tribune.* November 16. Reprint. *The Collected Essays, Journalism, and Letters of George Orwell Vol.4: In Front of Your Nose, 1945–50.* Sonia Orwell, ed. New York: Harcourt, Brace.

Outlook (London). 1914. [1970.] ["Novels,"] 24(Dec. 19): 795–96. Reprint. *D.H.Lawrence: The Critical Heritage.* R.P. Draper, ed. London: Routledge & Kegan Paul; New York: Barnes & Noble. 81–3.

Pritchard, R.E. 1971. *D.H. Lawrence: Body of Darkness.* Pittsburgh: University of Pittsburgh Press.

Rose, Shirley. 1975. "Physical Trauma in D.H. Lawrence's Short Fiction." *Contemporary Literature* 16: 73–83.

Sagar, Keith. 1979. *D.H. Lawrence: A Calendar of His Works with a Checklist of the Manuscripts of D.H. Lawrence by Lindeth Vasey.* Austin: University of Texas Press.

Sale, Roger. [1973] 1975. *Modern Heroism.* Berkeley: University of California Press. Reprint. Same.

Saturday Review (London). 1915. ["*The Prussian Officer and Other Stories*,"] 9 January: 42–43.

Schorer, Mark. 1956. "Introduction." *Poste Restante.* Harry T. Moore, ed. Berkeley: University of California Press. 1–18.

Scott, James F. 1977. "D.H. Lawrence's *Germania*: Ethnic Psychology and Cultural Crisis in the Shorter Fiction." *D.H. Lawrence Review* 10.2 (Summer): 142–64.

Seligmann, Herbert J. [1924] 1971. *D.H. Lawrence: An American Interpretation.* Freeport, N.Y.: Books for Libraries Press.

Shipp, Horace, ed. 1927. *The 'English Review' Book of Short Stories.* London: Sampson Low, Marston & Co.

Spilka, Mark. 1955. *The Love Ethic of D.H. Lawrence.* Bloomington: Indiana University Press.

Stewart, Jack F. 1986. "Expressionism in 'The Prussian Officer.'" *D.H. Lawrence Review* 18.2–3: 275–89.

Tedlock, E.W. 1963. *D.H. Lawrence: Artist and Rebel.* Albuquerque: University of New Mexico Press.

———, ed. 1964. *Frieda Lawrence: The Memoirs and Correspondence.* New York: Alfred A. Knopf, Inc.

Thornton, Weldon. 1985. "D.H. Lawrence." *The English Short Story: 1880–1945.* Boston: Twayne. 39–56.

Vickery, John. 1973. *The Literary Impact of 'The Golden Bough.'* Princeton, N.J.: Princeton University Press.

Weiss, Daniel. 1962. *Oedipus in Nottingham: D.H. Lawrence.* Seattle: University of Washington Press.

West, Anthony. [1950] 1977. *D.H. Lawrence.* Denver: Alan Swallow. Reprint. Norwood Editions.

Widmer, Kingsley. 1962. *The Art of Perversity: D.H. Lawrence's Shorter Fiction.* Seattle: University of Washington Press.

Wilt, Judith. 1980. *Ghosts of the Gothic.* Princeton: Princeton University Press.

Woolf, Virginia. 1947. "Notes on D.H. Lawrence." *"The Moment" and Other Essays.* London: Hogarth Press. 79–83.

Worthen, John. 1991. *D.H. Lawrence.* London: Edward Arnold.

———. 1989. *D.H. Lawrence: A Literary Life.* New York: St. Martin's Press.

———. 1983. "Introduction." *The Prussian Officer and Other Stories.* Cambridge: Cambridge University Press.

V

"The Horse Dealer's Daughter"

PUBLICATION HISTORY

In a letter of December 31, 1915, Lawrence confided in his friend Catherine Carswell that he was about to write a "midwinter story of oblivion" (Sagar 1979, 68; Boulton 1981, 493). Ten days later, he wrote another friend, Lady Ottoline Morrell, that he had completed the first part of a short story but found it difficult to continue. "You see," he wrote, "one must break into a new world and it is so difficult." Further describing this first draft of what would become "The Horse Dealer's Daughter," Lawrence went on to observe that one "always believe[d] in miracles" (Boulton 1981, 501), a revealing phrase considering "The Miracle" was the first title of "The Horse Dealer's Daughter."

It was November of 1916, however, before Lawrence again referred to the tale, this time as "another short story on hand" he planned to finish and send off to his agent J.B. Pinker just as soon as he had consigned his latest novel, *Women in Love*, to the publisher (Boulton 1984, 29). He finally posted "The Miracle" to Pinker on January 12, 1917. The accompanying letter, rather sullen in tone because of a publisher's recent rejection of *Women in Love*, described the short story as "beautiful" with a happy ending, "so the swine of people ought to be very thankful for it" (Boulton 1984, 74). The continuing horror of the first World War and the British government's refusal to allow him to leave England during the War may have further annoyed Lawrence. Nevertheless, the compassion in "The Horse Dealer's Daughter" is decidedly untypical of Lawrence's wartime tales (Delavenay 1972, 442–43).

Unhappy with Pinker's failure to sell the story in the preceding three years, on February 8, 1920, Lawrence asked the agent to return "The Miracle" along with eleven other unpublished tales (Boulton 1984, 472). Two days later Lawrence wrote New York publisher Benjamin Huebsch, with whom he had been negotiating the publication of *Women in Love*, and mentioned a number of short stories he would like to place in America (Boulton 1984, 473). But Huebsch "placed" none of them.

Eventually realizing that he would need an American agent, Lawrence enlisted the services of an acquaintance, literary agent Robert Mountsier, who in September of 1920 suggested the idea of a new volume of short fiction. Quickly concurring, Lawrence began to track down and recover his various manuscripts (Boulton 1984, 613).

Revising some of these stories the following year, Lawrence asked Edward Garnett on October 17, 1921, to send him "The Primrose Path" and any other of his stories still in his possession (Boulton 1987, 100). Then, in a letter of October 26, Lawrence noted that he had rewritten "The Miracle," and had changed its title to "The Horse Dealer's Daughter" (Sagar 1979, 115).

Lawrence wrote Mountsier on October 31, 1921, to say he had been revising some of his short fiction in somewhat desultory fashion and that "The Horse Dealer's Daughter," "a new story, or an old one rewritten [in] 7000 words," had just come back from the typist, Mrs. Carmichael, and would be posted to Mountsier in New York from Sicily, where the Lawrences were residing (Boulton 1987, 107).

The following month, Lawrence put his manuscripts in order so as to be free to leave Europe (Sagar 1979, 116). In a November 23 letter to British publisher Martin Secker, who had published *Women in Love* in June, Lawrence mentioned that he had almost finished readying their book of short stories, which he planned soon to have typed. That same day he informed Curtis Brown, an American newspaperman who had a large British agency, that "a batch of short stories for a volume: some unpublished" would arrive soon. Lawrence also said he hoped to sell some of the tales to magazines, especially in America, before the volume came out in England (Boulton 1987, 129).

On December 1, 1921, Lawrence sent "The Horse Dealer's Daughter" to Mountsier by registered post along with "The Fox," "The

Captain's Doll," "Samson and Delilah," "Fanny and Annie," "The Blind Man," "Hadrian" (the retitled "You Touched Me"), and "Monkey Nuts." He also noted that he would send duplicates to Curtis Brown when Mountsier acknowledged receipt of the manuscripts (Boulton 1987, 134). These tales, plus "Tickets, Please" and "The Primrose Path" were sent to Brown on December 7 with a note that the last tale to be included, "England, My England," was still being revised (Boulton 1987, 143–44). (Neither the manuscripts nor the typescripts of these tales sent to Mountsier and Brown have survived.)

Piqued by Secker's refusal to credit the volume of stories toward the five books he had contracted for, Lawrence asked Curtis Brown's office on January 3, 1922, to allow the unpublished tales ("The Horse Dealer's Daughter," "Monkey Nuts," and "The Primrose Path") to appear in magazines before they came out in Secker's collected format. Regretting that he could not time such journal publication of these stories to correspond with the publication of the volume in America, Lawrence felt differently about the British edition. He decided the forthcoming Secker volume could "wait awhile" (Boulton 1987, 155).

Brown succeeded where Pinker had failed; he sold "The Horse Dealer's Daughter," and it appeared in the *English Review* of April 1922. Lawrence wrote the editor, Austin Harrison, on April 11 from Ceylon that he had received the page proofs but saw no point in sending them back since the story would surely appear before the emended proofs arrived. This first variant was identical to the version that would appear in Lawrence's soon-to-be published collection (Boulton 1987, 226).

A June 1922 letter from Edward O'Brien and John Cournos requesting Lawrence's permission to include "The Horse Dealer's Daughter" in *The Best British Stories of 1923* followed in Lawrence's wake, missing him in Australia but reaching him that September in Taos, New Mexico. On September 12, Lawrence wrote to his American agent, Robert Mountsier, of his willingness to comply with the request, if legal matters could be worked out with Thomas Seltzer, who was to publish "The Horse Dealer's Daughter" in Lawrence's now titled second collection of short fiction, *England, My England and Other Stories*, the following month in America, and with Secker, who would eventually publish the English edition (Boulton 1987, 296).

October 24, 1922, saw Thomas Seltzer in New York publish this latest collection of Lawrence's short stories, which consisted of 273 pages and sold for two dollars (*N.Y. Times Book Review* 1922, 13). Eight months later, Lawrence received yet another letter from John Cournos, writing for the publishing firms of Jonathan Cape in London and Small, Maynard & Co., Boston, asking to place "The Horse Dealer's Daughter" in a collection of the best British stories of 1923. Lawrence dashed a letter off to Seltzer instructing the publisher to comply with Cournos immediately and to use the text from the *England, My England* volume, with the understanding that Cournos acknowledge Seltzer's earlier use of the story (Boulton 1987, 464– 465). Apparently all this came to pass, for *The Best British Stories of 1923*, which included "The Horse Dealer's Daughter," appeared in January, 1924 (McDonald 1925, 106). Also that January, a full fifteen months after the American edition, the British edition of *England, My England and Other Stories* reached the market, selling for 7s. 6d. (Jones 1924, 738).

In addition, "The Horse Dealer's Daughter" was published posthumously in 1934 in a two-volume edition titled *The Tales of D.H. Lawrence*. It was reprinted in 1971. *England, My England and Other Stories* was reprinted in its entirety by the London House, Heinemann Publishing Co., in 1950. In 1961, this story appeared again, this time in the second book of the Viking Press three-volume edition titled *The Complete Short Stories of D.H. Lawrence*. (All of Lawrence's major short stories were included in this Viking collection.) This edition went through fifteen reprintings before Penguin Books, which still reprints the three-volume set frequently, picked it up in 1976.

In 1974, yet another edition of Lawrence's short fiction appeared, from Heinemann: *The Complete Short Stories of D.H. Lawrence*. In 1990, Cambridge University Press published "The Horse Dealer's Daughter" in its slightly "corrected" form in a "revised" reissue of *England, My England and Other Stories*, edited by Bruce Steele. Most recently, in 1994, Knopf Publishing Co. put out an edition of Lawrence's short fiction, including this tale, entitled *The Collected Stories of D.H. Lawrence*. One of Lawrence's best-known short stories, "The Horse Dealer's Daughter" has also appeared in anthologies regularly through the years.

CIRCUMSTANCES OF COMPOSITION, SOURCES, AND INFLUENCES

Having come back to England in July of 1914, then their return to Europe blocked by the war raging on the continent, the Lawrences felt somewhat marooned. To make matters worse, Lawrence's fourth novel, *The Rainbow*, had been published on September 30, 1915, only to be suppressed by court order on November 13. In the words of a contemporary describing the debacle and the subsequent scramble by a number of Lawrence's associates to distance themselves from the suddenly controversial author, "The deafening silence, broken only by the sound of the white rabbits of criticism scuttling for cover will not soon be forgotten" (Goldring 1920, 70).

Despite these setbacks, in late December Lawrence and Frieda moved to Cornwall, where he felt temporarily rejuvenated. The Celtic, pre-Christian spirit of place and the restless wind off the gray sea agreed with him, and he began writing the first version of "The Horse Dealer's Daughter" while living at Padstow in "a calm, old, slightly deserted farmhouse" (Boulton 1981, 493).

By January 9, 1916, he had finished the first part of the story, but was uncertain how to proceed, for he knew that now he "must break into a new world" (Boulton 1981, 501). The very next day he grew ill with a lung inflammation—most likely an early stage of his tuberculosis—and it was February 12 before he again felt like himself. Moving in March from Padstow to Higher Tregerthen, Zennor, St. Ives, Cornwall, Lawrence received a medical examination in June to determine if he was fit for the western front, conscription being the order of the day. The medical board, however, granted him a full exemption from military service. This and subsequent physical examinations both humiliated and infuriated Lawrence. Recorded in the "Nightmare" chapter of his 1923 novel *Kangaroo*, his account of such examinations provides great insight into Lawrence's psyche during this dark period of his life.

Lawrence again mentioned "The Horse Dealer's Daughter," then "The Miracle," on November 13 as being "on hand," to be finished as soon as he sent off the novel *Women in Love* (Boulton 1984, 29). He at last sent the completed short story to his agent J.B. Pinker on January 12, 1917. The tone of the accompanying letter was dark—and no wonder. As if he had too few anxieties, publishers apparently preferred to avoid his latest novel and the small collection of poems, *Bits*. Lawrence grumbled that if the poems continued to be ignored, the publishers would make him glad, for he would put the verses into the fire (74).

The Lawrences' major concern at this time was, of course, their financial predicament. Money trickled in from the fiction, travel literature, and essays just barely permitting the pair to maintain themselves. Lawrence expressed his disdain for his native land in his January 1917 letter to Pinker, and he hoped America (his "untilled field") would alleviate his grinding poverty. His attempt to gain passports to America in January showed his determination to leave England, which he described as suffocating (Boulton 1984, 75–6). But his passport endorsement application for Frieda and himself was rejected in February, and it would be November of 1919 before he left Great Britain, Frieda having gone home to Germany the month before. That November, Lawrence sailed, not to America, but to Italy, where Frieda and he reunited on December 3. They went on to Capri, then Sicily, living at Fontana Vecchia, Taormina, from March of 1920 until February of 1922.

Lawrence revised "The Miracle" into its final form of "The Horse Dealer's Daughter" in October 1921 while in Sicily and had it typed in Palermo by a Mrs. Carmichael. A letter to the American agent Mountsier revealed Lawrence's difficult financial situation. With only about forty pounds in the bank, Lawrence asked the agent for a New York check book to tide him over until somebody in England paid him (Boulton 1987, 107). Meanwhile, he sent the typescript of "The Horse Dealer's Daughter" to England, where it appeared in the *English Review* for April, 1922.

By the time of its publication, the Lawrences had left Europe for Ceylon (in February) and then moved on to Australia, where they arrived on May 4. They lived in New South Wales until August 10, at which time they sailed for America, via New Zealand and Tahiti. They arrived in San Francisco on September 4, 1922, and reached Taos, New Mexico, September 11, Lawrence's thirty-seventh birthday (Sagar 1979, 116–26).

On October 24, 1922, "The Horse Dealer's Daughter" appeared in the American edition of *England, My England and Other Stories*, and a copy reached Lawrence in Taos on November 6. By the time that the

English edition of the collection came out, in January of 1924, the Lawrences were back in England.

Persistent travel like this hardly solved the Lawrences' money problem; in fact, they never would be wealthy. But they contented themselves with the spiritual enrichment their travels yielded.

Meanwhile, several locations in "The Horse Dealer's Daughter" resemble sites near Eastwood, the town of Lawrence's birth. For example, he based the Pervin farmhouse, Oldmeadow, on John Thomas Meakin's home, Hill Top House, on Nottingham Road in Eastwood. Meakin, a horse dealer, had a son, Duncan, who had been Lawrence's school friend. (In fact, the whole Pervin family seems modeled on the Meakin family.) Similarly, the Moon and Stars Pub, frequented by Jack Fergusson and Fred Henry Pervin, seems based on the Three Tuns, an Eastwood pub. As for the foundries and the smoke that polluted the wintry countryside, the Bennerley iron works were positioned just south of Eastwood (Steele 1990, :47).

World War I and the winds of change that propelled it exerted a major influence upon "The Horse Dealer's Daughter." In fact, Lydia Blanchard (1983) argued convincingly that World War I formed a watershed for Lawrence's fiction: just as Lawrence knew that positive social change could come about only through a rejection of the past, he realized that he must discover new ways to express the new thoughts change brings. Accordingly, he abandoned customary narrative constructs and traditional methods of character development as inadequate for presenting the ideas he must address (245).

Lydia Blanchard viewed *Women in Love* as the place where Lawrence began to experiment with themes and style. While many of these technical experiments—like the interruption of a narrative with an episodic structure, and a kind of flux-and-flow repetition device—were less than entirely effective in *Women in Love*, in the short fiction of *England, My England* they present Lawrence's themes more sharply. Style and theme complement one another in these tales as they had not in Lawrence's pre-war writing. For this reason, Blanchard viewed *Women in Love* as a kind of apprenticeship for these short stories (1983, 239).

To illustrate Lawrence's post-war change of style, Blanchard noted three characteristics in "The Horse Dealer's Daughter" and in other tales from that time: (1) both the readers and the characters themselves may find it difficult to understand motivation; (2) emotions are often inexplicable, and (3) stories are open-ended. Indeed, in the *England, My England* tales, the medium of touch frequently leads to emotional declarations, like Mabel and Jack's in "The Horse Dealer's Daughter" and Maurice's in "The Blind Man." The words "touch," "touched," and "dark" (where most of the touching occurs) appear more frequently in these and later tales. As such, they strengthen the stress upon what goes unsaid or is known as part of the process leading to verbal consciousness and one's development into a conscious being (Blanchard 1983, 241).

The Italian author Giovanni Verga also appears to have influenced "The Horse Dealer's Daughter." After reservations, Lawrence came to admire Verga's work to the point where in 1925 he translated Verga's *Little Novels of Sicily* into English. In October of 1921, while revising "The Horse Dealer's Daughter," he read Verga thoroughly. He especially admired Verga's ability to capture peasant life in dialect and to present the workings of the unsophisticated mind. The Italian writer instilled in Lawrence a desire to master the nuances of primitive life, and love's intuitive rituals that one finds in Verga also appear in "The Horse Dealer's Daughter" (Meyers 1982, 50–1, 71).

Another influence on this tale was Lawrence's own sense of life's mystery and his "power of using countries and landscapes and animals to interpret the human mind and its moods and tragedies" (Aldington, 1930, 33). The desolate wintry fields of Oldmeadow, the "horsey" natures of the Pervin brothers, and Mabel's "bulldog" temperament are cases in point.

THE RELATIONSHIP OF "THE HORSE DEALER'S DAUGHTER" TO OTHER LAWRENCE WORKS

Lawrence also used the setting, Oldmeadow—largely modeled on horse dealer John Thomas Meakin's Eastwood residence, Hill Top House—in his first novel, *The White Peacock*, where he called it The Hollies. The Meakins themselves, models for the Pervins, also appear in *The White Peacock*, as the Mayhews (Steele 1990, 247).

Connections also exist between "The Horse Dealer's Daughter" and some of Lawrence's earlier short fiction. For example, this tale resembles "Love Among the Haystacks" in its focus upon "initiation into desire" (Widmer 1962, 191) and its theme of "vitalistic death" and rebirth (Tedlock 1963, 114). The "ritualistic rubdown" the doctor gives Mabel in the rescue scene follows the pattern of other erotic scenes in *The White Peacock* (1911) and the 1922 novel, *Aaron's Rod* (Meyers 1989, 348). As they do in "The Thorn in the Flesh," a double rescue and a double vision of death and rebirth occur in "The Horse Dealer's Daughter" (Harris 1984, 126). Also, like "Daughters of the Vicar" and "Second Best," this tale focuses on the dangers of love and marriage (Vickery 1973, 313).

Lawrence's use of language also links this tale with such visionary fiction as "Daughters of the Vicar" and "The Prussian Officer." One might consider, for example, the way Lawrence compelled the verb of being to resound with meaning in the rescue scene—Fergusson gasped and knew that he *was* in the world, that he existed. Another connection between this tale and "The Prussian Officer" is the stark atmosphere that helps dramatize "the underself" of a protagonist. Accordingly, the characters in both tales are isolated and minimally delineated— "stripped down," as it were. Even their points of view get lost in the narrative (Harris 1984, 127–128).

The Rainbow and *Women in Love* also share similarities with "The Horse Dealer's Daughter." By means of touch, Mabel and Jack become aware of their love for one another that parallels in *The Rainbow* Lydia's transfiguration after she embraces Tom's knees and thighs, and in *Women in Love* Birkin's awakened feelings for Gerald in the "Gladiatorial" chapter and when he accidentally clasps Gerald's hand (Delavenay 1972, 443).

In addition, a strong similarity exists between Will and Anna's corn-shock building scene in *The Rainbow* and Jack and Mabel's coming together near the end of "The Horse Dealer's Daughter." Both works depict the sympathetic urge toward union and the desire to be separate in conflict. While gathering sheaves in the former work and coming to terms with their love in the latter story, the protagonists wage to-and-fro battles of wills—contests where the women triumph in the men's surrender. Following the capitulation of their mates, both Anna and Mabel draw away from their men, their victories having left them fearful (Schneider 1984, 151–2). In another comparison between these two works, Fergusson's descent into the cold, fetid, clay-bottomed pond is an act of love that fills him with fear and revulsion. Rupert Birkin of *Women in Love* advocates just such a descent into dissolution, toward death and subsequent rebirth, and in "The Horse Dealer's Daughter," Fergusson endures precisely this process "to chart a psychological progress" (Harris 1984, 127).

Such other stories in the *England, My England* volume as "Tickets, Please," "Monkey Nuts," "Samson and Delilah," and "You Touched Me" reflect what may have been Lawrence's growing need for male domination that would become fully developed in the early 1920's during what has been called his Leadership period. In this context, "The Horse Dealer's Daughter" seems to look back to the earlier period of *Women in Love* when Lawrence stressed passionate harmony between the sexes (Cushman 1980, 38).

Parallels between "The Horse Dealer's Daughter" and later novels also exist. In Lawrence's fiction man's essential aloneness is resolved when two vital lives form a connection. Such is the case with Mabel and Jack, and also with Ursula and Birkin in *Women in Love*, and with Connie and Mellors in *Lady Chatterley's Lover* (Ford 1965, 91). Moreover, Mabel and Jack's desire, like Yvette Saywell's in *The Virgin and the Gipsy*, come into being immediately after they nearly drown to form a pattern of "drowning and desire." In each case, waters of regeneration engender a salvific Eros (Widmer 1962, 27). In each case, water becomes a symbol for a "sex-giving and life-giving" force, and in each story a male rescuer rubs the warmth of life back into the body of a half-drowned woman (Moore [1954] 1962, 432).

In addition, "The Horse Dealer's Daughter," *The Virgin and the Gipsy*, and *Lady Chatterley's Lover* follow the "Sleeping Beauty" or "Little Briar Rose" theme where an enchanted princess can be awakened only by a brave prince who risks himself to break the spell. In each of these tales, too, the female protagonist, by means of a spontaneous will-less sexual experience, undergoes a magical awakening (Moore [1954] 1962, 411).

Finally, interesting parallels exist among "The Horse Dealer's Daughter" and some of Lawrence's later short stories. For example, both this story and "The Rocking-Horse Winner" are, in effect, updated fairy tales (Junkins 1969, 210); and in "Sun," "The Ladybird," and "The Woman Who Rode Away," Lawrence instilled in such phenomena as the sun, the moon, fire, and water magical properties that stem from myth. These transformed phenomena lie at the heart of "The Horse Dealer's Daughter" (Vickery 1973, 321).

CRITICAL STUDIES

The initial review of the American edition of *England, My England and Other Stories* appeared in *The New York Times Book Review* for November 19, 1922. Of "The Horse Dealer's Daughter" the reviewer noted that place was effectively conveyed fraught with "spiritual atmosphere." Thus, one knew the little town that Mabel Pervin hastened through on her way to the churchyard that gray wintry day (14).

Louis Kantor's review of the volume appeared in *The New York Tribune* on December 24, and Kantor proclaimed Lawrence England's most creative contemporary writer. With respect to this tale, he noted its "amazing love consummation" (23).

A review by Ben Lucien Burman appeared on January 17, 1923, in *The Nation* and one of his general impressions applies nicely to "The Horse Dealer's Daughter." The tale's characters were (he said) "naked humanity stripped bare of those three veils a super-civilized race wears to veil the animal within: convention, hypocrisy, repression" (73). Referring directly to this tale, Burman described how spiritual nakedness becomes physical nakedness—the tale's principal concern being the downhearted Mabel's "frenzied passion" for the doctor who saves her from suicide (74).

Rebecca West's *Yale Review* article on Lawrence's latest short story collection appeared in July of 1923. Her uncomplimentary review complained that Lawrence's use of foreign phrases (such as *museau* in "The Horse Dealer's Daughter") marred "the decorum of an English page." The main theme, the sudden development of love out of "sex-antagonism" as if "it were a chemical change" initiated by the antagonism's intensity, West termed monotonous. Ingrained in Lawrence's metaphysic, she wrote, this theme limited his scope (849).

Following the British publication of the *England, My England* stories in January of 1924, A.S. McDowall's review appeared that very month in the *Times Literary Supplement*. McDowall noted Lawrence's ability to describe powerful emotions felt in the blood before understood in the heart, thus barely apprehended by consciousness. With this method, Lawrence illustrated the close proximity of love and hate. Such perception, bolstered by Lawrence's "passionate sincerity," produced credibility. But the presence of "sudden, straining," paradoxical climaxes in the collection made such acquiescence difficult. Nevertheless, McDowall found the scenes and characters vivid and colorful. Despite a frequent focus upon instinct and "reactions of desire," Lawrence's expression was dynamic, and the most forceful story in the collection was "The Horse Dealer's Daughter." Therein, argued the reviewer, Lawrence effectively transfigured the "ugly and unlikely" with an intensity that burned away "their dross" (1924, 50).

Other contemporary reviews of *England, My England and Other Stories* failed to mention "The Horse Dealer's Daughter."

One of the most popular critical approaches to this tale, meanwhile, has been to examine it for symbols. Mark Schorer's (1950) comment explained how Lawrence used symbols to conjoin two distinct worlds: the objective world of everyday objects and activity, and the subjective world of psychic action. Lawrence's seamless fusion of this duality produced a verisimilitude that nevertheless presented characters whose speech and behavior only partially mimicked real-life dialogue and behavior (328).

This uniquely Lawrentian construct, Schorer attributed largely to the development of symbols that transfigured experience to a level of completely new psychic consciousness, returning Mabel and Jack to the everyday world in a kind of sanctified state at the story's end. Both had experienced a partial death of the self, had relinquished egoism, and having been receptive to life, awaken in love, as a loving couple might wake up to a new day. The imaginative view seemed to Schorer nothing less than eternal, for the work encompassed and illustrated "subjective realities" presenting the most important of themes: the central concept of "death in life" and life by means of death (1950, 328).

Ultimately, noted Schorer, the tale taught three important lessons about love. First, Lawrence had illustrated the way in which love was *alive*—it existed in physical life, was basic and dynamic, and represented "the final commitment" of the remaining self, the self transfigured above that self given up to death. Second, readers saw the *terrible* nature of love: part of oneself must die, resulting in moral disarray as one's being is exposed. Third, Lawrence treated love as *crucial*, illustrating the death experience from which life is rescued (1950, 329).

Three years later, Robert Davis (1953) termed Lawrence's description in this tale both vivid and natural. He viewed as "strange" and "symbolic," the scene that initiated the passion that united the two lovers before the blazing kitchen hearth. Such passion, Davis called unlikely, but genuine (306–7).

Ten years passed before the symbolism in "The Horse Dealer's Daughter again received scrutiny. E.W. Tedlock's (1963) brief study noted that Mabel's attraction to her mother's world of death, which seemed to her more real than life itself, resulted from her having known only rude, bestial men. Fergusson crosses the gulf to Mabel, whereby he leaves behind his impersonal role as doctor and his fear, through the sense of touch. The otherwise felicitous ending remains problematic through the couple's lingering fears of committing each to the other and of the work-a-day world that lies outside their connection. As with all of Lawrence's best work, this tale is characterized by "existential honesty" and a subtle, forthcoming creation of a "correlative natural symbolism" (114–15).

Jessie Rehder (1963) believed that the churchyard, pond, and final kitchen scenes were symbolic, but not in the traditional sense. Instead, each forms a rite involving both characters and readers, who walk with the hopeless Mabel and the distant doctor through the "falling dusk" into the pond's "obscurity" and then receive rebirth by means of "the water, the fire, the nakedness, and the new clothes of love" (241).

In fact, continued Rehder, the tale asks a reader to plunge into the pond with Fergusson, for only such behavior can divert the tale's earlier "drift toward death." The story, consequently, becomes quick with life and seems almost a religious parable of love's power, even though this love contains ambivalence (1963, 240).

George Ford's (1965) examination of "The Horse Dealer's Daughter" praised Lawrence's ability to render setting both symbolic and real. Throughout, for example, the gray, wintry landscape seems to absorb Mabel, and simultaneously the reader is made to "feel death's presence in our eyes and nostrils." The foul-pond smell in Mabel's hair serves a double function: to remind the reader of what has happened, and to portend what could again occur if the couple loses their vital connection (92).

For Jack's part—and Lawrence analyzed Jack's psychic transition much more thoroughly than Mabel's, whose development he suggested by means of the depth of her gaze and her behavior—the doctor undergoes a kind of "deathly baptism" when he rescues Mabel from the muddy water. In a Pauline sense, he dies into life, ready to turn to the vital having known its opposite. The tale concludes with Jack and Mabel's fears: both hesitate to yield to one another but are far more terrified of losing the other now that the other has presented a release from the previous sense of isolation. Two lonely people, the horse dealer's daughter and the doctor, find deliverance in each other that transfigures them from their daily selves, simultaneously revealing to each new self knowledge (Ford 1965, 91–4).

M.G. Krishnamurthi (1970) praised Lawrence's true grasp of that which made men and women "human." Mabel's "bulldog" expression indicates her withdrawal from the kind of life her brothers lead and signifies her protest against her father's remarriage and the distasteful life surrounding her—that is, signifies her death wish. Thus, the churchyard where her mother is buried provides a connection with lost love and security; Mabel's quest is for communion. As for Fergusson's momentary eye contact at the graveyard and his subsequent vital reaction, Lawrence's use of religious and magical imagery in that scene signifies the awakening Mabel effects of a lower repressed level of his being. Both are searching for something that lies beyond their present lives— that is, for a deeper relationship. Their commitment to one another is occasioned by a "reintegration" that occurs only after each reclaims the other: she from death, and he from "willed superficiality" (83–7).

Krishnamurthi defended as both naive and fitting Mabel's sudden question about Fergusson's love. The doctor's concern, so different from the coarse and brutal world she had experienced since her mother's death, is a novel experience. Fergusson's painful but vital gulf-crossing to Mabel, Krishnamurthi regarded as "the triumph of the tale," for Lawrence made it clear that Jack's commitment does not stem from feelings of charity (1970, 83–9).

R.E. Pritchard (1971) also saw the world of Mabel and Jack portrayed solidly and sensitively while at the same time infused with symbolic power. For example, he pointed to the departing horses at the tale's beginning as symbolic of a general dissipation of life energy prevalent until the rescue scene. Then, once the doctor has carried Mabel back to Oldmeadow, her assumption of Fergusson's impersonal sexual desire for her forces his need into open actuality, the impersonal desire having been increased by the new sense of death's dispassionate nature he experienced as he watched her try to kill herself. The shock and pain of having escaped death and of experiencing life anew with the added dimension of commitment—all are extreme emotions (110).

The psycho-sexual symbolism Sarah Betsky-Zweig discovered in "The Horse Dealer's Daughter" received thorough analysis in her 1973 article. She maintained that both the plot and its resolution stemmed from illnesses: Jack's head cold and Mabel's surrender to death. Following their reemergence from the pond (the rescue scene itself Betsky-Zweig interpreted as a subtle, precise, honest, and vivid description of coitus) the membrane of Jack's heart is ruptured by first love just as metaphorically was Mabel's hymen will be soon with the consummation of their marriage. With the blossoming of their love, the "brood mare" finds her mate: a man "alert to his own feelings," and the lovers' malady of living life is cured (163–65).

In a brief examination of "The Horse Dealer's Daughter," Alistair Niven (1980) praised Lawrence's sure control of atmosphere throughout the story and focused on the way that a reader could perceive the hearth fire before which Jack and Mabel surrender to one another as warming their love (84).

Janice Harris (1984) conducted a much more detailed examination of symbolism in "The Horse Dealer's Daughter." With regard to the pond scene, Harris commended Lawrence's ability to describe "the apocalyptic in the colloquial." The double immersion in the foul, frigid water is a descent from disability to death. But in that descent lie the initial steps of "an ancient rite of ascent," the cleansing bath of baptism. Both Mabel and Jack "rise from the waters of oblivion reborn" (127).

Sociological criticism of "The Horse Dealer's Daughter" is limited. E. W. Tedlock's (1963) study only mentioned in passing Mabel's having endured the society of coarse and brutish men that her brothers constitute. (114). But perhaps the dearth of sociological studies of this story was best explained in Keith Cushman's (1978) examination where he noted that unlike "Daughters of the Vicar," the surging tide of passion in "The Horse Dealer's Daughter" is absolutely unrelated to normal modes of social behavior (106). Next, George Becker (1980) noted that with the collapse of her male-dominated family, Mabel seeks out Fergusson through blind instinct (117). Concluding this short line of criticism, Jeffrey Meyers (1989) observed that the title suggests that Mabel's social role is defined by her father's occupation. He added that unlike Joe and their father, both of whom marry for security, Mabel refuses to plan for the future (346).

The psychological approach to "The Horse Dealer's Daughter" has proven much more rewarding than the sociological and began as early as 1926. Scottish poet Edwin Muir noted then that Lawrence's best quality consisted of "a kind of splendour, not of the spirit, nor of the mind, but of the senses and the instincts" (49). Muir's critique, the earliest instance of an extended psychological-philosophical examination, discerned acutely Lawrence's heavy emphasis upon man's instinctive nature over the mental. But he failed to notice Lawrence's goal of a balanced psyche with neither instinct nor reason dominating.

Muir's observations about the interchange between nature and human nature in Lawrence's work certainly seem prescient for 1926. (Muir's own fascination and experience with psychoanalysis surely contributed to his vision.) He discussed what Lawrence called objective and subjective responses between the unconscious plane of man's psyche and nature itself: "This out-and-in flowing communicates to everything a heightened life; the substance of experience is changed as if by alchemy. . . . For this unconscious communication all his characters strive: it is their fulfillment, and the intellect has hardly any part in it" (52–3).

Muir continued, "The responses of [Lawrence's] instincts are not merely phenomena to him, to be judged by the mind; they are truths whose force is conclusive. When the instinctive field of one character impinges on that of another. . . two vital principles are enraged, violated, or glorified by each other, while the mind looks on and knows its irrelevance" (1926, 54).

Muir next noted how Lawrence used dialogue as a "graph of the movement of the instincts," for it neither portrays character, nor describes situation. Lawrence's dialogue, like his narrative technique, has an "underlying content," and while words intimate it, they fail to contain it. Consequently, characters like Mabel sometimes say things that are senseless as "conscious statement," while nevertheless being true as "delineation of the unconscious" (Muir 1926, 55–6).

Thirty-five years later, the psychological examination of "The Horse Dealer's Daughter" resumed in earnest with Sean O'Faolain (1961). Perhaps influenced by Muir's earlier study, the Irish writer noted that this story exists on two levels: the opening contains glorious realism, and the love scene exists outside reason in the realm of human passion where moral issues fail to intrude and credulity and incredulity are beside the point. Unfamiliar as readers might feel themselves in this latter realm, Lawrence's own familiarity with it allows one to suspend judgment while following Lawrence "underground." The application of cold reason to the tale, O'Faolain argued, could only result in its—and a reader's—loss (1961, 461–3).

Kingsley Widmer (1962) ranked "The Horse Dealer's Daughter" among Lawrence's best works of fiction. He also decided that the story concerned "the impersonal unfolding of desire." The disintegration of the Pervin family offers Mabel the chance to escape forever her life of drudgery. Cast into a chaos that might also contain freedom, she seeks the world of death, where her dear mother abides. Desireless, Mabel's attempt to drown herself becomes, by a coincidence like those in fairy tales, "a moment of regenerative baptism." Having reemerged from the water, both Mabel and Jack leave death and a sense of hopelessness as they confront "the new agony of desire." Significantly, the liberation of this desire from structured society, as witnessed in Jack and Mabel's moment of revelation, stems from the chaos of the Pervin family's break-up. In the lovers' mutual desire at the story's end, one finds passion's most basic characteristic: love is not merely a triumph over death, it is a form of death itself (172–3).

Clyde Ryals (1962) produced the first psychological analysis to focus exclusively upon "The Horse Dealer's Daughter." Although Ryals mentioned Freud in connection with Mabel's desire to join her dead mother (a classic case of regression wherein her father's rejection of her by his taking a second wife awakened in her a longing for the security she once had with her mother), the examina-tion is, however, primarily Jungian. Focusing on Fergusson's rescue of Mabel from the pool, Ryals cited three phases of the rebirth archetype (1962, 40).

First, in the doctor-assistant's entry into the pond, Ryals saw a parallel to Jung's myth of the night journey beneath the sea where "slime" or some other objectionable elements in the water could represent unpleasant animal tendencies while simultaneously containing the germ of new life. Second, the suicide method Mabel chooses could be viewed as a "mythological enactment" of one's desire to return to the moist security of the womb. Third, both Mabel and Jack undergo a kind of rebirth, where each delivers the other psychically from a perception of the phenomenal world as meaningless. Both characters are transformed by their newly established organic connection with life (42).

In writing this vitalistic tale, Ryals concluded, Lawrence used a framing device. While the beginning and end focus on the characters' behavior in the everyday world, the heart of the work departs from this world, traveling to the interior world of their consciousness. With their psychic rebirth, they can rejoin the world's external reality and take part "in a larger circle of experience" (42).

Emile Delavenay (1972) furthered Ryals's analysis. Delavenay noted how the story illustrates that for Mabel and Jack to come face to face with each other and with their own inner beings, their everyday routines had to be disrupted dramatically. Only then could hidden emotions be acknowledged. Touch, the vehicle of "physical consciousness," when experienced in such a situation could for a time supersede "mental consciousness" (443).

In his study of "The Horse Dealer's Daughter," Steven Phillips (1975) acknowledged his debt to Kingsley Widmer's and Clyde Ryals' psychological approaches. Phillips then advanced the thesis that two rebirth patterns appear in the story: the first at the pond, the second at the farmhouse. This dual resurrection pattern divides the story into two halves. Phillips also pointed to Lawrence's use of directional words in each part as indicators of the beginning of rebirth. In both instances, Mabel is below Jack and draws him downward to herself (94–5).

Further parallels between the two sections exist in the fear that Fergusson experiences when approaching Mabel in the pond and in his later reluctance to commit himself to her. The transformation of the two characters in both situations is immediately preceded by Fergusson's yielding to powerful unconscious forces, and by his subsequent loss of his sense of time. The tentativeness of Jack and Mabel toward one another at the story's end suggests that the second "descent and rebirth," although reinforcing the first structurally, does not do so thematically. The second rebirth is incomplete, which implies that love must be confirmed continually if it is to grow and flourish. The pond experience would have to occur again in their personal relationship, Phillips asserted, for the second rebirth to be realized fully (1975, 96–7).

A study of "The Horse Dealer's Daughter" by D. Kenneth Mackenzie (1978) emphasized how the ennui that pervades the setting and the lives of Mabel Pervin and Jack Fergusson becomes transformed by a more than merely sexual "energy of sympathetic passion." In this marvelous course of events, the two lovers become completely human, become civilized, and thus, rise above the condition of heavy work horses (133–34).

Keith Cushman's (1980) interesting examination of "The Horse Dealer's Daughter" referred to it as a product of Lawrence's pre-leadership period, and, thus, as undogmatic in its openendedness. To Cushman, who pointed out that little actually is resolved in the story, it nevertheless seems to celebrate the redeeming aspects of a dark, mysterious sexuality. Contrary to earlier optimistic readings, Cushman observed that despite a reader's hope for Mabel and Jack's redemption through passion, uncontrollable and perhaps destructive forces have been loosed. Entering blindly into their relationship, Jack and Mabel might find a future together fraught with questions and dangers (34).

The most recent psychological study of this tale, Janice Harris's, came out in 1984. (A discussion of Harris's analysis of symbolism in the story appeared earlier in this chapter.) Harris saw the rescue scene functioning on three levels: the ritualistic, the literal, and the psychological. In reference to the latter, she saw Lawrence using the pond scene "to chart a psychological progress" in both Jack and Mabel. Fergusson's former impersonal, benevolent, and sensationalistic approach to love foundered during the rescue and thereafter, which fostered a fresh view of love as a personal force, seductive yet painful. Harris maintained that love threatened Fergusson's very psyche—the safe, secure world he had created—but, ultimately, he deems love to be vital (Harris 1984, 127).

Meanwhile, Mabel's love for the world of death, as exhibited by her sense of connection with her mother as she tends the grave, reverses direction toward the world of life once the young doctor delivers her from the pond. Drawn together by their "mutual need," Jack and Mabel are last seen in an embrace that might well be a metaphorical manifestation of the fleeting harmonious marriage of their psyches' conscious and unconscious planes (128).

Another helpful approach to "The Horse Dealer's Daughter" engaged the mythic facets of the tale. Harry T. Moore (1954) noted that the sense of touch and the Sleeping Beauty motif both become significant features (225).

In 1969, Donald Junkins approached the story as a contemporary dramatization of psychological truths found in myth. He noted that the story contains seven specific mythological motifs found in innumerable fairy tales, including "Snow Drop and Briar Rose": (1) the presence of three brothers; (2) a father's remarriage upon the death of the children's mother; (3) a protagonist who fails to grow and blossom; (4) soon-to-be lovers exchanging all-too-revealing glances prior to a recognition scene; (5) a girl encountering an unconscious-ness akin to death; (6) a hero risking his life to save her; and (7) the kiss that rouses the heroine from her death-in-life state. In Lawrentian fashion, Mabel is reborn of the flesh into life, her former isolated and uninitiated self having died (210–12).

The Andromeda myth in which a virgin princess is rescued from a sacrificial seaside death by a hero (Perseus) was seen as an ancient antecedent of "The Horse Dealer's Daughter" by John Vickery (1973). In this story, water purifies Mabel and fire revives her: two rites central to her salvation (322).

Sarah Betsky-Zweig's (1973) examination of the tale acknowledged Harry T. Moore's emphasis on touch and the Sleeping Beauty theme. Betsky-Zweig noted, however, noted that Lawrence's story deviates from the fairy tale in that Jack Fergusson, too, is awakened, not just Mabel (159). (Betsky-Zweig's focus upon psycho-sexual symbolism received earlier attention in this chapter.)

Seven years later, Keith Cushman's (1980) discussion of this story continued in the Moore vein, Cushman having detected a reworking of the Cinderella tale. The three sullen siblings and the industrious sister, Cushman saw as a standard of the Märchen. Lacking a fairy godmother, Mabel has to take her own salvation in hand. Paradoxically, it comes about as she is rescued by the prince figure, Jack Fergusson, from the waters of oblivion into which she has cast herself. Agreeing with Moore, Cushman observed that the "Sleeping Beauty" motif is also present in that as Mabel is brought back to life, Fergusson, himself, is revived (1980, 32).

Citing Freud's belief that the constant conflict between Eros, the instinct of life, and Thanatos, the instinct of destruction, accounts for life's energy, Jack Stewart's 1985 examination of "The Horse Dealer's Daughter" approached the story as a "reinvented myth" wherein mythic archetypes combine with realistic experience. Thus, a reader follows movements of Mabel and Jack from their individual states of isolation and alienation to mutual regeneration. To show this process, Lawrence presented Jack as a mythic-hero figure who must endure a descent into dissolution—the pond—before he can leave behind (and before Mabel can leave behind) separation. As part of the monomythic pattern, separation gives way to initiation, which leads to return (14, 18).

Stewart next noted how a reader sees Mabel and Jack at the beginning as yielding to Thanatos: Mabel worships death both literally and metaphorically, as we see in the churchyard scene. We also see that Jack's "workaholic" nature, purely mechanical, typifies a death-in-life existence. Yet even in characters in thrall to Thanatos, Eros is present. When their eyes meet at the graveyard, Fergusson feels temporarily revitalized, even though Mabel's eyes signaled to him "independent of her consciousness." Jack's subsequent descent into the foul muddy water epitomized a hero's need to know both the real and symbolic element of his and a heroine's death before he can form a connection with her "unconscious life" and restore her desire to live (1985, 14–5).

The water, Stewart suggested, is female and the symbol for both life and death, for "transformation and rebirth." Both Mabel and Jack having been delivered, Thanatos yields to Eros, but only after each protagonist is separated from the familiar world—literally by means of their immersion in the pond. Then, only through their initiation "into the otherness of death" could each return to begin a new life. Eros triumphs at the story's end, and the lovers must follow his vital direction, sacrificing will "to a larger, revitalized Being" (Stewart 1985, 15, 17).

Daniel Fraustino (1989) approached the story from the perspective of Christian mythology. He saw Mabel's original sin to be pride. Despite the loss of her social position and fortune, she seeks "spiritual transcendence through a bodiless orthodox puritanism" (106). Her experience in the pond, like the Christian baptism, redeems her of this sin; she is reborn by means of her recognition of her sexual nature, and she delivers Jack, as well, in the process. As Jack's redeemer, Mabel can be seen as a Christ figure. To this end, Fraustino contended that Lawrence established the savior motif by having Mabel, like Christ, sit at the head of a table as if "condemned," as after the Last Supper came death and resurrection. Fraustino also pointed out that Jack's name— John—suggests a parallel with John the Baptist, and that Mabel's father's name, another reference to Christ, is Joseph. Mabel's true feelings made obvious, Jack is saved by her from "his own enclosed, fallen self" (107).

In another 1989 examination of the story, Jeffrey Meyers reprised earlier studies focused on the theme of resurrection (notably Kingsley Widmer's 1962 analysis) and discussed their shortcomings. Meyers perceived in the tale a coalescence of both classical and Christian resurrection myths. As illustrations of the former mythology paralleling Jack's rescue of Mabel and their subsequent "resurrection," Meyers adduced Persephone's vernal return aboveground, and Orpheus's attempt to save Eurydice from the Underworld. Meyers discerned the same Christian mythos in God's creation of Adam (the parallel occurs when Jack massages Mabel's body to bring her to consciousness), and in Christ's raising of Lazarus from the dead, which required the removal of Lazarus's "grave clothes," just as the doctor relieves Mabel of her wet clothing following her rescue (348).

Meyers also contended that Lawrence presented the themes of this particular tale—acquiring knowledge through the sense of touch; ritualistic and ceremonial "release of primitive emotions"; self-realization; and rebirth through a regenerative love—by means of literary allusions and transformed analogues in earlier British literature. Thus, the effect of Jack and Mabel's exchange of glances at the cemetery resembles an episode in Keats's "Ode to a Nightingale," Mabel's suicide attempt resembles Ophelia's successful attempt in *Hamlet*, and Jack's "clairvoyant" vision resembles the vision Wordsworth described in "Tintern Abbey" (Meyers 1989, 346–8).

In 1956, F.R. Leavis noted that the form of "The Horse Dealer's Daughter" complemented its theme. Deeming this tale a work of "classical perfection," Leavis found it typical of Lawrence to concern himself with relationships between individual persons and to avoid clichés by examining fully the "delicate complexity" of such relationships. He presented Mabel Pervin objectively as impassive, sulky, and independent. He shunned pathos both in her description and when she tends her mother's grave. He conveyed her intensity in the churchyard, and her self-imposed distance masterfully. Similarly, he portrayed Jack Fergusson's dilemma at the farmhouse in its full complexity by means of an "unerring rightness of touch," the gift of only a very great artist. The doctor's reluctant response to Mabel's declaration is as positive as it is profound in a tale fraught with death but culminating in a victory for vitalism (311–15).

A much more detailed formalist approach to the work's text and its theme appeared with Thomas McCabe's (1972) study. McCabe noted how Lawrence used rhythm as form in "The Horse Dealer's Daughter." He also used two major devices to develop that rhythmic form, not only in this tale but in most of his short stories where the tension between potential participants in a relationship remains unresolved. The first device is the repetition of scenes, phrases, and characters. For example, "The Horse Dealer's Daughter" incorporates three important scenes in which Mabel and Jack exchange glances: initially in the Pervin kitchen, then in the churchyard where lay Mabel's mother, and finally by the hearthside after Mabel's rescue. Also, Lawrence repeated contrasting images of dampness and cold and of fire and warmth (64–5).

The second device, more uniquely Lawrentian according to McCabe, heightens the revelation of the characters' unconscious or psychic experience through characters' rhythmically alternating attitudes of attraction-repulsion toward one another, and through the use of repetition to expand rhythmic imagery. In this way, the story has a double rhythmic movement. The overall rhythm of the plot is progressive, moving ahead to an ever-closer relationship. But within this rhythm lies another: a "flux-and-flow" action that defines the battle between life and death, will and desire, man and woman. Thus, the major movement in this tale (the rhythm of which parallels nature itself) is lifeward, after its initial deathward impulse. Accordingly, Jack and Mabel abandon at least momentarily the world of willfulness and find their deeper essential selves, both having deferred to desire. At the story's conclusion, the balance between the soon-to-be husband and wife undergoes constant adjustment as they touch, then draw away (McCabe 1972, 66–7).

With regard to those images that disclosed psychic states, McCabe focused upon the metaphorical function of water in "The Horse Dealer's Daughter." Whereas the cold murky water of the pond represents the world of death Mabel embraces and against which Fergusson risks his life, the tears that later well up in Mabel's eyes affirm life, like the water of a fountain, portending the deliverance of Jack over to life. Consequently, the image denotes Mabel's psychic level: she has become part of the life force implicit in fountains, and Fergusson's transformation results from his looking deeply into them (68–9).

Thomas Gullason (1973) produced another excellent formalist study of "The Horse Dealer's Daughter." He began by disagreeing with Mark Schorer's adjudication that as a work of art "The Horse Dealer's Daughter" lacked "moral evolution." Schorer had found this specific quality only within the novel genre—the short story genre being better suited to presenting "moral revelation" (1950, 433). Gullason argued effectively against the idea that the brevity of a short story made it impossible for moral evolution to occur there. In fact, in "The Horse Dealer's Daughter" a reader watches the natures of Mabel and Jack, and their enigmatic and equivocal relationship evolve—that evolution being the very theme of the story. Lawrence developed these elements by the "cyclical, spiraling, and advancing structure of the work," as well as by a number of patterns and images that serve as a kind of "musical counterpoint" to one another. For example, the "falling action" that opens the tale readies the reader for the initial and subsequent "rising action" between Mabel and Jack, death often yielding new life in Lawrence (348–9).

Similarly, the various journeys in the story—Jack making his appointed rounds and Mabel's excursion to the churchyard and back to

Oldmeadow—as well as the "psychic journeys" at the cemetery, the pond, and in the kitchen at the story's end parallel the work's thematic movement toward independence and self-realization subsequent to the couple's rebirth (Gullason 1973, 349–51).

Contradictory motifs that illustrate further the puzzling nature of Mabel and Jack's relationship include elements of barrenness and generation, security and risk, control and helplessness, independence and entrapment, and mobility and immobility (351). The "moral revelation" in Mabel and Jack's affirmation of love neatly ties together the diverse narrative strands, but it also forces the action, as in a rite of catharsis, toward the most significant realm, "the level of evolution and universality." Thus, Gullason concluded, by means of both moral revelation and moral evolution, Mabel and Jack and their predicament are tried and provide "viable insights" into life's rhythm and the human condition (1973, 351–2).

Philip Hobsbaum's (1980) study of Lawrence's fiction character- ized "The Horse Dealer's Daughter" as "a poem of awakening" that contains one of Lawrence's major ideas: the sense of touch can convey both truth and knowledge. More than a mere naturalistic story, this allegory of a relationship's development uses visual, tactual, and audio images to describe Mabel's full awakening as a whole person. Her "new awareness" encourages Fergusson to cross the gulf and join her. Images of rising water and of shining eyes signify new love's intensity and suffering (35).

Janice Harris's (1984) examination of form and theme in "The Horse Dealer's Daughter" noted "a double vision of death and resurrection" and "a dual rescue." Harris perceived both Mabel and Jack as moving toward death up to the point of the rescue scene. Mabel had glorified her mother and her world of death. Jack, on the other hand, had struggled lonely and devitalized at a job that possessed him and offered him only "voyeuristic" excitement while he visited the homes of his working-class patients. Feeling ill and "done for," the weary doctor's deathward direction parallels the path of "impassive, blank" Mabel (126).

Jack's superior position (he is standing on a rise when he observes Mabel wade into the pond) recurs literally and metaphorically in the kitchen where Mabel embraces his knees and regards him in his male capacity as a potential lover rather than a physician. Thus, the literal descent he has made into the death-filled and life-giving pond water is repeated symbolically in the farmhouse when Mabel's pleas eventually wear down Jack's conscious idea of himself based on his doctor's sense of honor, his pride, and his wish to remain intact and apart. He then falls "into love and desire." Having rescued each other in a dual resurrection, Mabel and Jack can begin their new lives together, their feet firmly on the ground (Harris 1984, 126–28).

One finds little in the way of a linguistic focus on "The Horse Dealer's Daughter." But Garrett Stewart's (1976) linguistic analyses of Lawrence's prose style in such works as *The Rainbow, Women in Love,* and *Lady Chatterley's Lover* cast some light upon the thematic development of "The Horse Dealer's Daughter." Citing Lawrence's ability to use language allotropically so as both to say and do, Stewart suggested that Lawrence used as a signature "an ambiguous 'to be' variant" to highlight his characters' deaths and resurgences. Thus, such protagonists as Ursula in *The Rainbow* and Mabel and Jack in "The Horse Dealer's Daughter" metaphorically die "into the knowledge of life." Each passes away into a "new existence characterized by a revelation" created by life itself and their awareness of it (232–33).

For example, Lawrence's use of the verb "to rise" and verbal forms denoting descent in the rescue scene, in combination with the contradictory tenses of the verb "to be" therein, achieve linguistically what had actually occurred on the psychological and emotional levels in the characters, as well as what had developed thematically in the tale. From his initial position upon a prospect, Fergusson must descend to the pond and then plunge into its soft clayey foulness, from which both he and Mabel arise. His rescue of the suicidal woman is mirrored in the subsequent kitchen scene, where the doctor at Mabel's urging descends to the emotional level where he can experience and acknowledge the newborn love that has delivered them from their death-in-life existences. Thus, Lawrence's language in the narrative served a dual function: it became both expression and enactment (232–33).

Eighty years after its composition, "The Horse Dealer's Daughter" now ranks among the masterpieces of short fiction. The compelling interest the tale has attracted over the years among critics, scholars, and casual readers, testifies to its greatness. A model of Lawrence's "middle-period" fiction, "The Horse Dealer's Daughter" built upon the strengths of the earlier *Prussian Officer* stories. To his extraordinary sensitivity toward the plight of the individual in relation to others and to nature in a chaotic world, Lawrence added through his subtler precision in presenting symbols and psychology a deeper awareness of the need for vital relationships in which a mutual miracle of "rebirth" superseding a lonely death-in-life existence is not only possible, but also is imperative for the future of mankind.

WORKS CITED

Aldington, Richard. 1930. *D.H. Lawrence.* London: Chatto & Windus.

Becker, George. 1980. *D.H.Lawrence.* New York: Frederick Ungar Publishing Co.

Betsky-Zweig, Sarah. 1973. "Floutingly in the Fine Black Mud: D.H. Lawrence's 'The Horse Dealer's Daughter.'" *Dutch Quarterly Review* 3: 159–65.

Blanchard, Lydia. 1983. "Lawrence on the Fighting Line: Changes in Form of the Post-War Short Fiction." *The D.H. Lawrence Review* 16.3: 235–47.

Booklist: A Guide to the Best New Books. 1923. *"England, My England and Other Stories"* [A review], 19(April): 224.

Boulton, James T. ed. 1981. *The Letters of D.H. Lawrence.* Vol. 2. Cambridge: Cambridge University Press.

––––––. 1984. *The Letters of D.H. Lawrence.* Vol. 3. Cambridge: Cambridge University Press.

––––––. 1987. *The Letters of D.H. Lawrence.* vol. 4. Cambridge: Cambridge University Press.

Burman, Ben Lucien. 1923. "D.H. Lawrence." *The Nation* (January 17): 73–74.

Cushman, Keith. 1978. *D.H. Lawrence at Work: The Emergence of the Prussian Officer Stories.* Charlottesville: University of Virginia Press.

––––––. 1980. "The Achievement of *England, My England and Other Stories.*" *D.H. Lawrence: The Man Who Lived.* H.T. Moore and R.B. Partlow, eds. Carbondale: Southern Illinois University Press. 27–38.

Davis, Robert, ed. 1953. "D.H. Lawrence." *Ten Modern Masters: An Anthology of the Short Story.* New York: Harcourt, Brace & World, Inc. 305–07.

Delavenay, Emile. 1972. *D.H. Lawrence: The Man and His Work.* Carbondale, Illinois: Southern Illinois University Press.

Ford, George. 1965. *Double Measure: A Study of the Novels and Stories of D.H. Lawrence.* New York: Holt, Rinehart, and Winston.

Fraustino, Daniel. 1989. "Psychic Rebirth and Christian Imagery in D.H. Lawrence's 'The Horse Dealer's Daughter.'" *Journal of Evolutionary Psychology* 9(1–2): 105–08.

Goldring, Douglas. 1920. "The Later Work of D.H. Lawrence." *Reputations: Essays in Criticism.* New York: Thomas Seltzer. 65–79.

Gullason, Thomas. 1973. "Revelation and Evolution: A Neglected Dimension of the Short Story." *Studies in Short Fiction* 10: 347–56.

Harris, Janice. 1984. *The Short Fiction of D.H. Lawrence.* New Brunswick, New Jersey: Rutgers University Press.

Hobsbaum, Philip. 1980. *A Reader's Guide to D.H. Lawrence.* London: Thames & Hudson.

Jones, E.B.C. 1924. "Recent Fiction." *The Nation and the Athenaeum* 35 (Feb. 23): 738–40.

Junkins, Donald. 1969. "D.H. Lawrence's 'The Horse Dealer's Daughter.'" *Studies in Short Fiction* 6: 210–12.

Kantor, Lewis. 1922. "Lawrence Stories," *New York Tribune* (Dec. 24): Section 6, 23.

Krishnamurthi, M.G. 1970. *D.H. Lawrence: Tale as Medium.* Mysore: Rao & Raghavan.

Lawrence. D.H. 1922. "The Horse Dealer's Daughter." *English Review* 34(April): 308–25.

Leavis, F.R. [1956] 1979. *D.H. Lawrence: Novelist.* New York: Alfred A. Knopf. Reprint. Chicago: University of Chicago Press.

Mackenzie, D. Kenneth. 1978. "Ennui and Energy in *England, My England.*" *D.H. Lawrence: A Critical Study of the Major Novels and Other Writings.* A.H. Gomme, ed. New York: Barnes & Noble. 120–41.

McCabe, Thomas. 1972. "Rhythm as Form in Lawrence: 'The Horse Dealer's Daughter.'" *PMLA* 87.1(January): 64–9.

McDonald, Edward. [1931] 1969. *The Writings of D.H. Lawrence 1925–1930.* Philadelphia: Centaur Book Shop. Reprint. New York: Kraus Publishing.

McDowall, A.S. 1924. "Mr. Lawrence's Stories," *Times Literary Supplement* Jan 24: 50.

Meyers, Jeffrey. 1982. *D.H. Lawrence and the Experience of Italy.* Philadelphia: University of Pennsylvania Press.

————. 1989. "D.H. Lawrence and Tradition: 'The Horse Dealer's Daughter.'" *Studies in Short Fiction* 26: 346–51.

Moore, Harry T. [1954] 1962. *The Intelligent Heart.* New York: Viking Press. Reprint. New York: Grove Press.

Muir, Edwin. 1926. "D.H. Lawrence." *Transition: Essays on Contemporary Literature.* New York: Viking Press. 49–63.

New York Times Book Review. 1922. "*England, My England and Other Stories*" [A review,] (November 19): 13–4.

Niven, Alistair. 1980. *D.H. Lawrence: The Writer and His Work.* New York: Charles Scribner's Sons.

O'Faolain, Sean. 1961. *Short Stories: A Study in Pleasure.* Boston: Little, Brown and Co.

Phillips, Steven R. 1975. "The Double Pattern of D.H. Lawrence's 'The Horse Dealer's Daughter.'" *Studies in Short Fiction* 10: 94–7.

Pritchard, R.E. 1971. *D.H. Lawrence: Body of Darkness.* Pittsburgh: University of Pittsburgh Press.

Rehder, Jessie. 1963. *The Story at Work.* New York: Odyssey Press. 240–41.

Ryals, Clyde L. 1962. "D.H. Lawrence's 'The Horse Dealer's Daughter': An Interpretation." *Literature and Psychology* 12: 39–43.

Sagar, Keith. 1979. *D.H. Lawrence: A Calendar of His Works with a Checklist of the Manuscripts of D.H. Lawrence by Lindeth Vasey.* Austin: University of Texas Press.

Schneider, Daniel. 1984. *D.H. Lawrence: The Artist As Psychologist.* Lawrence: University Press of Kansas.

Schorer, Mark. 1950. *The Story: A Critical Anthology.* New York: Prentice-Hall, Inc.

Steele, Bruce. ed. 1990. "Introduction" and "Explanatory Notes." *'England, My England' and Other Stories.* D.H. Lawrence. Cambridge: Cambridge University Press. xix–li and 235–51.

Stewart, Garrett. 1976. "D.H. Lawrence and the Allotropic Style." *Novel* 9: 217–42.

Stewart, Jack F. 1985. "Eros and Thanatos in 'The Horse Dealer's Daughter.'" *Studies in the Humanities* 12 (June): 11–19.

Tedlock, E.W. 1963. *D.H. Lawrence: Artist and Rebel.* Albuquerque: University of New Mexico Press.

Vickery, John. 1973. *The Literary Impact of 'The Golden Bough.'* Princeton, N.J.: Princeton University Press.

West, Rebecca. 1923. "Among the Books: The Present Plight of the Artist." *Yale Review* July: 844–50.

Widmer, Kingsley. 1962. *The Art of Perversity: D.H. Lawrence's Shorter Fiction.* Seattle: University of Washington Press.

VI
"The Rocking-Horse Winner"

PUBLICATION HISTORY

Upon completing *The Plumed Serpent* in 1925, D.H. Lawrence had no desire whatsoever to begin another book. Rather, he decided between September of that year and October of 1926 to bolster his income by writing short stories for magazines and anthologies. Although he disliked the magazine format, the supplemental income, however modest, was welcome (Worthen 1989, 136–38).

In November of 1925, Lady Cynthia Asquith commissioned Lawrence to write a tale of the supernatural she planned to included in a ghost-story anthology she was editing. Lawrence, subsequently, wrote "Glad Ghosts," but Lady Asquith found it unsuitable, perhaps because it was insufficiently "ghostly" or, as critics like Harry T. Moore (1974) have suggested, because he had based the female protagonist— unfaithful to her husband with a Lawrence-like male—on Lady Asquith herself. Still another possible explanation for the rejection was that while Lawrence had begun "Glad Ghosts" with the anthology in mind, his story had grown too long (Worthen 1989, 138–9).

Lawrence composed "The Rocking-Horse Winner" in February 1926, and he mailed his handwritten manuscript to his London agent Curtis Brown on February 25. In an accompanying note, Lawrence suggested that this tale might be more suitable for Asquith's book since it was more "spectral" than "Glad Ghosts." Curtis Brown sent the now-typed manuscript on to Lady Asquith. It met with her approval, and in a letter of April 15, Lawrence told her that he was glad she liked it and added that his agent would work out the "terms" with her since he had written the story for her in the first place and not for the magazines. Having wished Asquith success with her anthology, Lawrence concluded with this caution, "You'd better ask somebody who is turfy if my racing and betting items are all right, in the 'Rocking Horse.' I'm by no means a dead cert!" (Boulton 1989, 400, 425).

Lady Asquith paid fifteen pounds for "The Rocking-Horse Winner." But before the tale could appear in her *The Ghost Book: Sixteen New Stories of the Uncanny* (published in September of 1926 in London by Hutchinson and Co. Ltd.), it appeared first in the July 1926 issue of *Harper's Bazaar*, which paid fifty pounds for the tale (Worthen 1989, 138–39). In an August 1926 letter to a friend with family in America, Lawrence asked for a copy of "that *Harper's*" (Boulton 1989, 508).

A year later, September 3, 1927, Lawrence asked Curtis Brown if he had a copy of the tale or of Asquith's *The Ghost Book* that he could send him. His sister-in-law, Else Jaffe, had offered to translate the story into German for the journal *Jugend*, and Lawrence thought "it would do very well." Although he received the requested copy on September 20, the translation never materialized (Boulton 1991, 140, 154).

On September 17, 1927, in a letter to publisher Martin Secker concerning a new collection of Lawrence's short fiction being assembled, Lawrence proffered as a title *The Woman Who Rode Away* and suggested that Secker include in its volume "The Rocking-Horse Winner," "Glad Ghosts," "The Man Who Loved Islands," "Two Blue Birds," "In-Love," "Sun," "The Last Laugh," "Jimmy and the Desperate Woman," "Smile," "The Lovely Lady," and the title story. *The Woman Who Rode Away and Other Stories* appeared in May of 1928 but did not include "The Rocking-Horse Winner," "The Man Who Loved Islands," or "The Lovely Lady." In April of 1928, Lawrence offered a manuscript of several short stories, including "The Rocking-Horse Winner," to Harry Crosby, a wealthy American, but Crosby expressed no interest in it (Boulton 1991, 152, 348, n. 5). Thereafter, the tale languished until the 1933 posthumously published collection of Lawrence's short fiction entitled *The Lovely Lady and Other Stories*.

Lawrence's hand-written manuscript of "The Rocking-Horse Winner," a thirty-page holograph on ruled paper, is owned by a private collector. Its pages measure six and three-quarters by eight and one-quarter inches, and they are bound in marble boards (Powell 1937, 26). The University of California at Berkeley owns a twenty-four page carbon typescript of the tale (Sagar 1979, 253). The text of this typescript is identical with that found in *Harper's Bazaar, The Ghost Book, The Lovely Lady and Other Stories*, and the May 1933 issue of *The Golden Book Magazine*.

The textual differences between the holograph and the typescript are negligible, so one can safely assert that no variants of this tale ever existed. Moreover, no early drafts exist, and all evidence indicates that Lawrence never significantly revised the story after sending it to Curtis Brown in February, 1926.

"The Rocking-Horse Winner" has, of course, became one of Lawrence's best-known and most frequently anthologized short stories. It perhaps reached its zenith of popularity with the general public in the 1950's and 1960's when it seemed ubiquitous in British literature collections. Some criticism from British quarters began to emerge to the effect that the tale was respected much more in America than in Britain (Leavis 1956, 371). This assertion was unfounded, but "The Rocking-Horse Winner" did lose its place in some anthologies in the 1970's and 1980's as other Lawrence masterpieces began to attract admiration. Nevertheless, only changing tastes can explain why this still-popular tale no longer serves as the "capstone" of Lawrence's later short fiction, the position it held for at least two decades.

Further evidence of the immense popularity of "The Rocking-Horse Winner" lies in the fact that it has passed beyond the boundaries of the printed page. A January 29, 1948, letter of Frieda Lawrence's mentioned "a contract in England with 'Pictor' for 'The Rocking-Horse Winner'" (Tedlock 1964, 310), and indeed, a film of "The Rocking-Horse Winner" was released in 1949. With John Mills producing, the film's cast included Mills as Bassett, Valerie Hobson as Paul's mother, and John Howard Davies as Paul (Nehls 1959, 661, n. 66). Presenting a kind of gothic horror story, director Anthony Pelissier took screenplay liberties with the tale, enlarging it, but "losing some of the story's grace" (Whitebait 1949, 757).

Finally, in 1996 Bethan Scourse Jones and Andrew McBirnie wrote an opera entitled *The Rocking-Horse Winner* based closely on Lawrence's tale.

CIRCUMSTANCES OF COMPOSITION, SOURCES, AND INFLUENCES

Following the January 1926 publication of *The Plumed Serpent*, a book that had severely tried Lawrence's health, he caught the flu and suffered consequent hemorrhaging. Although he regained his strength, his health remained fragile. Thus he began to write some short stories rather than embark upon the formidable task of another novel (Worthen 1989, 136–38).

To speed his recuperation, Lawrence decided to travel. Leaving Frieda and her two daughters behind in the Lawrences' primary place of residence at the time, Villa Bernarda, Spotorno, Italy, he visited Monte Carlo on February 22 with his sister Ada. From there he proceeded to Nice, where he mailed the handwritten manuscript of "The Rocking-Horse Winner" to Curtis Brown on February 25. He next traveled to Rome before returning to Spotorno. On April 3 he and Frieda went to Florence, where they stayed at Pensione Lucchesi until May 6, at which time they moved over to Villa Mirenda, Florence, where they lived until June of 1928. In the interim they took additional trips, notably to England from July 30 to September 28, 1926, and twice to Germany in July and August of 1927. They stayed, as well, in Switzerland from late January until March 6, 1928 (Sagar 1979, 149–74).

Lawrence wrote "The Rocking-Horse Winner" in February of 1926 during that period of ill-health. Critic Carol Sklenicka (1991) echoed the opinion of several earlier critics that Lawrence seemed to have had little enthusiasm for the tale, writing it only because Cynthia Asquith, to whom he had promised a ghost story, had rejected his first offering, "Glad Ghosts" (158). Closer investigation, however, would seem to contradict those critics.

In view of Lawrence's penchant for basing fictional characters on actual acquaintances, critics have tried to determine the real identities of Paul and his family in "The Rocking-Horse Winner." In 1967, G.R.Turner thought he had discovered the models for these characters. A 1966 biography by Leonora Thompkins, *My Lovely Days*, suggested to Turner that Lawrence had patterned Hester and her husband after Lady Sylvia and Sir Charles Brooke (the "White Rajah of Sarawak"), the sister and brother-in-law of Lawrence's close friend Dorothy Brett. Paul resembled their daughter Leonora, who secretly bet on horse races with a family servant. The gardener, Bassett, had in real life been Brooke's bootman, Willy, and the source for Uncle Oscar had been no less a personage than Dorothy Brett herself, the only family member to know about Leonora's betting. Turner concluded his argument with the point that Leonora had a rocking horse as a child (72).

Rosemary Reeves Davies (1981) criticized G.R. Turner's argument, noting that its evidence was almost impossible to corroborate. After all, Lawrence never mentioned the Brookes in any of his letters, and Davies doubted that Dorothy Brett, who had little contact with her relatives, would have mentioned them to Lawrence. Also, the memoir G.R. Turner had based his article on possessed no parallels to the "The Rocking-Horse Winner," leaving Davies to wonder if the similarities Turner noted had been the result of correspondence between Turner and Thompkins (320).

Two years later, Davies (1983) built upon an idea first presented but incompletely developed in 1978 by Paul Delany (106) regarding the sources for Paul and his family. Davies suggested that Lawrence had based Hester on Lady Cynthia Asquith, Paul on Asquith's oldest son John, and the family on the Asquiths (121). An autistic child, John's "freakishness" appears to have fascinated Lawrence and evoked his sympathy during a 1915 visit with the Asquiths. The diagnosis Lawrence gave to the boy's mother included an indictment of her skeptical and cynical nature, as well as her hard, cold spirit (123). Davies also reported that Charles Koban's 1978 examination of the story (a discussion of Koban follows shortly) arrived at conclusions close to Lawrence's own "analysis." Although indifferent to materialism per se, the Asquiths took an interest in possessions that Lawrence saw as potentially enslaving to the spirit. Moreover, like Hester, the Asquiths were better titled than monied; and during World War I, Cynthia, like Hester, had once received a humiliating summons for a small debt (124).

During a 1917 visit with the Asquiths, Lawrence continued to assert that John's illness was spiritual rather than psychological. He even volunteered to take John for a while to see if he and Frieda could help. Tragically, Lady Cynthia gradually stopped loving her son; she came to find it unbearable to be in the same room with him. Lawrence certainly knew of the sense of horror John evoked in Asquith, just as he must have sensed the guilt her reaction to her son evoked in her (Davies 1983, 125).

Next, Davies pointed out that John's autistic behavior would have paralleled Paul's: "his wildness, his self-absorption, his uncanny faces, his non-human quality," and his sense of separation from the rest of the household (126). The to-and-fro rocking motion so often associated with the autistic emerges in Paul's incessant rocking horse riding. Lastly, Davies noted that Lawrence's slip of the pen—he described Paul as Hester's "first born" when Paul actually has an older sister— perhaps revealed further the Asquith family as the model for Hester's, for Lady Asquith had three children, and John was the oldest (126).

As regarded other potential sources for and influences upon this short story, critic Robert Davis (1953) noted that the magic in the tale had ancient sources. Folklore compendia contain frequent references to hobbyhorses, and there is mention, too, of rituals wherein their riders gain powers of prophecy by means of rocking themselves into dervish-like trances (307).

Frank Amon (1953), too, discussed folklore and ritual as possible sources for "The Rocking-Horse Winner," but with more specificity. Amon noted connections between Lawrence's use of the rocking horse and (1) hobbyhorse riders in the English morris and the Abbots Bromley antler dances; (2) the hobbyhorse dance of Padstow, Cornwall; (3) the *maiyanyi*, the New Mexican Pueblos' saints impersonation; and (4) the Balinese *sanghang djanar*, during which a rider enters a trance (233).

Harry T. Moore ([1954] 1974) agreed with Amon, and pointed out that Lawrence's infusion of ritualistic aspects into "The Rocking-Horse Winner" demonstrated his "modernness of method," for Lawrence was one of the first writers of his time to draw upon anthropology. Lawrence also drew upon something closer to home: his recollections of an Uncle Herbert who apparently had been an inveterate horse player (422).

As a possible source for an aspect of the tale's form, Dominick Consolo (1969) adduced the traditional English ballad. Lawrence's repetition in the story of words such as 'luck,' 'love,' and 'knew' occurs in the incrementally repetitive style often found in the ballads. In Lawrence's tale, this reiteration produces the effect of an incantation (3).

Irish author Frank O'Connor (1963) discerned a sociological influence upon Lawrence in "The Rocking-Horse Winner." He argued that Lawrence's deep sense of social inferiority resulted in his need to escape his background and, consequently, to dream of an independent income. As a "serious prophet," Lawrence most assuredly detested money worship; on the other hand, no normal person could read of Paul's riding for a winner without avariciously wondering exactly how much money had been won (1963, 154).

Knowing as we do today about Lawrence's attempts in the late 1920's to leave Frieda financially comfortable after his death, including investments in the stock market, it would probably be more accurate to say that Lawrence distrusted rather than detested material wealth. He made this point at least twice in conversations shortly after finishing "The Rocking-Horse Winner." The first time, in March 1926, while chatting with Achsah Brewster and others in Capri about the "curse of money," he retold "The Rocking-Horse Winner" to illustrate his point (Nehls 1959, 44). Six months later, he told his friend Catherine Carswell he believed riches had a "magical touch" that made people unfeeling and "wicked" (Moore [1956] 1974, 422). This deep-seated mistrust certainly must have influenced this story.

Also an influence upon "The Rocking-Horse Winner," Lawrence had become aware that the vision expressed during his "Leadership period" in such works as *The Plumed Serpent* and *Aaron's Rod* had become "untenable." Thus, he turned to a different literary form and subsequently spoke through fable and satire. "The Rocking-Horse Winner" is the first of these fables written in the latter part of his career (Harris 1984, 204, 224).

THE RELATIONSHIP OF "THE ROCKING-HORSE WINNER" TO OTHER LAWRENCE WORKS

Some facets of "The Rocking-Horse Winner" appeared in Lawrence's earlier short fiction. For example, "The Prussian Officer" contains the description of the officer's eyes filled with a cold blue fire, which corresponds to Paul's gaze after the corruption of his world view and psyche. In each case, cold, blue eyes are symptomatic of repression and perversity (Ford 1965, 79).

In another early tale, "The Thorn in the Flesh," a connection may exist between the allusion to St. Paul's "thorn in the flesh" in Corinthians that was resolved in the short story by Bachmann's vital sexual initiation, and the characters named Paul in *Sons and Lovers* and "The Rocking-Horse Winner." All three works involve male protagonists who struggle with strongly Oedipal emotions. Bachmann's "solution" may represent a compromise with Lawrence's autobiographical personae in these works and Lawrence's limited understanding of psychology (Cowan 1990, 164).

Tedlock (1963) noted that "The Rocking-Horse Winner" deviated from Lawrence's later work in that, like much of his earlier fiction, it displays a considerable warmth for children (209). "Odour of Chrysanthemums" (especially in its early variants) and *Sons and Lovers* offer affecting portraits of youngsters.

Other commonalities include Lawrence's interest in difficult child-parent relationships and their devastating impact on the development of the child. The protagonist of "The Rocking-Horse Winner," Joyce of "England, My England," and Paul of *Sons and Lovers* are all children cast in such roles (Coveney 1957, 320–36).

Then, too, mother figures form a connection between "The Rocking-Horse Winner" and other works. Lawrence's description of Paul Morel's focus on his mother in *Sons and Lovers* where he is overly conscious of her feelings, finding no peace when she frets, his soul continually attentive to her, describes equally well young Paul's response to his mother in "The Rocking-Horse Winner" (Delavenay 1972, 9).

Additionally, the mother's unspoken household proclamation "there must be more money," and Paul's ensuing efforts to satisfy his mother's desire play out in a subtly different form in *Sons and Lovers*, where a mother's dissatisfaction registers with Paul Morel, who turns single-mindedly to gratifying her desire. Accordingly, just as a restless mother plants the "incest germ" within Paul Morel, so is Paul's seed of destruction—mechanistic and abnormal—sowed by his avaricious mother in "The Rocking-Horse Winner" (Spilka 1955, 80–81).

A frequent pattern among Lawrence's protagonists is, in fact, a son's victimization by his mother (Amon 1953, 232). Like "The Rocking-Horse Winner," Lawrence's novel *Sons and Lovers*, and his stories "The Lovely Lady" and "Mother and Daughter" focus on a sort of matriarchy where a mother attempts to draw sustenance from her son, to the detriment of all, literally or metaphorically or both (Widmer 1962, 92). A similar pattern appeared in *The Virgin and the Gipsy*, where the Mater attempts to rule the household with an implacable will (Draper 1964, 141).

Another correlation, this one between "The Rocking-Horse Winner" and *Women in Love*, involves form. Style embodies meaning in this story in much the same way it does in the novel. In both, Lawrence continually repeated words, sometimes in slightly modified form. In "The Rocking-Horse Winner," the words include "luck," "love," "dust," and "knew", repeated so as to approach an emotional, passionate, or cognitive climax by means of frictional, to-and-fro, pulsating language (Consolo 1969, 3).

Form also links this tale with two others, "The Man Who Loved Islands" and "The Princess," each of which combines fabular and ironic methods of style. All three works contain two voices, one implicit in the other; and although one voice turns away from the other, it relies on the other to be correctly interpreted (Padhi 1983, 53). (Other fables from late in Lawrence's writing career include "The Man Who Died" and "The Lovely Lady.")

Mythology and psychology, too, associate this short story with such other Lawrence works as "The Blind Man," "Glad Ghosts," and "St. Mawr," where characters show an affinity with *Golden Bough* primitivism in their "modes of thought and belief" and where levels of consciousness extend from the logical to the farthest reaches of the intuitive (Vickery 1973, 306). Moreover, in "The Rocking-Horse Winner," *Women in Love*, *The Plumed Serpent*, and the short story "Jimmy and the Desperate Woman," the psychic condition of characters is implicit in "imposed or induced" trances of varying durations (309). Also, as in the short stories "The Blind Man," "The Last Laugh," and "Glad Ghosts," "The Rocking-Horse Winner" concentrates upon the myth of a supernatural world populated by supernatural beings with which humans try to cope by means of magical rites of appeasement and prediction and by spiritualism (Vickery 1973, 323).

Still another connection between "The Rocking-Horse Winner" and other Lawrence works involves the figure of a horse, typically presented as a vital creature living in harmony with nature but living in discord with willful man. The colt that easily outraces the locomotive at the beginning of "Odour of Chrysanthemums," or the massive shire horses, vestiges of a bygone era, departing Oldmeadow at the beginning of "The Horse Dealer's Daughter" are two prominent cases in point. Lou Witt's stallion, St. Mawr, in the novel with the same name probably stands as Lawrence's best developed presentation of horse as metaphor, but countless Lawrence works summon up this natural representation of vitalism. In "The Rocking-Horse Winner," however, the horse is wooden: a man-made imitation. As such, it becomes the obverse of the vital horse symbol for man's lower psyche where the dark vital unconscious lies. This hobbyhorse upon which Paul willfully enters the realm of the unconscious is unvital to the point of deadliness; in fact, it becomes the means to Paul's death. A Lawrentian anti-horse, Paul's steed symbolizes the lad's own artificial (thus, fatal) approach to his vital unconscious plane. Once there, he plunders it, then hoists it upward into the conscious plane, all for material gain.

Lawrence's use of "the intrusive knock" also unites this tale with "The Prussian Officer," *The Trespasser*, *Sons and Lovers*, and *The First Lady Chatterley*. Like Thomas De Quincey's well-known 1823 essay "On the Knocking at the Gate in *Macbeth*," Lawrence used the intrusive knock to alert a character to the irreversible division between an ordinary and a nightmare world. With the knock comes the intrusion of the ordinary world upon the nightmare world, and the subsequent revelation to a character—in this instance, to Paul's mother, Hester—that a person is trapped there unable to escape (Appleman 1957–1958, 328–32).

Familiar story features also link some of Lawrence's work. A similar plot device appears in both "The Rocking-Horse Winner" and the drama *David* Lawrence finished in May of 1925. Saul and David form a dichotomy in the play: Saul is associated with blood prescience—David with the intellect. Refusing to acknowledge God's urging, Saul is punished and subsequently experiences a "clairvoyant madness" (Clark 1980, 324). Paul's clairvoyance in "The Rocking-Horse Winner," written nine months after *David*, is analogous.

If, in fact, Lawrence based Hester on Lady Cynthia Asquith, she shared this employment with other characters in Lawrence's fiction. For example, Lady Ottoline Morrell and Philip Heseltine serve as models for Hermione and Halliday in *Women in Love*. John Middleton Murry appears as a ridiculous figure in the short stories "The Last Laugh" and "Smile." Compton Mackenzie became "the man who loved islands" in the tale of the same name, and Percy Lucas, as well as his in-laws, the Meynells, became Lawrence's satiric target in "England, My England." In addition, Lady Cynthia served as the model for the protagonist in Lawrence's short story "The Thimble," for Lady Daphne in "The Ladybird," and for Carlotta in "Glad Ghosts" (Davies 1983, 121–22).

In yet one more link between "The Rocking-Horse Winner" and "Glad Ghosts," like Hester, Carlotta had married into an unlucky family and predicted that she would have "luck for two." Both characters, moreover, wear green dresses at an important juncture in their respective tales (Davies 1983, 122 n.9). Both tales explore the supernatural, and Hester's loss of a son at the end of the story obversely mirrors the birth of a son to Carlotta at the conclusion of "Glad Ghosts."

Finally, Lawrence's world view unites "The Rocking-Horse Winner" with various Lawrence works—notably, those critical of the modern death-in-life world like "Two Blue Birds," "The Man Who Loved Islands," "The Lovely Lady," "The Blue Moccasins," and "Things" (Vickery 1973, 324).

Other works Lawrence wrote in 1926 include *The Virgin and the Gipsy*, "Two Blue Birds," "The Man Who Loved Islands," "In Love," the poems "Fireworks" and "The Nightingale," and the first version of *Lady Chatterley's Lover*. Lawrence also began work in 1926 upon the lengthy prose piece, *Etruscan Places* (Sagar 1979, 149).

CRITICAL STUDIES

Critics neglected "The Rocking-Horse Winner" until its 1933 publication in *The Lovely Lady and Other Stories*. Although the reviewers tended to disparage the collection overall, most wrote favorably of "The Rocking-Horse Winner." The review by Mercury Patten (1933), David Garnett's pen name, expressed high praise for the tale (75) as did Ben Redman (1933), who proclaimed the story "remarkable" (478). Ferner Nuhn's (1933) review called the tale "strange and powerful" (324).

Most of the scholarly explications of this popular tale took either a psychological approach or a formalist approach, which involved stylistic and textual analyses. But other critical methods also used sociology, mythology, Marxism, and linguistics.

The earliest formalist study of "The Rocking-Horse Winner," a 1949 critical commentary by Wallace Douglas and his fellow editors, preceded the tale in their anthology. Douglas and his colleagues noted that while thematically the story concerns a boy's sacrifice in an ineffectual effort to gratify his mother's avarice, symbolically, in a family that knows neither luck nor love, luck comes to represent the obverse of love and then takes its place. In this light, one can view Paul's quest for luck as his search for love (416–21).

Carolyn Gordon and Allen Tate (1950) illustrated the effective way that Lawrence used: (1) a concealed narrator whose objectivity disappears only occasionally when the reader hears Paul's thoughts: (2) complication, which stems from Paul's situation; (3) enveloping action, guided by Hester's world view, which pervades the house in the form of obsessive materialism; (4) resolution, as portrayed by Paul's efforts to satisfy both his and his mother's quite different desires by means of riding for a winner on his link between visible and invisible worlds, his rocking horse; and (5) tonal unity, established by means of Lawrence's "carefully chosen cadences," in the whispering voices, and in the strange name Malabar, its short and broad "a's" combining to form "a tragic sound" (227–30).

Frank Amon's (1953) formalist examination illustrated Lawrence's success in melding method, technique, and form. Written primarily as a Märchen, or fairy tale, the short story has two major parts: a moralistic narrative, and a moral clearly stated as a proverb at the end. Similarly, the opening paragraph employs the syntax and rhetorical formulae found in fairy tales. Specifically, the character goes unnamed, and some explanation serves to introduce the complication of the plot the tale itself will illustrate. Thus in an ironic version of the rags-to-riches theme, Lawrence established the tone and milieu for a "modern moral fable" (Amon 1953, 232).

Philip Appleman's (1957–1958) study of "The Rocking-Horse Winner" noted how Lawrence, much as Thomas De Quincey described in his essay "On the Knocking at the Gate in *Macbeth*," used the device of "the intrusive knock" whereby a character apprehends the gulf between the "normal" world and the nightmare world. In "The Rocking-Horse Winner," Hester, representing the real world, throws open the door to Paul's room to witness in horror the full extent of her son's "madness." By means of this mechanism, according to Appleman, Lawrence revealed "two violently opposed [unbridgeable] orders of experience": the human and the "fiendish" world (328).

W.R. Martin's (1962) analysis took issue first with F.R. Leavis's (1956) cursory criticism of the story as a minor thing (371) and with Graham Hough (1957), who thought it laudable despite his conclusion that Lawrence had invested more fancy than imagination in its creation (188). Martin (1962) expounded on the skill Lawrence used to incorporate, by means of objective correlatives, one of his central themes—"the nature and nemesis of unlived lives" (65). As an example, he noted that the mother's deadness and the boy's deathward direction find expression in images involving stones: the mother's dress is crystal, at the center of her heart is a hardness, and by the tale's end her heart has turned into a stone. Paul's feverish eyes, meanwhile, are like blue stones. The horses, both animate and the inanimate, are also objective correlatives. The quick racing horses represent the possibilities of a vital existence; whereas, the mechanical wooden horse parallels the mimetic, unlived existence of Paul's parents. Like Paul and the unnamed rocking horse, Paul's parents are astride a hobby horse—obsessive materialism—rendering them mere faces in a crowd of money-lusting bourgeoisie (64–5).

Kingsley Widmer (1962) perceived the story as both a satiric inverted romance and a sardonic fairy tale based upon the old saw "lucky in money, unlucky in love." In keeping with the fairy-tale motif, the protagonist, fittingly enough, is a child, and his mother is the familiar Märchen figure of the beautiful lady with the cold heart. Widmer pronounced "The Rocking-Horse Winner" technically "well-made," possessing such stylistic strengths as effective dialogue, the economical portrayal of characters within their society, skillful use of allegory with the images of the whispering house and the extraordinary rocking horse, an unintrusive narrator, and the ironic presentation of Paul's luck as the means to his death. Widmer did, however, consider the story limited because Lawrence had drawn upon his own "magical perception of reality" to present a strong moral. Ultimately, then, the tale promoted "the rather extreme convention" of a cannibalistic mother (1962, 92–5).

Frank O'Connor (1962) closely examined the story's form and observed that with its suspension of the sense of actuality, "The Rocking-Horse Winner" seemed nearer to Poe and Pushkin's tales than to Chekhov or Maupassant's. O'Connor liked Lawrence's supernatural stories, for "the miraculous" in all of Lawrence's work lifted them above mere dabblings in the occult. O'Connor saw as "something of a problem," however, punishing young Paul for his mother's avarice (153–4).

William D. Burroughs's (1963) article on the story agreed with Gordon and Tate's much earlier adjudication that it came close to technical perfection. Burroughs noted such stylistic strengths as plot, diction, and allegorical characterization, but he agreed with Hough and Leavis that what might have been a tale of true tragedy had become, in Lawrence's hands, a tale of mere pathos. The major weakness of the work, Burroughs thought, lay in a mild didacticism in opposition to the fantastical tenor of the tale. Burroughs also expressed disappointment in Lawrence's failure to illustrate just how man's dark level of consciousness "[could] be, or should be applied to life" (323).

Praising W.R. Martin's article, Robert Lawrence (1963) proffered two more suggestions to reinforce the contribution of unity the rocking horse made to the tale. First, Robert Lawrence saw the wooden horse as an allusion to the Trojan Horse—both symbols of deception. In the short story, Paul perceives the horse as the answer to the household problem but, in fact, it leads him ever deeper into a trap. The second suggestion was that the presentation of a boy far enough out of the nursery to study Latin and Greek yet still riding a hobbyhorse represented a regression into infancy so as to escape the problems seen to accompany adulthood (324).

Six years elapsed before the next formalist study of "he Rocking-Horse Winner" appeared. Dominick Consolo (1969) examined Lawrence's consistent employment of two major motifs: eyes and hardening. At the story's climax, Paul's blazing eyes flood his mother with an intense, triumphant, accusatory, and condemnatory light. An ironic meaning is implicit: Hester has finally apprehended Paul's blaze, and it thaws her frozen heart. At long last, she feels real concern for her son, but her enlightenment has arrived too late to save him. As the light leaves Paul's eyes, life itself leaves his mother's heart. Thus, Lawrence's development of the two main motifs resulted in an intensification of "the final effects of lovelessness and misplaced values" (3–5).

Robert G. Davis (1969) developed the observations first presented in Amon's 1953 and Widmer's 1962 examination of the tale. Davis noted how "The Rocking-Horse Winner" starts like a fairy tale, and how Lawrence's style, simple and quick-flowing, complemented this narrative of the supernatural. Unwittingly linking "luck" with "money," Paul uses his luck—his psychic power—to make money for his materialistic mother. As is often the case in Märchen, wishes come true only to be paid for in unanticipated ways. In this instance, payment is made in the forfeiture of Paul's life (41).

Despite the tale's focus on magic, its theme, structure, and circumstances are wholly realistic, continued Davis. Paul's monetary gift to his mother, rather than solving her problem, exacerbates it. Just as the mother's money lust intensifies, thus increasing the lad's desperation, so mounts the tale's dramatic tension. The figure of the rocking horse itself is especially apt, for not only does it imply frantic activity leading nowhere, but it also is an instrument of magic that clairvoyants use in folk ritual to help them attain knowledge (42).

The following year, James Cowan (1970) observed that the horse placed in the service of Mammon as Paul tries to satiate his mother's avarice leads to the death of his instinctual being (88).

Three 1980 assessments of "The Rocking-Horse Winner" were brief, but to the point. Despite the tale's popularity, Philip Hobsbaum found it barely worth mentioning, except for the fact that it was fueled by Lawrence's detestation of money and the so-called respectability of the bourgeois life. Ultimately, Hobsbaum concluded, the story was "crude in its means" (129). Calling the story an unsuccessful venture into the occult, George Becker viewed the tale as fantastical, "amusing and acceptable" (1980, 120). Keith Cushman noted how Lawrence frequently revised fairy tales to suit his own purposes, and in "The Rocking-Horse Winner," he had managed to create an original story of this kind (1980, 33).

Developing Cushman's idea, Bibhu Padhi (1983) characterized the story as an "inverted fairy tale." It has two basic components of the genre: (1) a knight on horseback who tries to save a distressed damsel despite overwhelming odds, and (2) attendant adventures. No happy ending occurs in this instance, however, for the acquisition of a fortune, though it might have set the damsel free, is fatal to the knight. Padhi also observed that the voice behind the narrative voice repudiates everything the tale tells. A reader is thus urged to look beyond the "nervous, hurried" explicit voice to find Lawrence's true feelings and thus judge the case more wisely. Ultimately, the master of luck is, in fact, its slave—the victim of his own imperatives (54–5).

Janice Harris (1984) pursued still further the Märchen aspect of the tale, noting how it begins "with the distant, singsong voice of a fairy tale." It is an age-old story: a young protagonist strives to acquire the secret to conveying riches to the woman he loves. Countering this "wish fulfillment narrative," however, is the tale of "the devouring mother" whose child can never satisfy her. Paul, in fact, resembles the young girl in Rumpelstiltskin who continually had to spin straw into gold. Unlike the young girl in the German fairy tale, however, Paul has no savior, and he spins out his very life (224–5).

In the most recent formalist approach applied to "The Rocking-Horse Winner," James Scott (1989) focused on Lawrence's use of imagery to illustrate how an obsessive pursuit of material wealth resulted in petrified emotions. Scott noticed a "sheen-petrification motif" in such images as Hester's green glittering sequined gown, the varnished rocking horse, the mother's stony heart, and Paul's eyes, first ablaze with blue fire, then turning to blue stones. These appropriate images recall new coins, as well as hard-heartedness. The mother's final appearance as "heart-frozen" culminates this process of hardening sensibilities, for she shows that a mad race for wealth can lead to the heart's "glaciation" (175–76).

With its focus on the inner lives of Paul, his relatives, and even their house, "The Rocking-Horse Winner" lent itself nicely (and frequently) to psychological criticism. The earliest of such studies, Roy Lamson's (1949) discussion of the tale, effectively illustrated how Lawrence had patterned the facets of character and symbol, theme and plot tension, as integral parts of his story. To study only one of these elements separately from the rest, Lamson suggested, would be to do "violence to the particular and individual character" of the work (547).

Lamson went on to observe that Lawrence presented the moral concern in the tale as a psychological development; Hester's insatiable appetite for more money Paul attributes to the whispers he hears coming from the house and from behind the new toys. This foreboding force against which Paul pits himself was Lawrence's clever creation—an antagonist that strengthens as Paul's confidence grows. The climax had thus been prepared, a climax Lamson viewed as tragic rather than maudlin or pathetic. Noting that this tale centered on symbol more than character, Lamson focused on the confusion between luck and love—each irrational, each something that can be experienced only through feelings. In that Paul experienced only luck, never love, Lamson considered Uncle Oscar's epitaph for Paul particularly apposite: to be out of such a loveless and materialistic world, Paul was luckier than he knew (546–7).

One of the most thorough treatments of this story was W.D. Snodgrass's (1958) psychological study. Snodgrass perceived Paul as a representative of modern civilized man in frantic and frenzied pursuit of what would kill him were it ever apprehended. Money, literal in the tale, could also be seen as a surrogate for love, affection, and sperm. In fact, the Snodgrass study analyzed how the rocking horse extended symbolically into the area of sex. For example, Snodgrass was convinced that Paul's ecstacy while riding for a winner, although religious, was also onanistic, part of a pattern of loving implicit in a household where family members withdrew into themselves, withholding from the others vital emotions and connections. Money and luck became the substitutes for love to which this family committed itself. Just as riding a hobbyhorse imitates the real feat, so Paul's masturbatory clairvoyance imitates coition and true unconscious intuition (192–6).

Snodgrass contended that from both masturbation and forced prophecy, Paul's substitutes for real sex and familial affection, a yet stronger craving for the authentic feeling arose. But Paul found no reciprocity in either activity, only dissipation. Ultimately, maintained Snodgrass, "The Rocking-Horse Winner" implicitly condemns Christian idealism, which Lawrence saw as reinforcing a falsehood about the nature of purity—namely, that it is less sinful to indulge in self abuse than in coitus, and that the material world of "getting-on" is superior to the world of man's dark unconscious. The tale, for Snodgrass, thus encouraged mankind to acknowledge the vital value of "the greater urge within us and beyond us" (1958, 198–200).

James Hepburn (1959) took a Freudian approach to "The Rocking-Horse Winner." First stating his awareness of the limitation of Freudian literary criticism, Hepburn nevertheless extolled the pleasure in its inherent complexity and proceeded to analyze the strategies and forms of Sherwood Anderson's "Death in the Woods" and Lawrence's "The Rocking-Horse Winner," both of which he found to contain "the evocation of a sense of the uncanny" (9).

Illustrating, rather cryptically, that Freud's conditions concerning the formulation and presentation of uncanniness in literature were met in Lawrence's tale—a tale defying adequate explication—Hepburn again cautioned against single solutions. He closed his essay by suggesting that more studies be conducted that focus on other Lawrence short stories with fairy-tale qualities in an endeavor to determine "how their style and tone function as literary strategies" (12).

Eliseo Vivas (1960) concluded that "The Rocking-Horse Winner" was a "constitutive symbol" through which one could grasp reality directly. In the final analysis, the rocking horse surpassed any kind of explanation that ineffectual language might offer it. For this reason, critical attempts to analyze the tale, ingenious and deceptively sound as they might be, were ultimately failures (280).

Nevertheless, E.W. Tedlock (1963) discussed how the story's fairy-tale tone suited the social and psychological facets of the tale, signaled the price Paul would pay to satisfy his mother's materialism, and directed the exposition toward the "archetypical." Tedlock traced Lawrence's presentation of Paul's eyes as steadily harder and colder to the point where they resembled the eyes of the rocking horse. With Paul's eyes like blue stones in the climactic scene, and his mother's sense that her heart had turned to stone, the "rhythmic terror" of life's dehumanization comes to an end—finally and dramatically. Tedlock closed with the observation that "The Rocking-Horse Winner" was characteristic of Lawrence in that all of the adults stand indicted (1963, 209–10).

In 1964, Ronald Draper noted that no true "blood connection" existed between Paul and his mother. Thus, Paul overcompensates by means of his forays into the unconscious designed to win her love. Echoing earlier studies, Draper observed that because of a perversion of the mother-child's natural flow, Hester absorbed life from her son (141).

In another 1964 study, Donald Junkins's faulted such earlier critics as F.R. Leavis, Graham Hough, Caroline Gordon, Allen Tate, and William Burroughs for their limited readings. Like W.R. Martin, Junkins judged "The Rocking-Horse Winner" successful, but he assessed it as a story of meaning more than morality. Junkins believed it addressed the failure of modern man to reconcile his Oedipal conflict with the woman-mother. Dealing with myth, Lawrence incorporated a style and symbols that reinforced the story's mythic qualities. Its first lines, for example, juxtaposed the mythical and the modern—a tension that exists throughout the story. On the level of myth, Paul represents the would-be knight who rides to rescue an unhappy fairy princess. His stallion but a wooden hobbyhorse, Paul seems impotent, his manhood repressed by the insatiable needs of the woman-mother. Laid low by "the relentlessly unsatisfied woman-mother," the unrealized man-boy's quest is doomed from its start, suggested Junkins (88–9).

In 1965, W.S. Marks III published a fascinating psychological examination of this story. Following in W.D. Snodgrass's footsteps, Marks's analysis diverged in that he based it on Freud's studies of children's autoerotic fantasies and uncanny behavior. Translated into English in 1920, 1922, and 1925, these studies might well have been familiar to Lawrence (382).

Marks noted how Paul's behavior parodies primitive myth and ritual transferred to "the bourgeois nursery." This pattern parallels the idea Freud expressed in "Obsessive Acts and Religious Practices"— namely, that obsessional actions parody ritual. From a Freud case history of the phobia of a five-year-old lad, Marks drew an interesting analogy to "The Rocking-Horse Winner." Noting Freud's belief that daydreams or fantasy, usually being Oedipal and autoerotic, could lead to obsessive actions that serve to conceal or repress these longings, Marks argued that compulsive gambling might be such an endeavor. Then, too, he continued, Carl Jung had noted that horses ridden in dreams were common symbols for the repressed libido. Thus, Paul's incessant rocking-horse riding became the objectification of what he was doing to his libido (1965, 382–83).

Yet another of Freud's studies focused on how an Oedipal child's fantasy might take the form of a family romance wherein the child plays the knight errant who rescues the princess (his mother) from imminent danger (the threat of financial insecurity), thereby symbolically achieving his repressed desire to woo and win the mother from the father. As for Paul's prophetic ability, Marks noted that Freud's essay "The Uncanny" established a close link between the uncanny and animism. In a universe apprehended animistically, magical powers reside among various people and objects. With these powers, man endeavored "to withstand the inexorable laws of reality" (383–84).

Freud's essay "From the History of an Infantile Neurosis" led Marks to a still more illuminating comparison with Paul's Oedipal nature. Freud described the following four phases of neurosis: (1) experiencing a sense of the uncanny about horses, (2) in adolescence, desiring masochistically to become a passive means to his father's pleasure, (3) developing enthusiasm for nationalism and horses (Marks perceived this facet as having been presented satirically through various connections between horses' names in the tale and the British colonialization of India), and (4) viewing his deceased father's inheritance as filth—an inadequate replacement for a once-living father. With regard to this last phase, the critic discerned a parallel unacceptable substitute: money for "primitive phallic values" and patriarchal authority in Paul's home (384–85).

Marks next used Freud's essay "From the Neurosis of Demoniacal Possession in the Seventeenth Century" to compare Lawrence's short story with Lawrence's analysis of Hawthorne's *The Scarlet Letter* in his collection of essays, *Studies in Classic American Literature*. At the heart of both the novel and of short story lay witchcraft and infanticide, presented by Hawthorne through Hester Prynne's relationship with Pearl, and presented by Lawrence in Hester Cresswell's treatment of Paul (388). In a direct parallel with his essay on Hawthorne's tale, Lawrence condemned in his short story the mother as a devilish matriarchal figure—a well-deserved scourge of modern man, who was too weak to "assert his phallic divinity" (Marks 1965, 388–89).

In the final analysis, Marks believed "The Rocking-Horse Winner" to be satiric in its depiction of mankind as having lost touch with vital living, accepting "a mechanically organized environment" in its stead. Thus, in a parallel closer to Jung than to Freud, he believed that Lawrence's story implied that the modern race of mankind had lost the living universe still present for "the unreflective child and the savage" (391).

Perhaps because of Marks's thoroughness or a waning critical interest in the psychological approach, some fifteen years passed before Judith Wilt (1980) noted in her brief look at this tale that Paul travels to the "place of power" within him, but the outside world discourages his quest for full placement in the body. Consequently, one could only reach the place "hampered, corrupted, or driven." For this reason, Wilt argued, something within Paul is destroyed, and he dies (280).

Soon after Wilt, L.D. Clark (1980) wrote that Lawrence had finished his play *David* by May 7, 1925. In that play, Saul is associated with blood prescience—David with the intellect, forming a polarity. Losing God's flame because he ignored its urging, Saul experiences a "clairvoyant madness" that is akin to Paul's experience in "The Rocking Horse Winner," composed only nine months after the play. Clark saw this split as evidence that Lawrence was turning away from the idea expressed in *The Plumed Serpent* that raised blood consciousness over intellect. David would take over after Saul's passing, which illustrated for Clark Lawrence's belief in the need for a human consciousness both instinctive and mental. Since Paul dies as the result of the abuse of his blood consciousness, the same theme concerning the importance of a balanced psyche where intuition and intellect complement one another seems implicit in both works (343–45).

John F. Turner's (1982) study of this tale drew upon Snodgrass and Marks, but moved beyond their Oedipal interpretations. Turner saw

Lawrence presenting a child's and a culture's inability to play. The impulse had been perverted and arrested by an adult world that had made the child feel inadequate or unworthy. Thus, his anxiety shifts from a frightening unseen aspect of his life, like a sense of being unloved, to a highly visible aspect that can be improved, like enhancing the family's financial situation. In this case, the shift involves the use of a plaything as a vehicle to force knowledge from the unconscious (sensual) level. Although victimizing himself in and by the process whereby the conscious level exploits the unconscious plane, the child achieves his desired result—a temporary reduction of anxiety. The dual goal of healthy play—to improve skills needed for the future and to escape the pressure to possess such skills—becomes perverted by the second facet of fantasy when it becomes central in the development of the first facet, living successfully in an adult world (Turner 1982, 250–55).

In essence, Turner maintained, Lawrence presented an archetypal figure of horse and rider as an inharmonious image of soul and body. It also became the embodiment of Paul's need to win—to triumph—a need he had acquired from the adult world. Turner disagreed with Snodgrass and Marks' Oedipal analyses, for Paul turned to his horse for consolation to try and heal the wound made by his mother's rejection of him for his father (257–60).

Turner next asserted that for Lawrence, creativity involved the construction of one's world by means of the infusion of valued personal symbolism into both objective reality and the subjective experience of labor. Thus, Paul's self abuse, though having its sexual side, also involves the ability to play and to create. Nor does it stop there. Lawrence saw in gambling a perversion of religious instinct. Thus, Paul's ritual that employs prophecy for pounds rather than for spiritual illumination perverts religious spirit, destroying the lad's sense of wonder and his capacity to create. Ultimately, Paul provides much, but creates nothing (260–65).

Turner concluded his examination by observing that "The Rocking-Horse Winner" uses the parable idiom, or more accurately, the fairy-tale idiom, wherein all the major elements of Märchen appear: a journey involving magic, a "supernatural gift" from an animal, and the hope of rescue from a "persecuting figure of heartless authority." In the unhappy ending, of course, Lawrence deviated from the fairy-tale formula, for he intended a "tale of experience, not of innocence" presenting an image of a culture's repressed anxieties. No consolation was forthcoming, for the loss of Paul paralleled a loss within all too many members of modern culture (Turner 1982, 269).

Janice Harris's (1984) psychological study of this tale developed Snodgrass's reading in one respect. Harris recalled Lawrence's condemnation of masturbation in the essay "Pornography and Obscenity," where he observed that onanism's absence of reciprocity or exchange with a lover's "otherness" rendered it, like Paul's hobbyhorse riding, "an endless and futile circle of self-stimulation, analysis, gratification." Encouraged by his mother to "ride" obsessions learned from her, Paul spouts prophecies that lead to no awareness of "other" and diminish "his field of intercourse to a vanishing point." Consequently, Paul's wooden horse never constitutes an "otherness" he could appreciate, rather than merely exploit. Paul is never afforded "a glimpse into all that is beyond him." Thus, Harris saw embedded in the theme the idea that "the quest for absolute control leads to the loss of control" (226–27).

John J. Clayton's (1984) engaging psychological study of the tale examined Lawrence's interest in rebirth. Viewing the male and female characters as facets of Lawrence's own psyche, Clayton argued that the apparent capitulation of female to male in Lawrence's fiction resulted from a need in Lawrence's female, dominant side "to be broken down, to be entered and changed by male force." Lawrence's problem, as Clayton saw it, was that his unresolved Oedipal urges left him haunted by a mother figure which made it impossible for him, as with Paul, to be reborn by means of touching a woman. Clayton was convinced that Lawrence could not escape his own internalized fixation of "woman as mother-goddess." Thus, woman, for Lawrence, was never to be touched "as separate, as other." The constant struggle between man and woman in Lawrence's work represents his attempt to leave behind his own projections and to be reborn. But he never overcame the contradiction of the internalized woman figure versus the external (205, 220).

In "The Rocking-Horse Winner," Clayton continued, Lawrence attacked the mother as devouring and destructive; for Paul, the son-lover, lived and died in her service. Also, the rocking itself might be perceived as both "an Oedipal activity" and a regression to infancy.

Feeling emotionally deserted by his mother, Clayton noted (perhaps drawing upon Rosemary Davies's study from the preceding year), the riding became "an autistic ritual to regain wholeness." Citing what he perceived to be the tale's angry tone, Clayton inferred that Lawrence intended the mother to be a modern, materialistic, narcissistic, evil stepmother (1986, 204, 218).

Hugh Ingrasci (1985) stated that the names of the race horses and of such major characters as Paul, Oscar, and Hester provided a symbolic basis or foundation for the story that linked the supernatural facets of the tale—the whispering house and the magic wooden horse—with Paul's "psychological dilemma." Consequently, these names symbolically consolidated two facets of the tale—the occult and the psychological—that some critics considered unbalanced and disparate (3, 17).

Although Ingrasci struggled to make each name symbolic, as in the cases of Singhalese ("single-ease," implying Hester's cold independence and Paul's onanism) and Sansovino ("without wine," suggesting the partially lived life), other names, indeed, seemed to be "symbolic crowns" serving to combine the occult and the psychological sides of the story (6–8). As the best example of this process, Ingrasci adduced the name of the last horse Paul chooses to win, Malabar, the etymology of which is mal(a): evil, Latin; and bar: son of, Hebrew. Son of the evil Hester, perhaps named after Hester Prynne of *The Scarlet Letter* (Lawrence designated her a man-devourer in his study of American fiction), Paul is, indeed, a "poor devil" and a "devil of a son" who sacrifices himself for his mother by means of the only kind of love he has ever known—the one-sided kind (15–22). Accordingly, Lawrence stressed modern man's unvital tendency to live from an unbalanced psyche, for in too many people the separatist battles the sympathetic urge to become one with another, resulting in alienation and isolation, and no winners (17).

The most recent psychological study of "The Rocking-Horse Winner" was Carol Sklenicka's (1991). She pointed out that in his long essay *Fantasia of the Unconscious*, Lawrence classified an illness typified by one's living willfully and depletingly from the upper centers of consciousness—much in the manner of Hester Cresswell—as "neurasthenia of the heart." Thus, in her greed Hester endeavors to satisfy her "impoverished heart." The story also illustrates that the absence of a vital connection between people results in an individual's slow but inevitable descent into corruption. Finally, Sklenicka noted that Lawrence expressed allegorically in this story his belief that without the parents' unconditional, egoless love, the child must die (1991, 158–59).

Only three primarily sociological examinations of "The Rocking-Horse Winner" have appeared. First, Frank Amon (1953) discerned that in the course of the story Paul becomes the victim of his mother's confusing luck with money. The whole family, in fact, sits astride a hobbyhorse, riding frantically and furiously to nowhere. The fact that Paul's divinations occur on a rocking horse seems apposite, however, for the artificial horse symbolically embodied "humanity's trance-like and mechanistic plunging onward to nowhere." In this way, Lawrence captured Paul's moment of transition, which transforms the boy and his mother forever. The value of Lawrence's art, for Amon, is the new meaning it provides to our experiences through illustrations of more vital realms of being that lie beneath the social surface (233).

Second, Michael Goldberg's (1969) analysis asserted that the tale is best read as "a Dickensian social fable," for its principal themes of parental negligence, and the loss of humanity involved in Mammon's glorification were of major interest to Dickens. As in Dickens's *Dombey and Son* so in Lawrence's tale, an aura of "brittle gentility" pervades both house and household. In Lawrence's story, Paul's mother and the rocking horse establish only tenuous contact with reality, and their movement resembles a sort of "directionless frenzy." Thus, Paul's withdrawal from reality exemplifies in him as in Hester a denial of "natural instinct" that alone offers a kind of fulfillment. Concluding his comparison between "The Rocking-Horse Winner" and *Dombey and Son*, Goldberg observed that in both tales children must yield to a spurious adult logic since they cannot oppose it. In both stories, this yielding leads to the abuse of the children's humanity. Both works ultimately explore the degree to which the entire human personality is marred by a "primary misconception of human goals" (525–35).

Third, Janice Harris (1984) conducted a social examination of "The Rocking-Horse Winner," calling the tale a satire "on the equation of money, love, luck, and happiness." Such equations are fatal, she argued, and as a symbol of a society that most values a money ethic, the mother has imposed upon the younger generation "a murderous education." Harris also mentioned Lawrence's presentation of a mother who molds her son into "a desirable opposite" of her husband. Unable to change her husband, and unsuccessful in the business world herself partly because of "the lack of opportunities available to her," Hester places demands upon her son that largely result from her inability to satisfy her boundless desires directly. Consequently, Paul's death is attributable less to the specific nature of Hester's demands than to "the strength of those demands" (1984, 225–26).

Several scholarly studies of "The Rocking-Horse Winner" utilized the mythological approach. The earliest, the aforementioned 1964 Oedipal study by Donald Junkins, relied on both psychology and myth but more heavily on psychology.

Frederick W. Turner's (1969) study observed that Lawrence turned away from ego-centrism in the late 1920's, after becoming increasingly aware of its restraints upon individual, social, and human development. Lawrence believed that the "little self" must die in a process that leads to a selfhood of selflessness wherein one becomes aware of one's relationship with all mankind and of one's greater connection with the cosmos. Paul achieves such an "apotheosis of selfhood" through his death, which Turner viewed as a symbolic rebirth through which Paul is released into this superior, more generous kind of selfhood. Simultaneously, Paul's demise might have led to the reader's rebirth, argued the critic, for the reader had witnessed the lad's willing sacrifice to help those he loved (97, 105).

Turner supported his thesis by means of a mythological interpretation of the tale that focused upon Paul and the rocking horse as modern representatives of Bellerophon and Pegasus. Both tales fit two specific types classified under the heading "Magic Flight" in Stith Thompson's *The Types of Folklore*. The plot has a tripartite structure: (1) the hero is removed from his natural environment, (2) he performs several tasks with the aid of a magic horse, and (3) the lad escapes imprisonment astride his magical steed. The fatal nature of the boy's escape indicts the greedy, selfish, egocentric society for which he dies. In the manner of the mythic hero and willing scapegoat, Paul attains his full humanity, having dedicated himself to something greater than self (Turner 1969, 100, 102).

Concluding his argument, Frederick Turner noted Lawrence's interpretation of the vision in "Revelations" where a white horse appears after the heavens have split—an image repeated when Paul's mother suddenly switches on the light and sees him entranced on his horse. Lawrence interpreted the rider on the white horse in the vision as his holy ego riding forth to conquer his old self and to make way for the birth of his new self. Turner argued persuasively that in "The Rocking-Horse Winner," Lawrence presented Paul just this way: his death, consequently, is both achievement and triumph (104).

The next application of myth to this tale came from John Vickery (1973), who asserted that this story used myth to emphasize the mystery of existence. Accordingly, the tale illustrated that the world of myth and ritual is too vital to treat frivolously (324).

The following year, L.T. Fitz's (1974) mythological approach focused on how the names of race horses developed themes implicit in the tale. Thus, the name of Daffodil, considered with the flower imagery in other Lawrence works, might be "sexually charged." Another horse's name, Lancelot, suggested to Fitz "ritualized, artificial love," the destructive nature of which the story illustrates. Fitz found most interesting three horses whose names both denote primitive tribes or places, and appear in James Frazer's *The Golden Bough*: Singhalese, Malabar, and Mirza—the last of which Fitz identified as a shortened variant of Mirzapur (199).

Lawrence most likely used these three names from Frazer's book because they evoked cultures that possessed "primitive magical power" akin to the tale's magical occurrences. But in the name of Malabar, Paul's last winner, Fitz found direct correlations between Frazer's account and Lawrence's use of the name. Frazer had described how the people of Malabar transferred their sins to a scapegoat, which parallels Paul's scapegoat role in the tale (200).

Perhaps more importantly, Fitz maintained, was the tradition of the King of Calicut in Malabar compelled to commit suicide following a twelve-year reign during which he had possessed godlike power. Like the king, Paul is permitted for a time to exercise magical power, but ultimately must pay for it with his life. By incorporating myth into the tale, Lawrence revealed an affinity for the tragic opposite of the dying-

and-reborn god figure that appears in much of his work (Fitz 1974, 200).

Although skirting the mythological approach per se, Charles Koban's (1978) study of "The Rocking-Horse Winner" did focus on its religious nature. Crediting first Snodgrass's contributions, Koban suggested that the mystical side of the story had yet to be fully explicated. He went on to cite Lawrence's deep religious nature, and then to set forth his own "religious" argument: human feeling in this tale is sublimated "in the form of money as a mystical force in family life." Koban next summarized Lawrence's religious understanding of the matrimonial relationship. For a marriage to be vital, Lawrence had stressed the need for a mystical relationship only in part sexual. Paul's parents' marriage, Koban noted, is in "the process of disaffection," and greed had replaced what once might have been a "mystical energy" (391–93).

Koban's thesis revolved around his reading of the tale as a climactic account of the demise of love in Paul's mother, a narrative that delineates "the death of her heart," which thus made the story an allegorical depiction of the demise of the child in Hester, a work portraying the expiration of love and innocence. The "mystifying of greed" is the culprit. Caught in this net cast by Hester, she and Paul become one "in their self-destructive mystical union." Paul's insanity is hers, and his death parallels her "living death." In disagreement with what he saw as Snodgrass's condemnation of Paul for his immorality, Koban perceived Paul's efforts to please his tormented mother, and his subsequent death, as "the supreme sacrifice" (393–95).

Koban concluded his argument with the observation that even the prose style Lawrence used had the deceptive simplicity of a Biblical parable. As an example, Koban compared the story's first paragraph with the *King James* version of the Good Samaritan parable. Both contained "succinctness," terse "clipped clauses," and a "reliance on coordination." Such similar styles, inferred Koban, certainly suggest the tale's allegorical nature (395–96).

Only one scholar, Keith Wilson (1987), has published a linguistic reading of "The Rocking-Horse Winner." Wilson began his examination somewhat defensively by disparaging earlier critical approaches to the tale. For example, he suggested that those earlier analyses classifying the tale as parable ignored the manner its structure, not just its style, is "parabolic." Referring to the aforementioned Koban study that found the Good Samaritan parable implicit in parallels between the opening lines of the two stories, Wilson noted that both works refer to anonymous characters in the past tense to begin what promises to be a narrative with a "defined closure" (Wilson 1987, 439).

The structure of the tale, Wilson argued, relies upon the typical text and subtext of parable and the conflict between them experienced by Paul. The lad accepts language literally, failing to perceive the latent meanings. Indeed, his inability to decipher the subtext of language correctly—the part of language that contains emotional reality and remains unspoken—leads directly to the secretive, terminal path he takes to win his mother's love. He communicates successfully with Bassett and Oscar because of "a linguistic trust" among them: the verbal and inaudible-unsaid joined in "an act of communicative trust." But the secret Paul keeps from his mother—a good example of how language is a function of a relationship's nature—ensures that the spoken and unspoken languages therein remain irreconcilable (445).

Having perceived the Parable of the Talents as implicit in the tale, Wilson maintained that Paul's gift may have been heaven sent. To this end, he cited several religious references from dialogue, like Bassett's, "It's as if he had it from heaven." Consequently, one could see Paul's misreading of the messages, his hiding the gift for fear of its loss, and his effort to cure a "concealed illness of the spirit" with filthy lucre, as integral facets of the parabolic subject matter and structure of "The Rocking-Horse Winner." Like biblical parable, Lawrence balanced contradiction and presented profound meaning within an apparently simple narrative (449–50).

One Marxist examination of this tale has appeared in print, Daniel Watkins's (1987) analysis. Watkins acknowledged Snodgrass's earlier perception that "The Rocking-Horse Winner" indicts capitalist culture, but he believed much of the socioeconomic dimension of the work had gone uninvestigated. As Watkins read it, the tale is a symbolic creation of social life in capitalism's grasp; and the two constituting facets of a capitalist society —labor and religion—became the focus of his examination (295).

Basing many of his observations upon *The Nature and Logic of Capitalism* by Robert Heilbroner, Watkins argued that all capitalist labor exploits underlings, as the story illustrates when Paul becomes a laborer for his mother. Later in the tale, as a successful capitalist himself, Paul symbolically invests himself, selling his gift so as to acquire the money he cannot possess, but which is necessary for him to maintain established relationships (1987, 297).

Departing from Snodgrass's assessment of the occult in the tale, Watkins saw instead orthodox religion, supported primarily by the presentation of Paul as a Christ figure. When Uncle Oscar and Bassett join Paul in the mutual money-making scheme clothed in secrecy, Watkins perceived a Lawrentian allegory for the trinity (299).

Watkins prepared his closing argument with the assertion that orthodox religion was, after all, "firmly committed to the money ethic," which became "the basis for all human value and the key to all human exchange." Thus, Paul's self sacrifice for love is, on one level, the epitome of his Christ-like role, but on a deeper level, Paul's seemingly selfless act illustrates Lawrence's further condemnation of Christianity as a religion of true demonic character that encourages the sacrifice of human life in the effort to gain personal excellence and to afford personal advancement. The monetary foundations of Christianity, concluded Watkins, contributed greatly to the society's materialistic values so that the ultimately pointless labor of underlings like Paul could be exploited for personal gain by those who control them (299–300).

The great amount and wide diversity of critical attention that Lawrence's "The Rocking-Horse Winner" received bespeaks the lasting significance of the work. Recognized early as "one of Lawrence's most unusual stories" (Powell 1937, 26), it has come to be regarded as "among the best short stories in the English language," having achieved "real grandeur" (West 1950, 105). Despite being embraced by so many scholars as "a great work of art," (a declaration that often confers the kiss of death upon a work among the general reading public), "The Rocking-Horse Winner" maintains a strong universal appeal. Among other critics, Nicholas Joost and Alvin Sullivan (1970) judged it to be the most popular of all Lawrence's stories (96).

So long as such keen interest remains in this powerful work—as illustrated by Jones and McBirnie's 1996 British opera named for and based on the tale and by its continued inclusion in literature anthologies—readers will continue to be drawn into its subtleties. Meanwhile, scholarly examinations of "The Rocking-Horse Winner," as perceptive and ingenious as they have been so far, seem sure to discover more nuances and offer new interpretations.

WORKS CITED

Amon, Frank. 1953. "D.H. Lawrence and the Short Story." *The Achievement of D.H. Lawrence.* F.J. Hoffman and H.T. Moore, eds. Norman: University of Oklahoma Press. 222–234.

Appleman, Philip. 1957–1958. "D.H. Lawrence and the Intrusive Knock." *Modern Fiction Studies* 3 (Winter): 328–32.

Becker, George. 1980. *D.H.Lawrence.* New York: Frederick Ungar Publishing Co.

Boulton, James T. ed. 1989. *The Letters of D.H. Lawrence.* Vol. 5. Cambridge: Cambridge University Press.

———. 1991. *The Letters of D.H. Lawrence.* Vol. 6. Cambridge: Cambridge University Press.

Burroughs, William D. 1963. "No Defense for 'The Rocking-Horse Winner.'" *College English* 24: 323.

Clark, L.D. 1980. *The Minoan Distance: The Symbolism of Travel in D.H. Lawrence.* Tucson: University of Arizona Press.

Clayton, John J. 1984. "D.H. Lawrence: Psychic Wholeness through Rebirth." *The Massachusetts Review* 25: 200–21.

Consolo, Dominick. 1969. "Introduction." *D.H. Lawrence: 'The Rocking-Horse Winner.'* Columbus, Ohio: Charles E. Merrill Publishing Co. 1–6.

Coveney, Peter. [1957] 1967. *Poor Monkey: The Child in Literature.* London: Rockliff. Reprinted and revised as *The Image of Childhood.* Harmondsworth: Penguin Books.

Cowan, James. 1982. *D.H. Lawrence: An Annotated Bibliography of Writings About Him.* Dekalb: Northern Illinois University Press.

———. 1990. *D.H. Lawrence and the Trembling Balance.* University Park: The Pennsylvania State University Press.

———. 1970. *D.H. Lawrence's American Journey.* Cleveland: Case Western Reserve University Press.

Cushman, Keith. 1980. "The Achievement of *England, My England and Other Stories.*" *D.H. Lawrence: The Man Who Lived.* H.T. Moore and R.B. Partlow, eds. Carbondale: Southern Illinois University Press. 27–38.

Davies, Rosemary Reeves. 1983. "Lawrence, Lady Cynthia Asquith, and 'The Rocking-Horse Winner.'" *Studies in Short Fiction* 20: 121–26.

Davies, Rosemary Reeves. 1981. "'The Rocking-Horse Winner' Again: A Correction." *Studies in Short Fiction* 18: 320–22.

Davis, Robert, ed. 1953. "D.H. Lawrence." *Ten Modern Masters: An Anthology of the Short Story.* New York: Harcourt, Brace & World, Inc. 305–07.

———. 1969. "Observations on 'The Rocking-Horse Winner.'" *D.H. Lawrence: The Rocking-Horse Winner.* Dominick Consolo, ed. Columbus: Charles E. Merrill Publishing Co. 41–43.

Delany, Paul. 1978. *D.H. Lawrence's Nightmare: The Writer and His Circle in the Years of the Great War.* New York: Basic Books, Inc.

Delavenay, Emile. 1972. *D.H. Lawrence: The Man and His Work.* Carbondale, Illinois: Southern Illinois University Press.

Douglas, Wallace, Roy Lamson, and Hallett Smith, eds. 1949. "Introduction" to "The Rocking-Horse Winner." *The Critical Reader.* New York: Norton. 416–21.

Draper, Ronald. 1964. *D.H. Lawrence.* Boston: Twayne Publishers, Inc.

Fitz, L.T. 1974. "'The Rocking-Horse Winner' and *The Golden Bough.*" *Studies in Short Fiction* 11: 199–200.

Ford, George. 1965. *Double Measure: A Study of the Novels and Stories of D.H. Lawrence.* New York: Holt, Rinehart, and Winston.

Goldberg, Michael. 1969–70. "Lawrence's 'The Rocking-Horse Winner': A Dickensian Fable?" *Modern Fiction Studies* 15: 525–36.

Gordon, Carolyn, and Allen Tate. [1950] 1960. "'The Rocking-Horse Winner': Commentary." *The House of Fiction: An Anthology of the Short Story.* New York: Charles Scribner's Sons. 348–51. Reprint. 227–30.

Harris, Janice. 1984. *The Short Fiction of D.H. Lawrence.* New Brunswick, New Jersey: Rutgers University Press.

Hepburn, James G. 1959. "Disarming and Uncanny Visions; Freud's 'The Uncanny' with Regard to Form and Content in Stories by Sherwood Anderson and D.H. Lawrence." *Literature and Psychology* 9: 9–11.

Hobsbaum, Philip. 1980. *A Reader's Guide to D.H. Lawrence.* London: Thames & Hudson.

Hough, Graham. 1957. *Dark Sun: A Study of D.H. Lawrence.* New York: The Macmillan Company.

Ingrasci, Hugh J. 1985. "Names as Symbolic Crowns Unifying Lawrence's 'The Rocking-Horse Winner.'" *Festschrift in Honor of Virgil J. Vogel.* Edward Callary, ed. Dekalb: Illinois Name Society. 1–22.

Jones, Bethan and Andrew McBirnie. 1996. *The Rocking-Horse Winner.* Nottingham: University of Nottingham.

Joost, Nicholas, and Alvin Sullivan, eds. 1970. *D.H. Lawrence and the 'Dial.'* Carbondale: Southern Illinois University Press.

Koban, Charles. 1978. "Allegory and the Death of the Heart in 'The Rocking-Horse Winner.'" *Studies in Short Fiction* 15: 391–96.

Lamson, Roy. 1949. "A Critical Analysis of 'The Rocking-Horse Winner.'" *The Critical Reader.* New York: W.W. Norton & Company, Inc. 542–47.

Lawrence, Robert. 1963. "Further Notes on D.H. Lawrence's 'Rocking-Horse.'" *College English* 24: 324.

Leavis, F.R. [1956] 1979. *D.H. Lawrence: Novelist.* Alfred A. Knopf. Reprint. Chicago: University of Chicago Press.

Marks III, W.S. 1965–66. "The Psychology of the Uncanny in Lawrence's 'The Rocking-Horse Winner.'" *Modern Fiction Studies* 11: 381–92.

Martin, W.R. 1962. "Fancy or Imagination? 'The Rocking-Horse Winner.'" *College English* 24: 64–65.

Moore, Harry T. [1954] 1974. *The Priest of Love: A Life of D.H. Lawrence.* New York: Farrar, Straus and Giroux. Reprinted and revised edition of *The Intelligent Heart.*

Nehls, Edward. 1959. *D.H. Lawrence: A Composite Biography.* Vol. 3. Madison: The University of Wisconsin Press.

Nuhn, Ferner. 1933. "Lawrence and the Short Story." *Nation(NY)* 136 (March 22): 324.

O'Connor, Frank. 1962. *The Lonely Voice: A Study of the Short Story.* New York: The World Publishing Co.

Padhi, Bibhu. 1983. "Lawrence's Ironic Fables and How They Matter." *Interpretations: A Journal of Ideas, Analysis, and Criticism* 15: 53–59.

Patten, Mercury. 1933. "Books in General," *New Statesman and Nation* 5 (January 21): 75.

Powell, Lawrence Clark. 1937. *The Manuscripts of D.H. Lawrence.* Los Angeles: The Ward Ritchie Press.

Redman, Ben Ray. 1933. "Here Are Ladies," *Saturday Review of Literature* 9 (March 11): 478.

Sagar, Keith. 1979. *D.H. Lawrence: A Calendar of His Works with a Checklist of the Manuscripts of D.H. Lawrence by Lindeth Vasey.* Austin: University of Texas Press.

Scott, James B. 1989. "The Norton Distortion: A Dangerous Typo in 'The Rocking-Horse Winner.'" *The D.H.Lawrence Review* 21.2: 175–77.

Sklenicka, Carol. 1991. *D.H. Lawrence and the Child.* Columbia: University of Missouri Press.

Snodgrass, W.D. 1958. "A Rocking-Horse: The Symbol, the Pattern, the Way to Live." *The Hudson Review* 11.2: 191–200.

Spilka, Mark. 1955. *The Love Ethic of D.H. Lawrence.* Bloomington: Indiana University Press.

Tedlock, E.W. 1963. *D.H. Lawrence: Artist and Rebel.* Albuquerque: University of New Mexico Press.

Thompkins, Leonora. 1966. *My Lovely Days.* New York: Carlton Press.

Turner, Frederick W. 1969. "Prancing in to a Purpose: Myths, Horses, and True Selfhood in Lawrence's 'The Rocking-Horse Winner.'" *D.H. Lawrence: The Rocking-Horse Winner.* Dominick Consolo, ed. Columbus: Charles E. Merrill Publishing Co. 95–107.

Turner, G.R. 1967. "Princess on a Rocking Horse." *Studies in Short Fiction* 5: 72.

Turner, John F. 1982. "The Perversion of Play in D.H. Lawrence's 'The Rocking-Horse Winner.'" *The D.H. Lawrence Review* 15: 249–70.

Vickery, John. 1973. *The Literary Impact of 'The Golden Bough.'* Princeton, N.J.: Princeton University Press.

Vivas, Eliseo. 1960. *D.H. Lawrence: The Failure and the Triumph of Art.* Bloomington: Indiana University Press.

Watkins, Daniel. 1987. "Labor and Religion in D.H. Lawrence's 'The Rocking-Horse Winner.'" *Studies in Short Fiction* 24: 295–301.

West, Anthony. 1950. *D.H. Lawrence.* Denver: Alan Swallow.

Whitebait, William. 1949. "'The Rocking-Horse Winner,' at the Marble Arch Odeon," *New Statesman and Nation* 38 (December 24): 756–57.

Widmer, Kingsley. 1962. *The Art of Perversity: D.H. Lawrence's Shorter Fiction.* Seattle: University of Washington Press.

Wilson, Keith. 1987. "D.H. Lawrence's 'The Rocking-Horse Winner': Parable and Structure." *English Studies in Canada* 13: 438–50.

Wilt, Judith. 1980. *Ghosts of the Gothic.* Princeton: Princeton University Press.

Worthen, John. 1989. *D.H. Lawrence: A Literary Life.* New York: St. Martin's Press.

Index